Garfield
swallows his pride

BY JIM DAVIS

Ballantine Books • New York

2006 Ballantine Books Trade Paperback Edition

Published in the United States by Ballantine Books, an imprint of The Random House Publishing Group, a division of Random House, Inc., New York.

BALLANTINE and colophon are registered trademarks of Random House, Inc.

Originally published in slightly different form in the United States by Ballantine Books, an imprint of The Random House Publishing Group, a division of Random House, Inc., in 1987.

ISBN 978-0-345-91386-9

Printed in China

www.ballantinebooks.com

9 8 7 6 5 4 3 2

First Colorized Edition

GARFIELD'S 10 ALL-TIME FAVORITE
BAD CAT JOKES

1 What do you get when you cross a cat with a fish?
A carp that always lands on its feet.

2 What does a cat take for a bad memory?
Milk of amnesia.

3 Did you hear about the two cats who were inseparable?
They were Siamese twins.

4 Why did the cat climb the drapes?
He had good claws to.

5 Did you hear about the cat who was an overachiever?
He had ten lives.

6 Why do cats eat fur balls?
They love a good gag.

7 Did you hear about the cat who made a killing in sports?
He was in the tennis racket.

8 I knew a cat who was so rich . . .
he had his mice monogrammed.

9 What do you get when you cross a cat with a dog?
A badly injured dog.

10 Can cats see in the dark?
Yes, but they have trouble holding the flashlight.

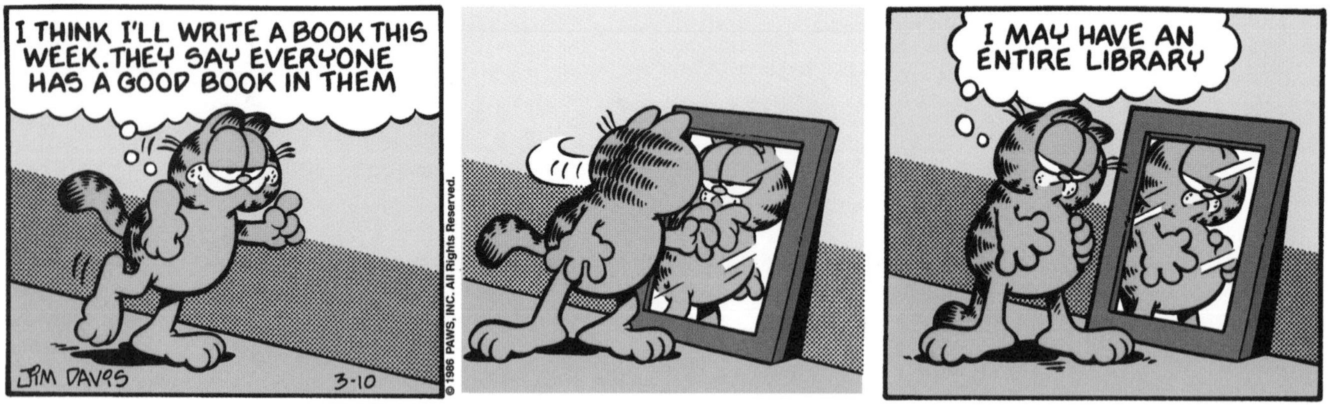
I THINK I'LL WRITE A BOOK THIS WEEK. THEY SAY EVERYONE HAS A GOOD BOOK IN THEM
JIM DAVIS 3-10
© 1986 PAWS, INC. All Rights Reserved.
I MAY HAVE AN ENTIRE LIBRARY

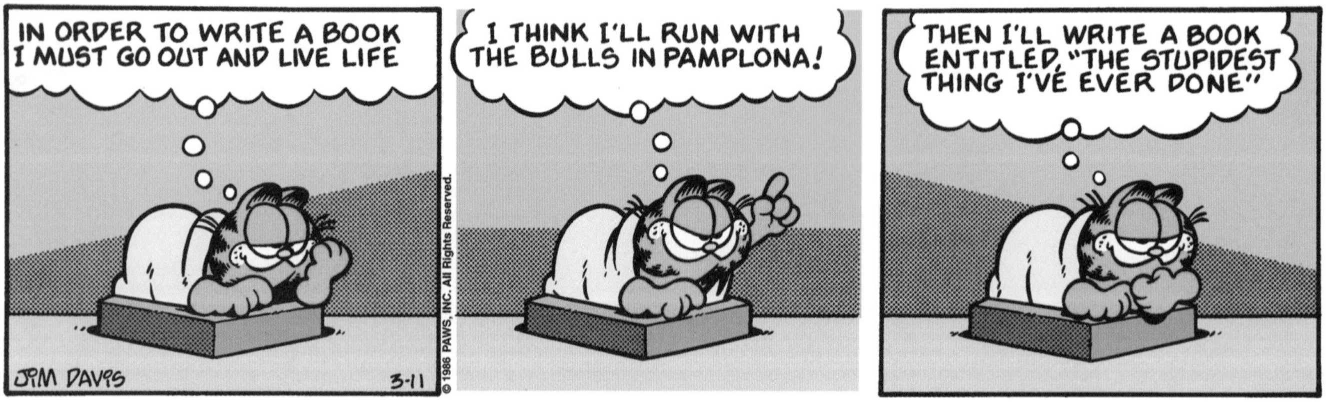
IN ORDER TO WRITE A BOOK I MUST GO OUT AND LIVE LIFE
JIM DAVIS 3-11
© 1986 PAWS, INC. All Rights Reserved.
I THINK I'LL RUN WITH THE BULLS IN PAMPLONA!
THEN I'LL WRITE A BOOK ENTITLED, "THE STUPIDEST THING I'VE EVER DONE"

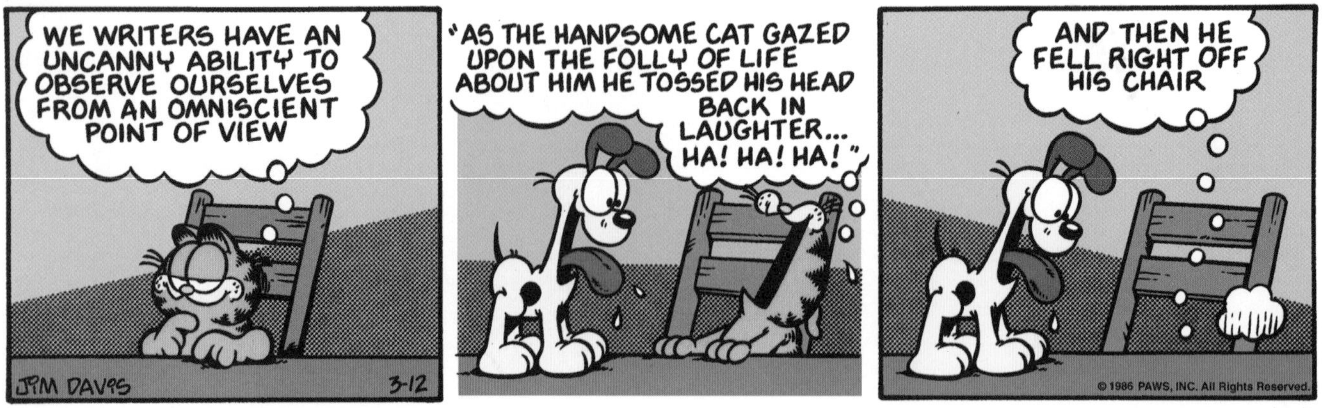
WE WRITERS HAVE AN UNCANNY ABILITY TO OBSERVE OURSELVES FROM AN OMNISCIENT POINT OF VIEW
JIM DAVIS 3-12
"AS THE HANDSOME CAT GAZED UPON THE FOLLY OF LIFE ABOUT HIM HE TOSSED HIS HEAD BACK IN LAUGHTER... HA! HA! HA!"
AND THEN HE FELL RIGHT OFF HIS CHAIR
© 1986 PAWS, INC. All Rights Reserved.

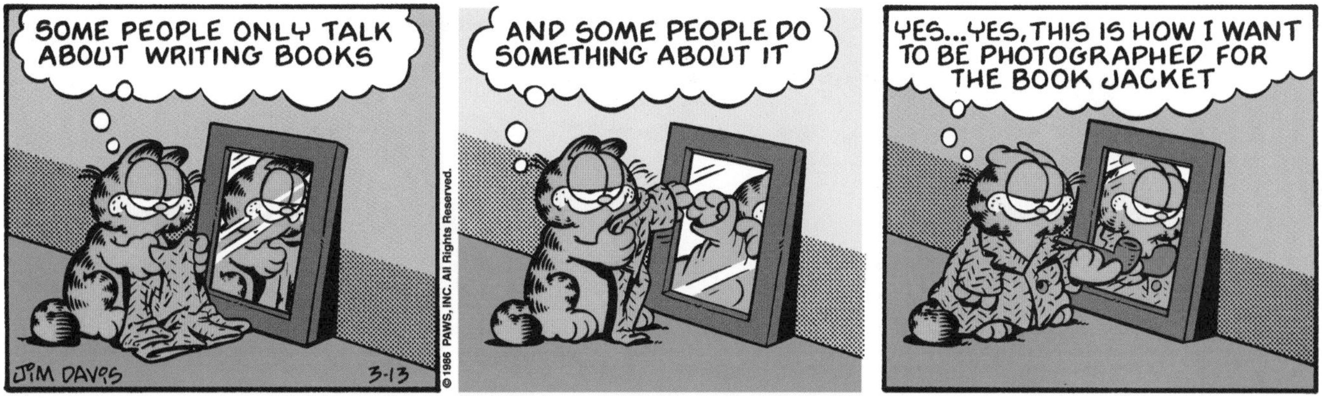
SOME PEOPLE ONLY TALK ABOUT WRITING BOOKS
JIM DAVIS 3-13
© 1986 PAWS, INC. All Rights Reserved.
AND SOME PEOPLE DO SOMETHING ABOUT IT
YES...YES, THIS IS HOW I WANT TO BE PHOTOGRAPHED FOR THE BOOK JACKET

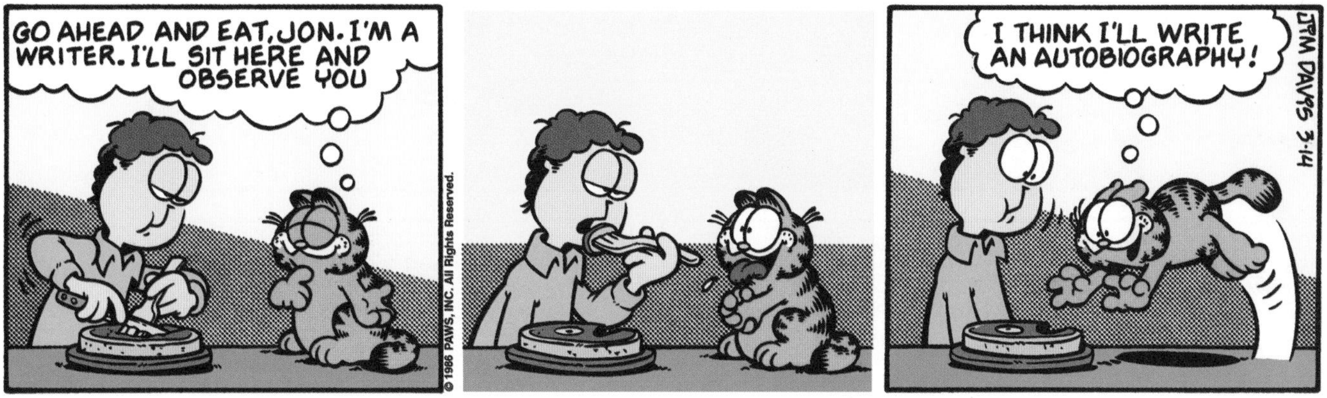
GO AHEAD AND EAT, JON. I'M A WRITER. I'LL SIT HERE AND OBSERVE YOU
© 1986 PAWS, INC. All Rights Reserved.
I THINK I'LL WRITE AN AUTOBIOGRAPHY!
JIM DAVIS 3-14

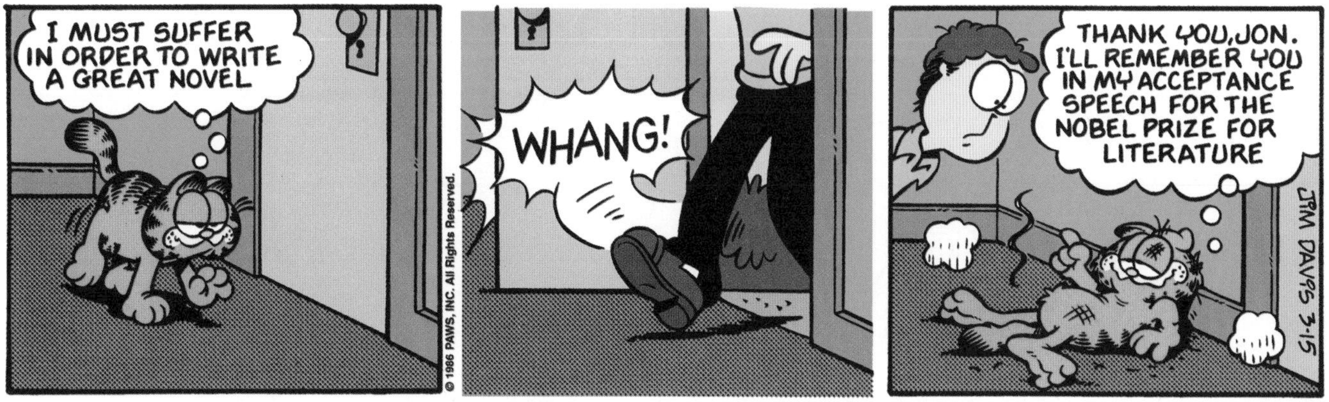
I MUST SUFFER IN ORDER TO WRITE A GREAT NOVEL
© 1986 PAWS, INC. All Rights Reserved.
WHANG!
THANK YOU, JON. I'LL REMEMBER YOU IN MY ACCEPTANCE SPEECH FOR THE NOBEL PRIZE FOR LITERATURE
JIM DAVIS 3-15

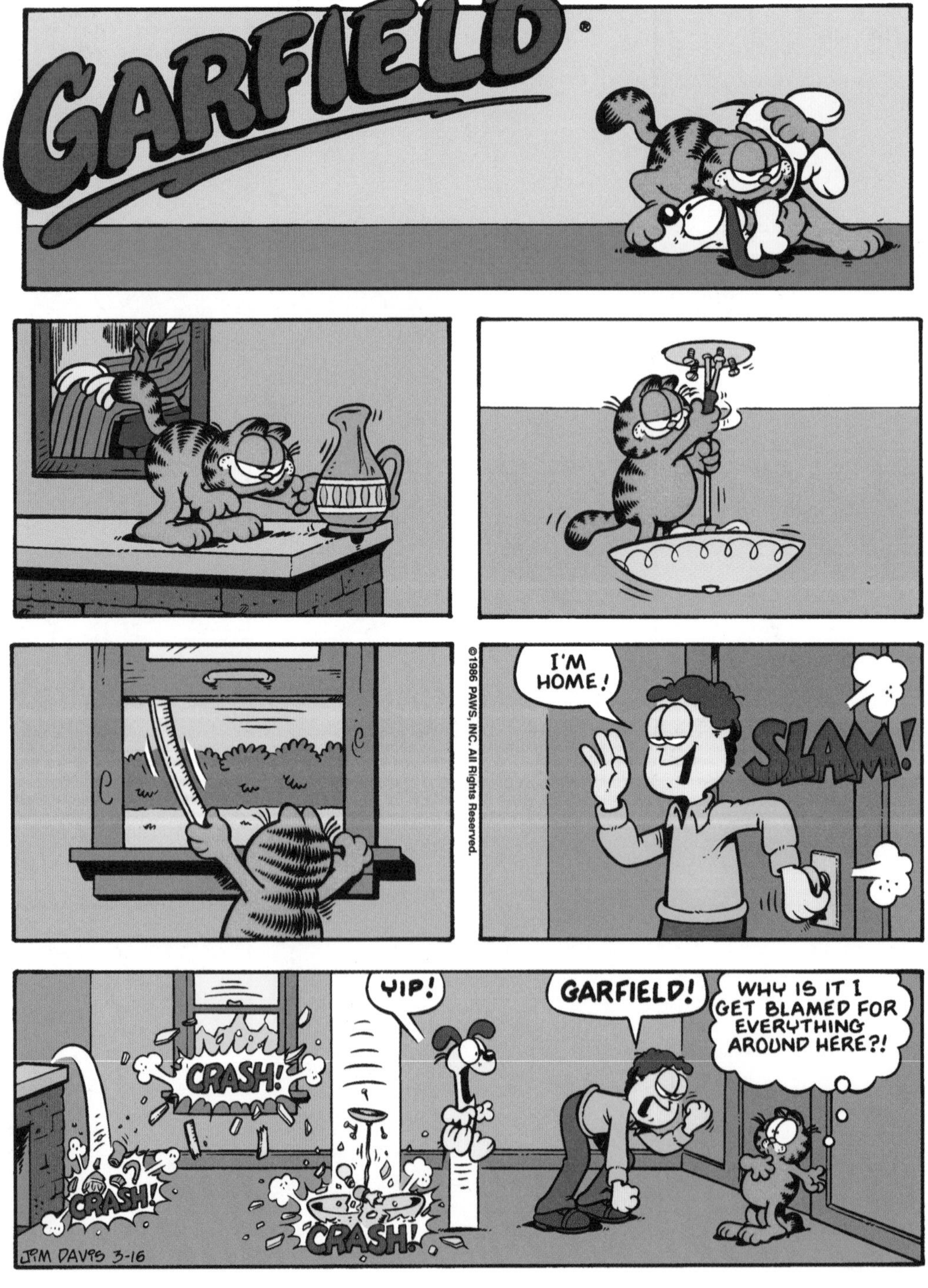
GARFIELD®
I'M HOME!
SLAM!
CRASH!
CRASH!
CRASH!
YIP!
GARFIELD!
WHY IS IT I GET BLAMED FOR EVERYTHING AROUND HERE?!
JIM DAVIS 3-16

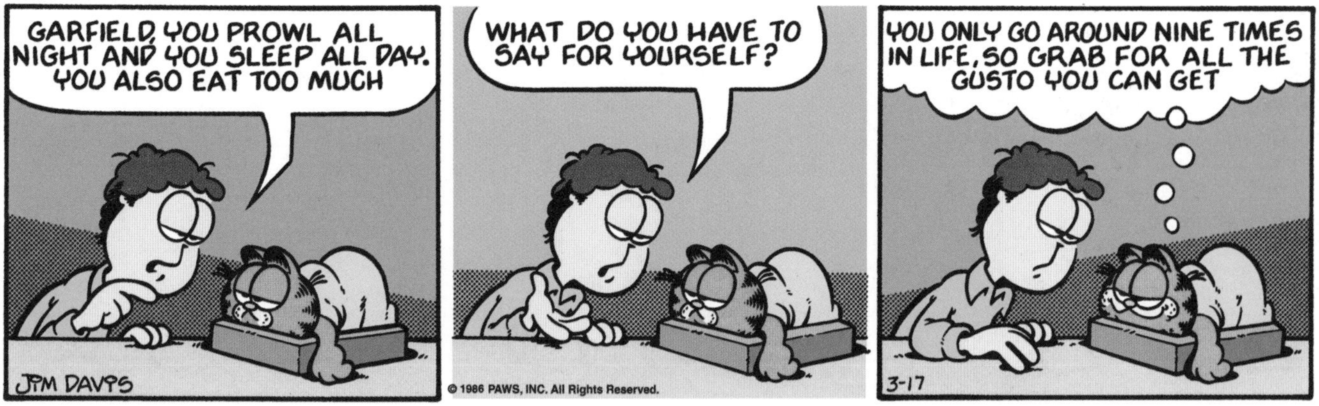
GARFIELD, YOU PROWL ALL NIGHT AND YOU SLEEP ALL DAY. YOU ALSO EAT TOO MUCH
WHAT DO YOU HAVE TO SAY FOR YOURSELF?
YOU ONLY GO AROUND NINE TIMES IN LIFE, SO GRAB FOR ALL THE GUSTO YOU CAN GET
JIM DAVIS
© 1986 PAWS, INC. All Rights Reserved.
3-17

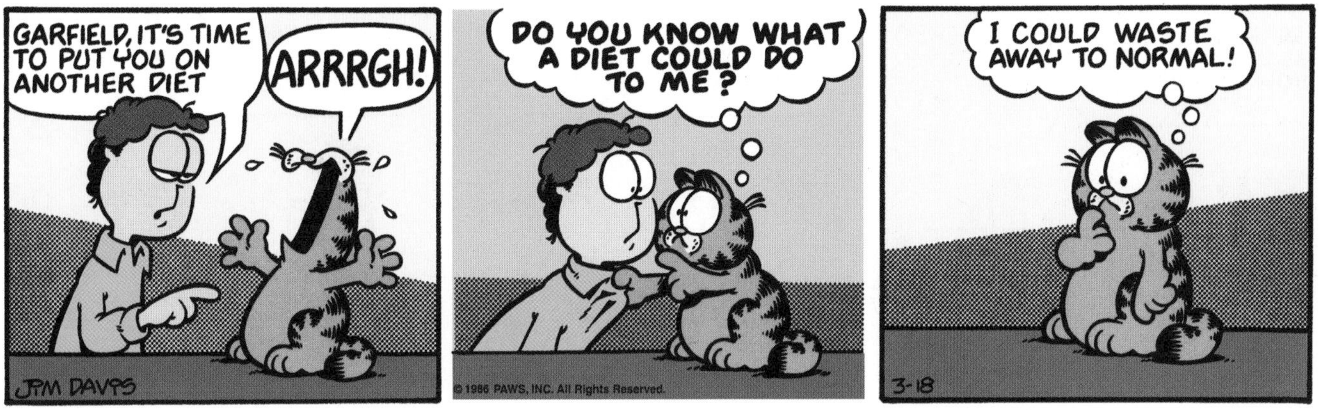
GARFIELD, IT'S TIME TO PUT YOU ON ANOTHER DIET
ARRRGH!
DO YOU KNOW WHAT A DIET COULD DO TO ME?
I COULD WASTE AWAY TO NORMAL!
JIM DAVIS
© 1986 PAWS, INC. All Rights Reserved.
3-18

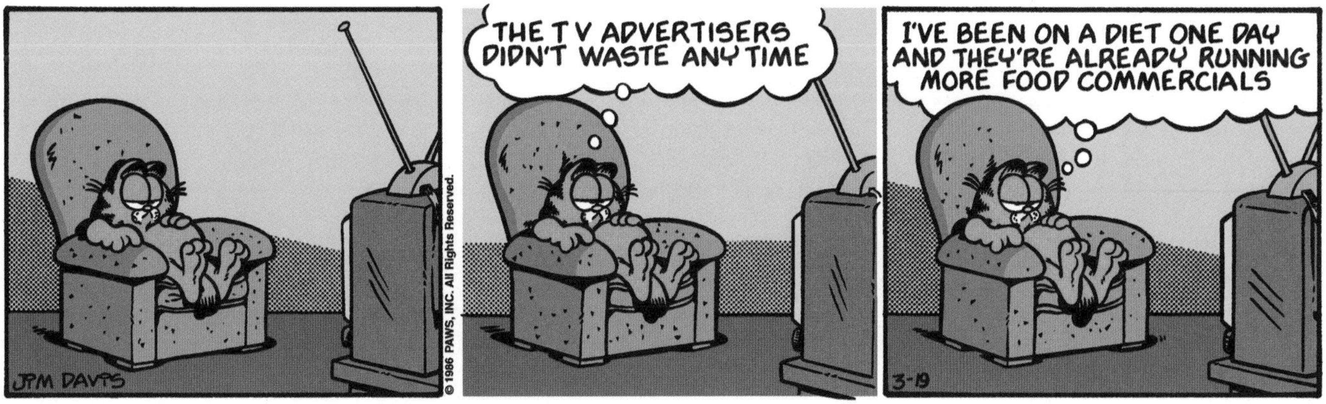
THE TV ADVERTISERS DIDN'T WASTE ANY TIME
I'VE BEEN ON A DIET ONE DAY AND THEY'RE ALREADY RUNNING MORE FOOD COMMERCIALS
JIM DAVIS
© 1986 PAWS, INC. All Rights Reserved.
3-19

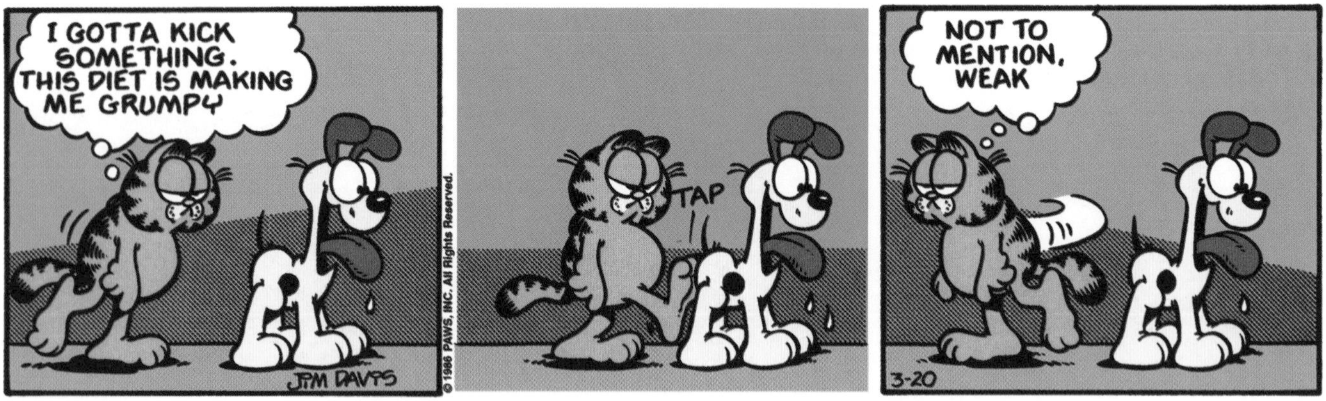
I GOTTA KICK SOMETHING. THIS DIET IS MAKING ME GRUMPY
JIM DAVIS
© 1986 PAWS, INC. All Rights Reserved.
TAP
NOT TO MENTION, WEAK
3-20

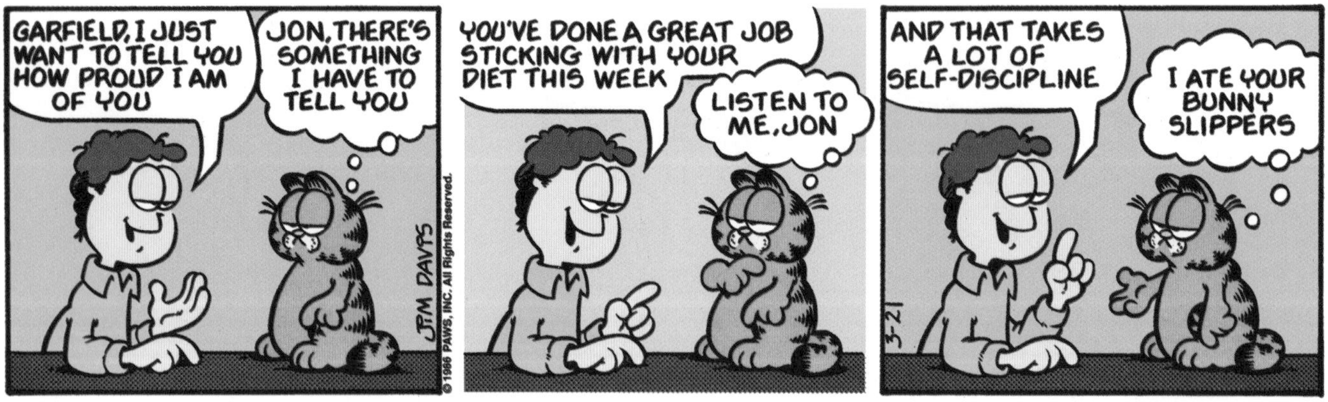
GARFIELD, I JUST WANT TO TELL YOU HOW PROUD I AM OF YOU
JON, THERE'S SOMETHING I HAVE TO TELL YOU
JIM DAVIS
© 1986 PAWS, INC. All Rights Reserved.
YOU'VE DONE A GREAT JOB STICKING WITH YOUR DIET THIS WEEK
LISTEN TO ME, JON
AND THAT TAKES A LOT OF SELF-DISCIPLINE
I ATE YOUR BUNNY SLIPPERS
3-21

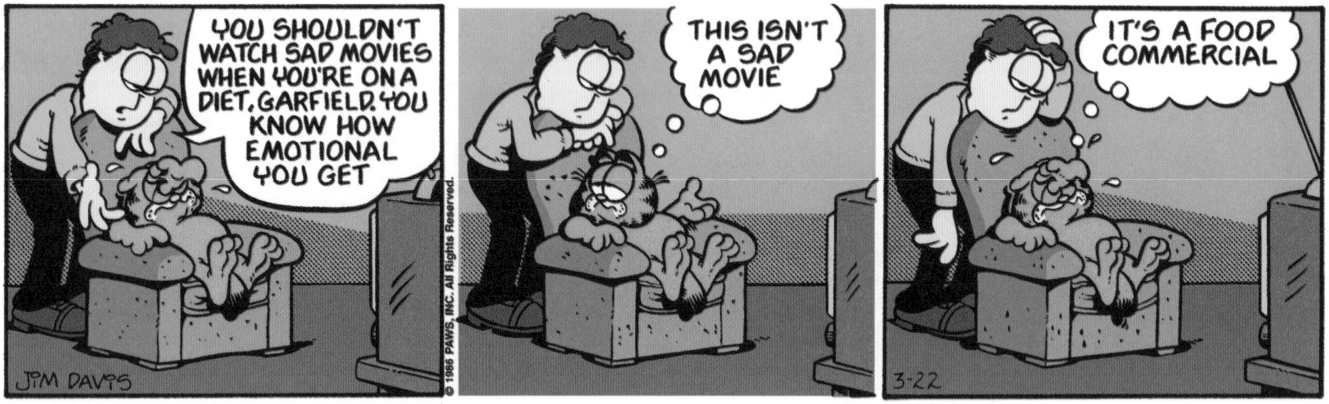
YOU SHOULDN'T WATCH SAD MOVIES WHEN YOU'RE ON A DIET, GARFIELD. YOU KNOW HOW EMOTIONAL YOU GET
JIM DAVIS
© 1986 PAWS, INC. All Rights Reserved.
THIS ISN'T A SAD MOVIE
IT'S A FOOD COMMERCIAL
3-22

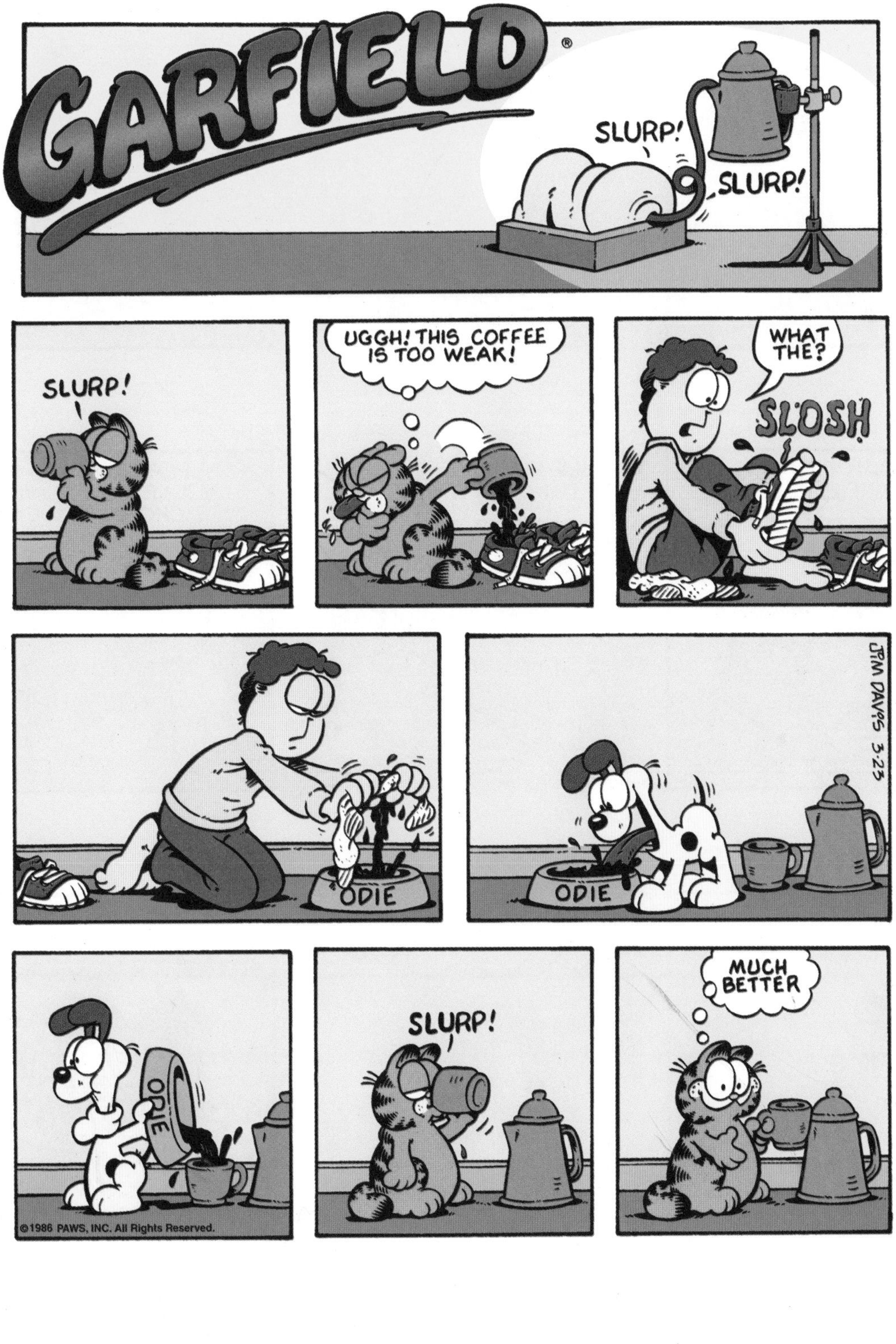
GARFIELD®
SLURP!
SLURP!
SLURP!
UGGH! THIS COFFEE IS TOO WEAK!
WHAT THE?
SLOSH
ODIE
JIM DAVIS 3-23
ODIE
ODIE
SLURP!
MUCH BETTER

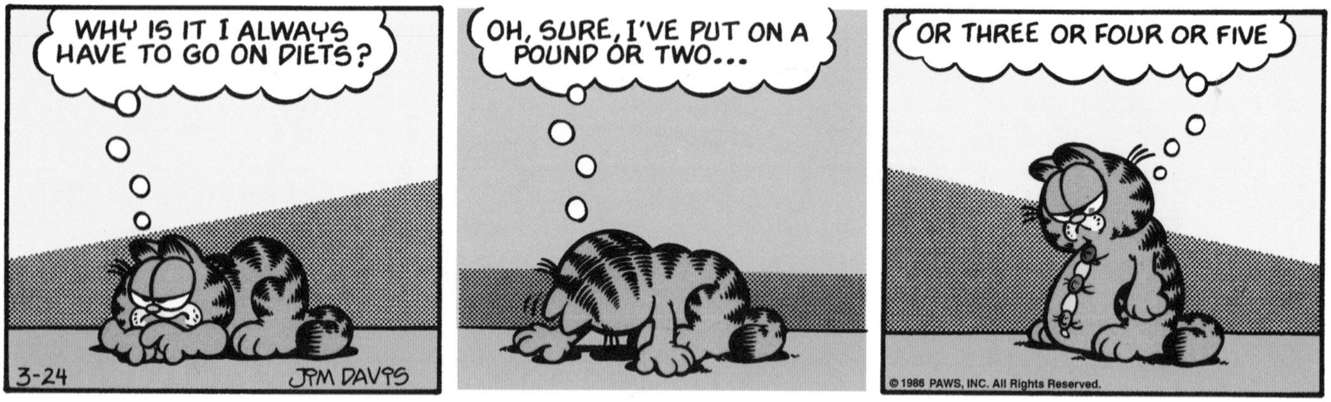
WHY IS IT I ALWAYS HAVE TO GO ON DIETS?
OH, SURE, I'VE PUT ON A POUND OR TWO...
OR THREE OR FOUR OR FIVE
3-24
JIM DAVIS
© 1986 PAWS, INC. All Rights Reserved.

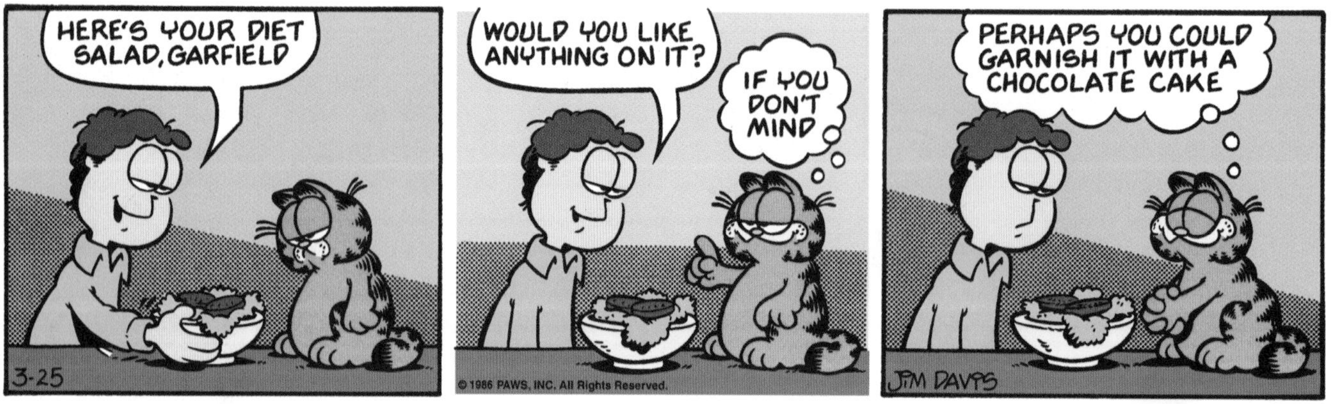
HERE'S YOUR DIET SALAD, GARFIELD
WOULD YOU LIKE ANYTHING ON IT?
IF YOU DON'T MIND
PERHAPS YOU COULD GARNISH IT WITH A CHOCOLATE CAKE
3-25
JIM DAVIS
© 1986 PAWS, INC. All Rights Reserved.

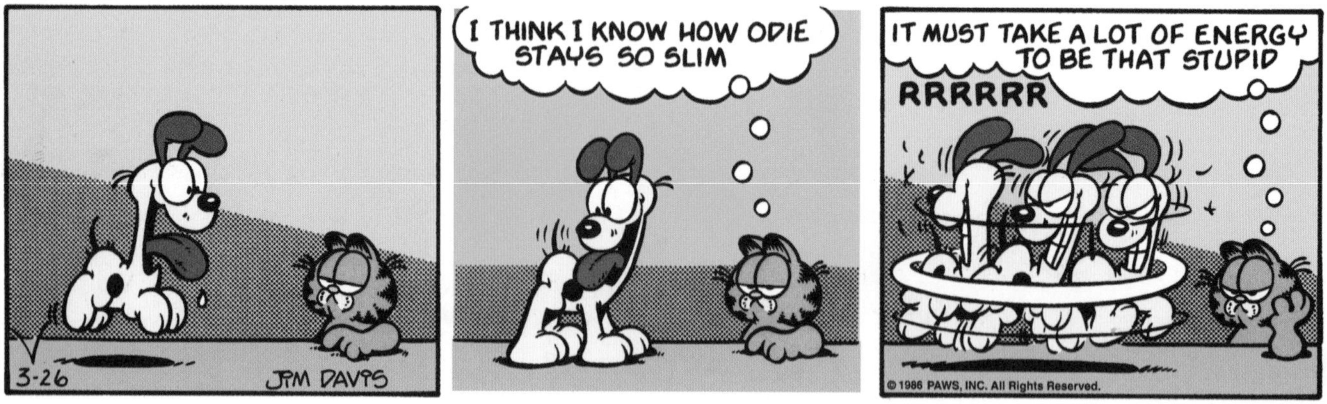
I THINK I KNOW HOW ODIE STAYS SO SLIM
IT MUST TAKE A LOT OF ENERGY TO BE THAT STUPID
RRRRRR
3-26
JIM DAVIS
© 1986 PAWS, INC. All Rights Reserved.

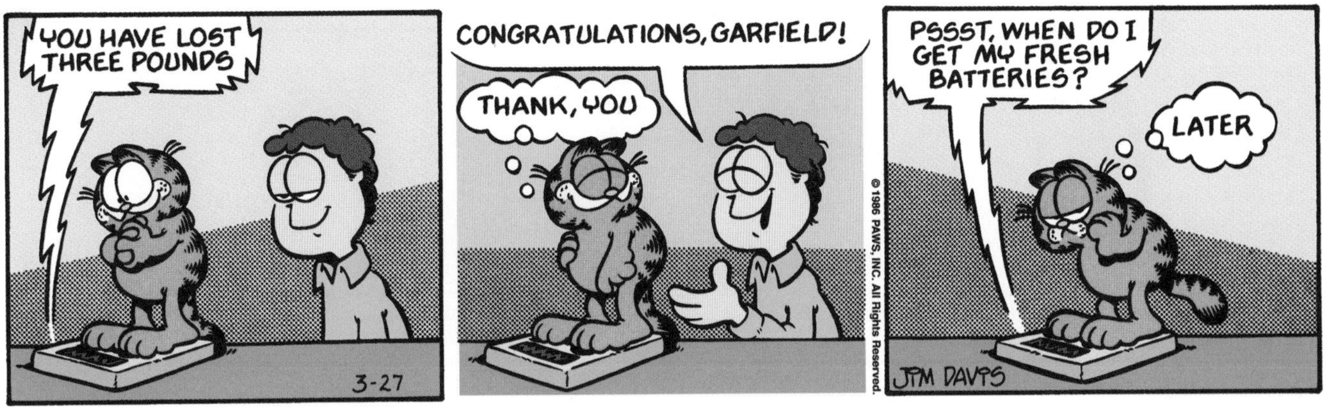
YOU HAVE LOST THREE POUNDS
3-27
CONGRATULATIONS, GARFIELD!
THANK, YOU
© 1986 PAWS, INC. All Rights Reserved.
PSSST, WHEN DO I GET MY FRESH BATTERIES?
LATER
JIM DAVIS

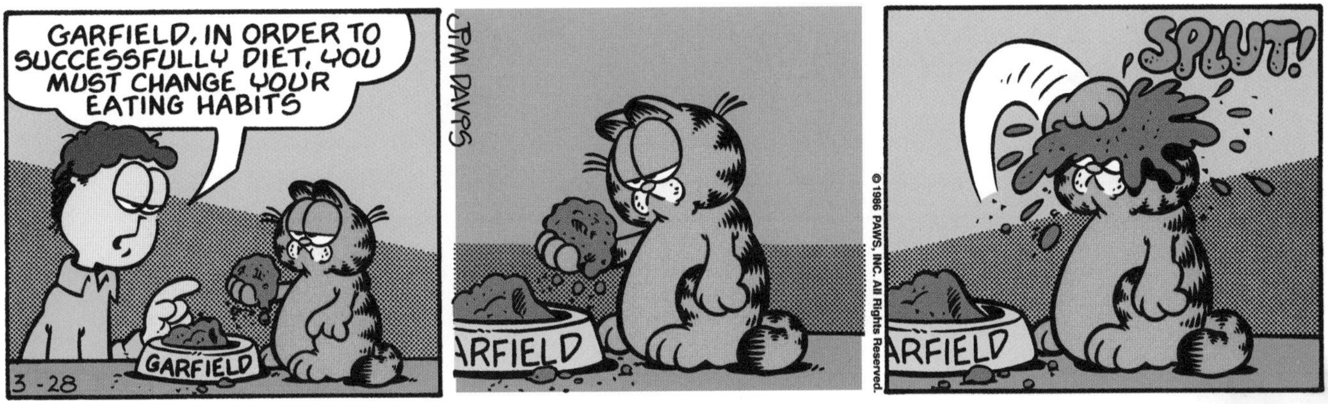
GARFIELD, IN ORDER TO SUCCESSFULLY DIET, YOU MUST CHANGE YOUR EATING HABITS
GARFIELD
3-28
JIM DAVIS
RFIELD
© 1986 PAWS, INC. All Rights Reserved.
SPLUT!
RFIELD

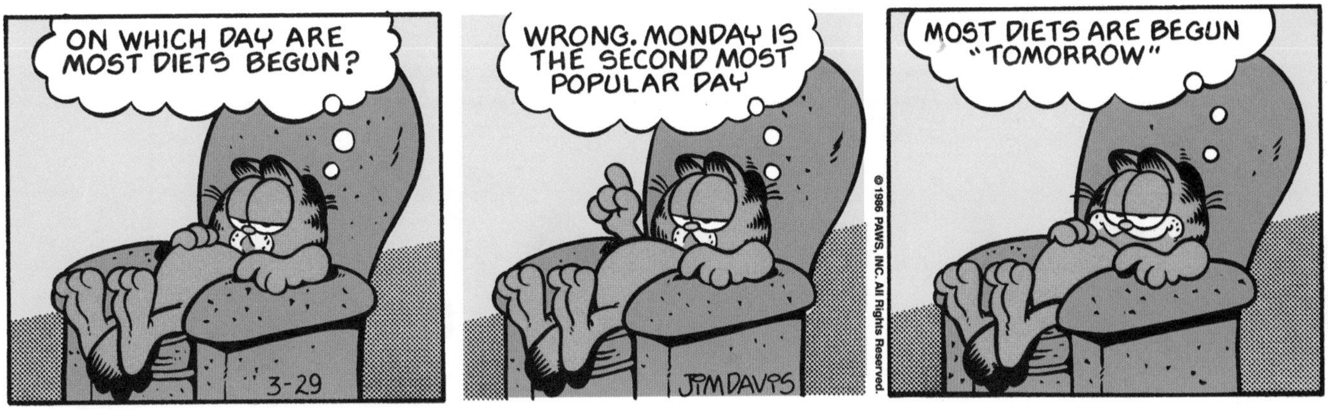
ON WHICH DAY ARE MOST DIETS BEGUN?
3-29
WRONG. MONDAY IS THE SECOND MOST POPULAR DAY
JIM DAVIS
© 1986 PAWS, INC. All Rights Reserved.
MOST DIETS ARE BEGUN "TOMORROW"

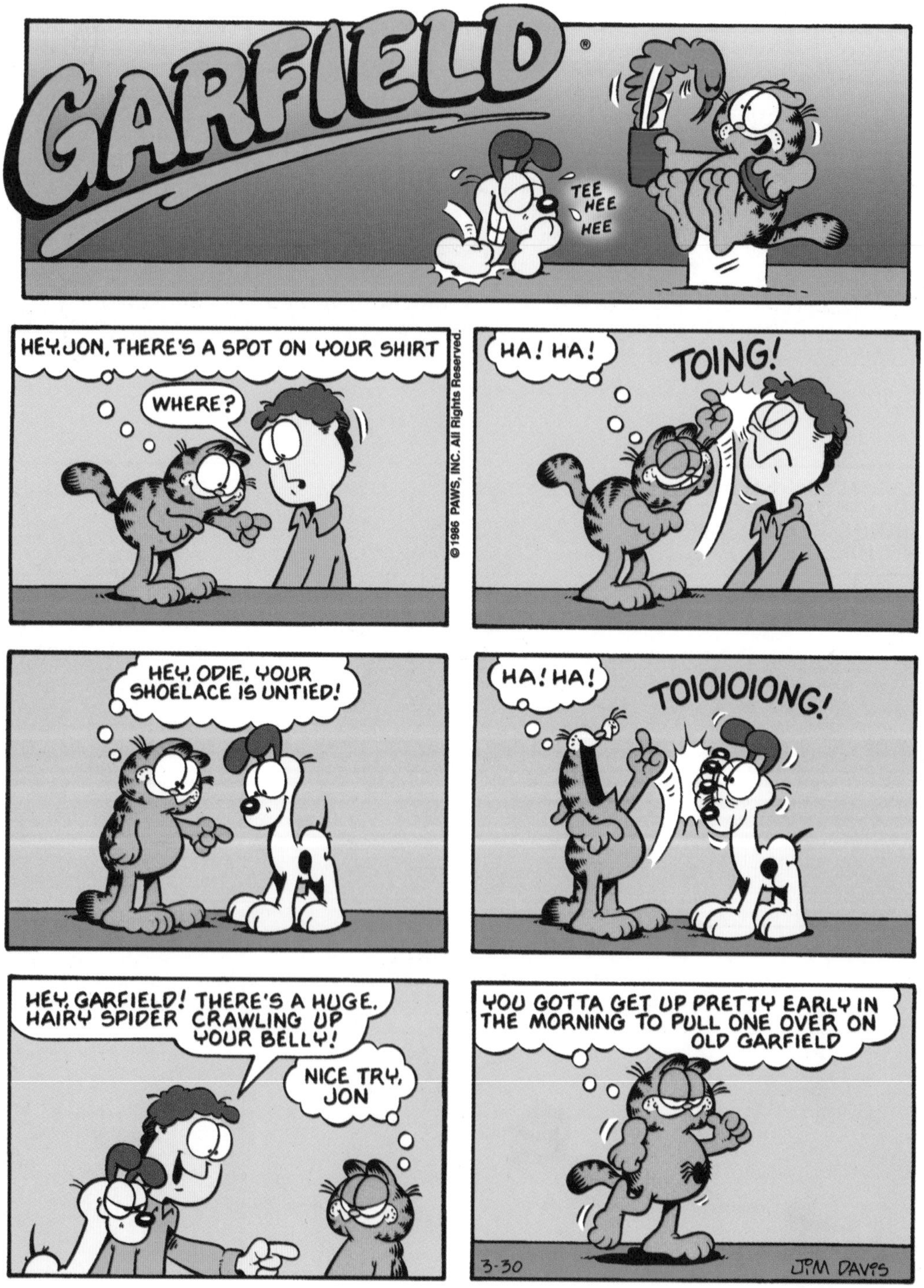
GARFIELD®
TEE HEE HEE
© 1986 PAWS, INC. All Rights Reserved.
HEY, JON, THERE'S A SPOT ON YOUR SHIRT
WHERE?
HA! HA!
TOING!
HEY, ODIE, YOUR SHOELACE IS UNTIED!
HA! HA!
TOIOIOIONG!
HEY, GARFIELD! THERE'S A HUGE, HAIRY SPIDER CRAWLING UP YOUR BELLY!
NICE TRY, JON
YOU GOTTA GET UP PRETTY EARLY IN THE MORNING TO PULL ONE OVER ON OLD GARFIELD
3-30
JIM DAVIS

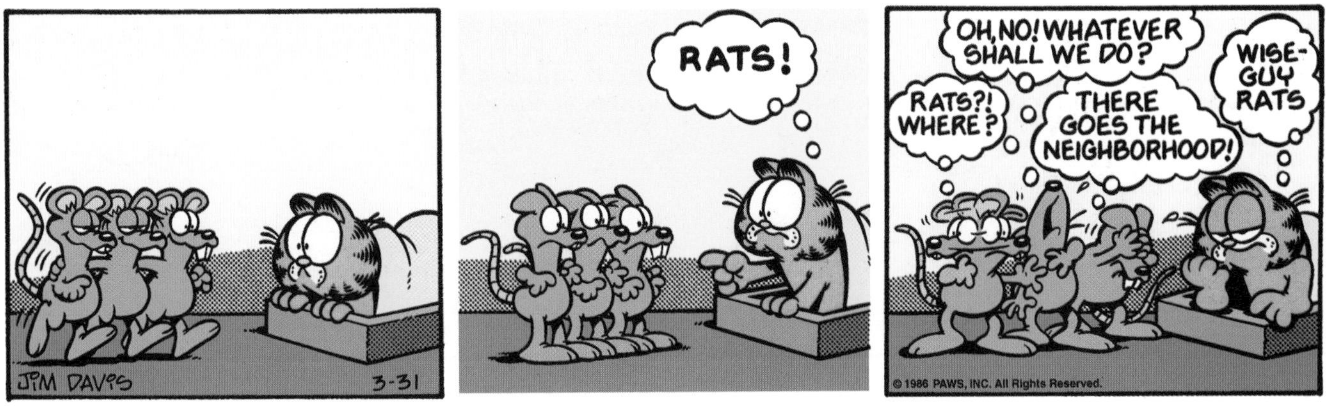
JIM DAVIS
3-31
RATS!
OH, NO! WHATEVER SHALL WE DO?
RATS?! WHERE?
THERE GOES THE NEIGHBORHOOD!
WISE-GUY RATS
© 1986 PAWS, INC. All Rights Reserved.

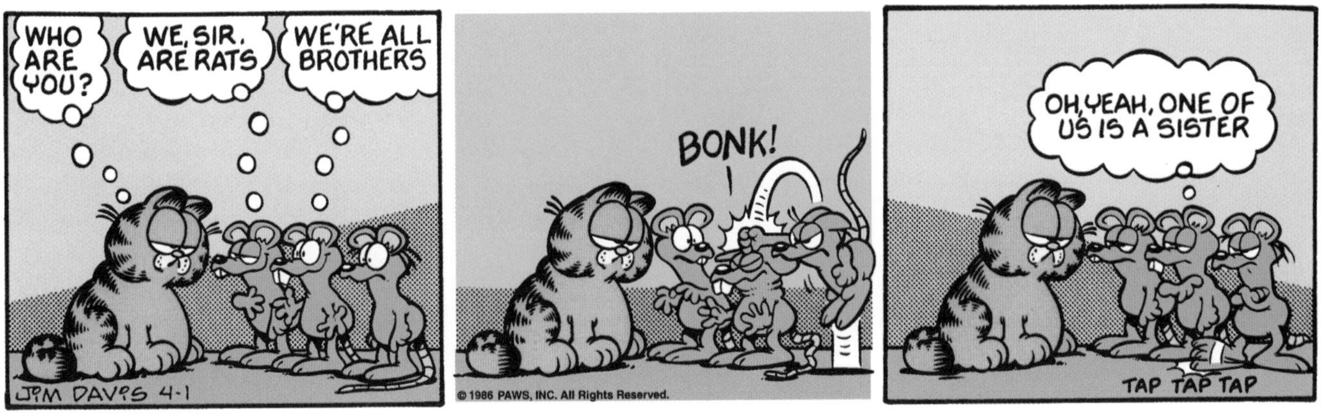
WHO ARE YOU?
WE, SIR, ARE RATS
WE'RE ALL BROTHERS
JIM DAVIS 4-1
BONK!
© 1986 PAWS, INC. All Rights Reserved.
OH, YEAH, ONE OF US IS A SISTER
TAP TAP TAP

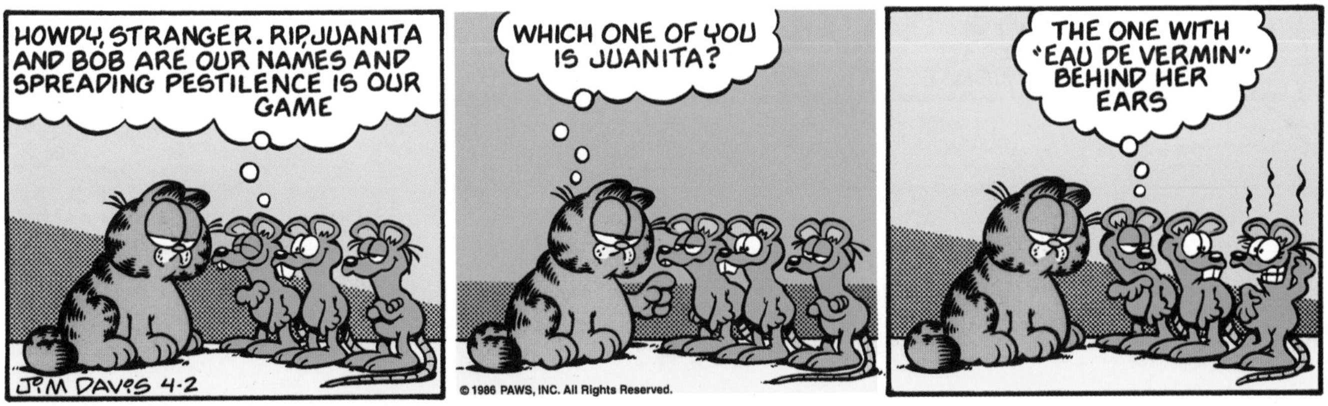
HOWDY, STRANGER. RIP, JUANITA AND BOB ARE OUR NAMES AND SPREADING PESTILENCE IS OUR GAME
JIM DAVIS 4-2
WHICH ONE OF YOU IS JUANITA?
© 1986 PAWS, INC. All Rights Reserved.
THE ONE WITH "EAU DE VERMIN" BEHIND HER EARS

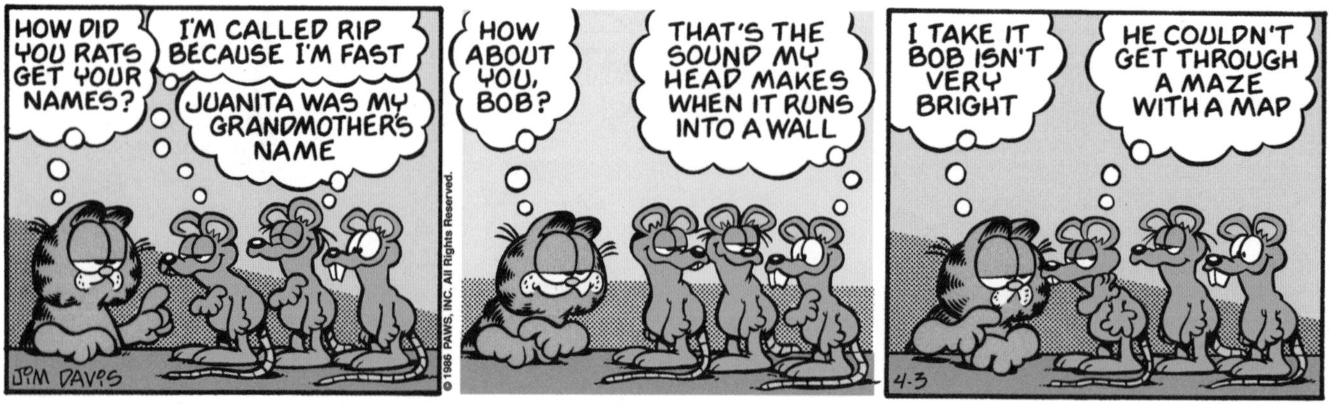
HOW DID YOU RATS GET YOUR NAMES?
I'M CALLED RIP BECAUSE I'M FAST
JUANITA WAS MY GRANDMOTHER'S NAME
JIM DAVIS
© 1986 PAWS, INC. All Rights Reserved.
HOW ABOUT YOU, BOB?
THAT'S THE SOUND MY HEAD MAKES WHEN IT RUNS INTO A WALL
I TAKE IT BOB ISN'T VERY BRIGHT
HE COULDN'T GET THROUGH A MAZE WITH A MAP
4-3

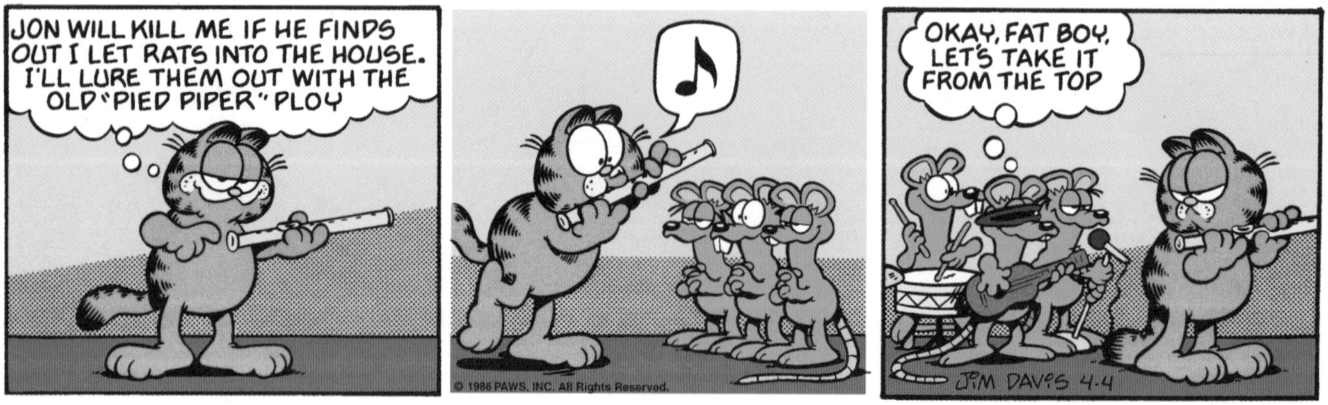
JON WILL KILL ME IF HE FINDS OUT I LET RATS INTO THE HOUSE. I'LL LURE THEM OUT WITH THE OLD "PIED PIPER" PLOY
♪
© 1986 PAWS, INC. All Rights Reserved.
OKAY, FAT BOY, LET'S TAKE IT FROM THE TOP
JIM DAVIS 4-4

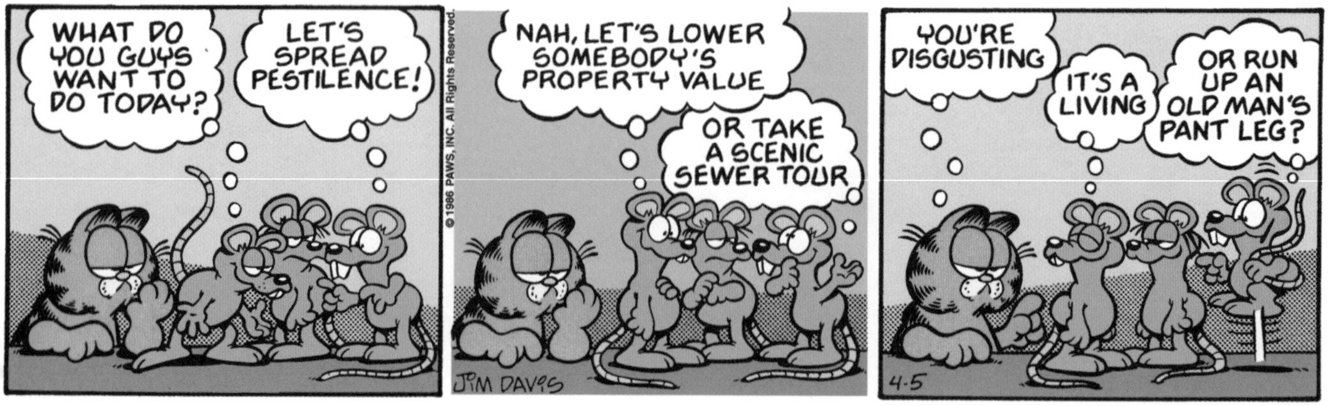
WHAT DO YOU GUYS WANT TO DO TODAY?
LET'S SPREAD PESTILENCE!
© 1986 PAWS, INC. All Rights Reserved.
NAH, LET'S LOWER SOMEBODY'S PROPERTY VALUE
OR TAKE A SCENIC SEWER TOUR
JIM DAVIS
YOU'RE DISGUSTING
IT'S A LIVING
OR RUN UP AN OLD MAN'S PANT LEG?
4-5

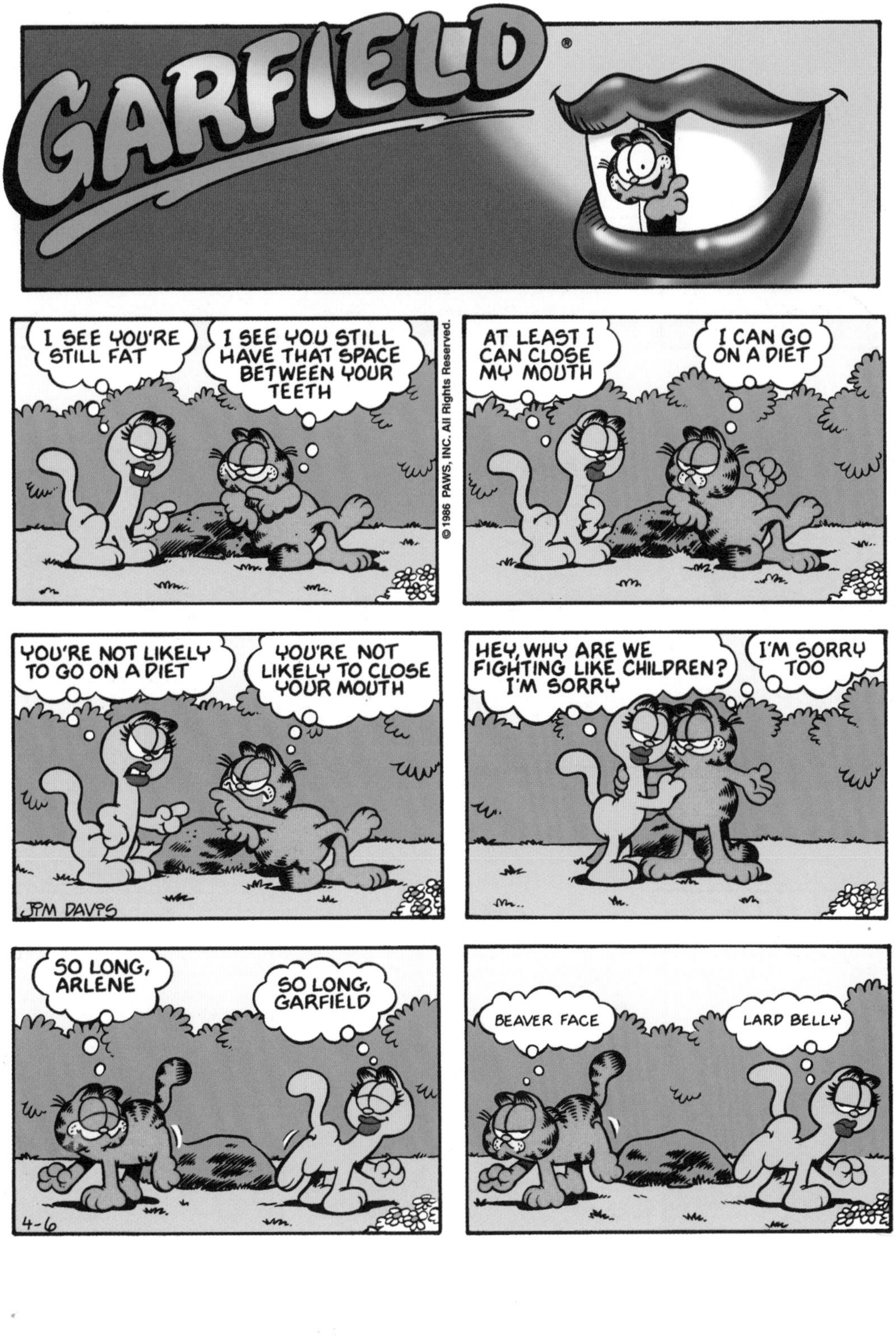
GARFIELD®
I SEE YOU'RE STILL FAT
I SEE YOU STILL HAVE THAT SPACE BETWEEN YOUR TEETH
© 1986 PAWS, INC. All Rights Reserved.
AT LEAST I CAN CLOSE MY MOUTH
I CAN GO ON A DIET
YOU'RE NOT LIKELY TO GO ON A DIET
YOU'RE NOT LIKELY TO CLOSE YOUR MOUTH
JIM DAVIS
HEY, WHY ARE WE FIGHTING LIKE CHILDREN? I'M SORRY
I'M SORRY TOO
SO LONG, ARLENE
SO LONG, GARFIELD
4-6
BEAVER FACE
LARD BELLY

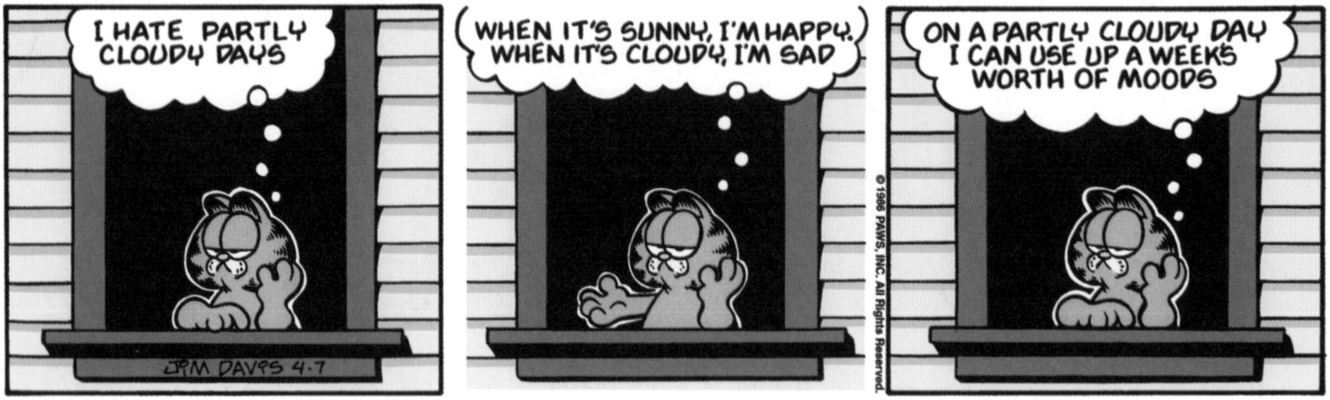
I HATE PARTLY CLOUDY DAYS
WHEN IT'S SUNNY, I'M HAPPY. WHEN IT'S CLOUDY, I'M SAD
ON A PARTLY CLOUDY DAY I CAN USE UP A WEEK'S WORTH OF MOODS
JIM DAVIS 4-7

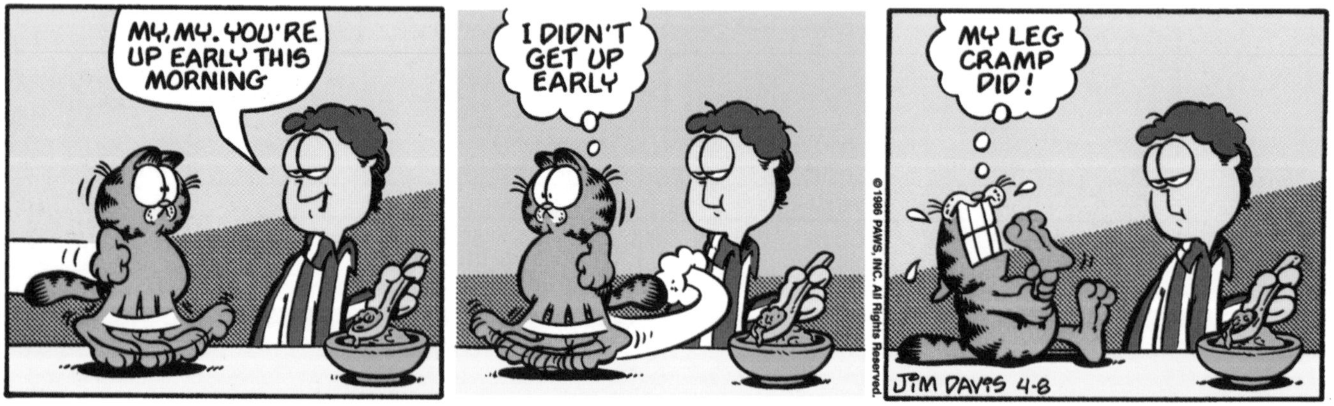
MY, MY. YOU'RE UP EARLY THIS MORNING
I DIDN'T GET UP EARLY
MY LEG CRAMP DID!
JIM DAVIS 4-8

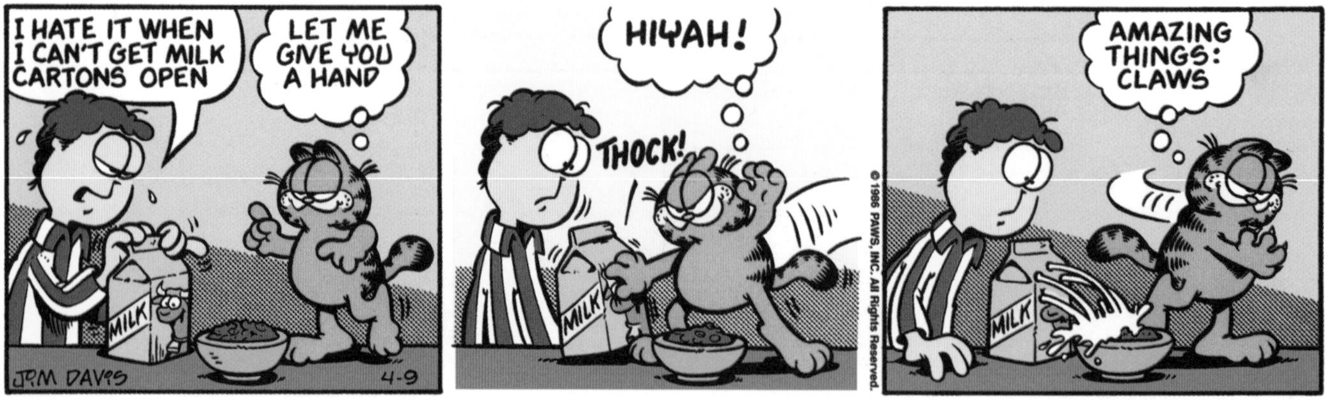
I HATE IT WHEN I CAN'T GET MILK CARTONS OPEN
LET ME GIVE YOU A HAND
MILK
JIM DAVIS 4-9
HIYAH!
THOCK!
MILK
AMAZING THINGS: CLAWS
MILK

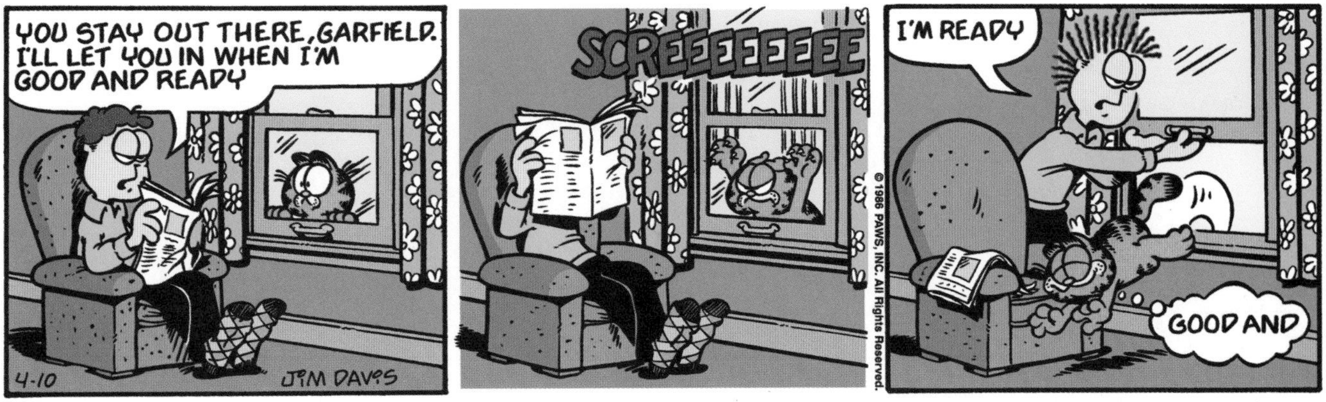
YOU STAY OUT THERE, GARFIELD. I'LL LET YOU IN WHEN I'M GOOD AND READY
4-10
JIM DAVIS
SCREEEEEEEEE
© 1986 PAWS, INC. All Rights Reserved.
I'M READY
GOOD AND

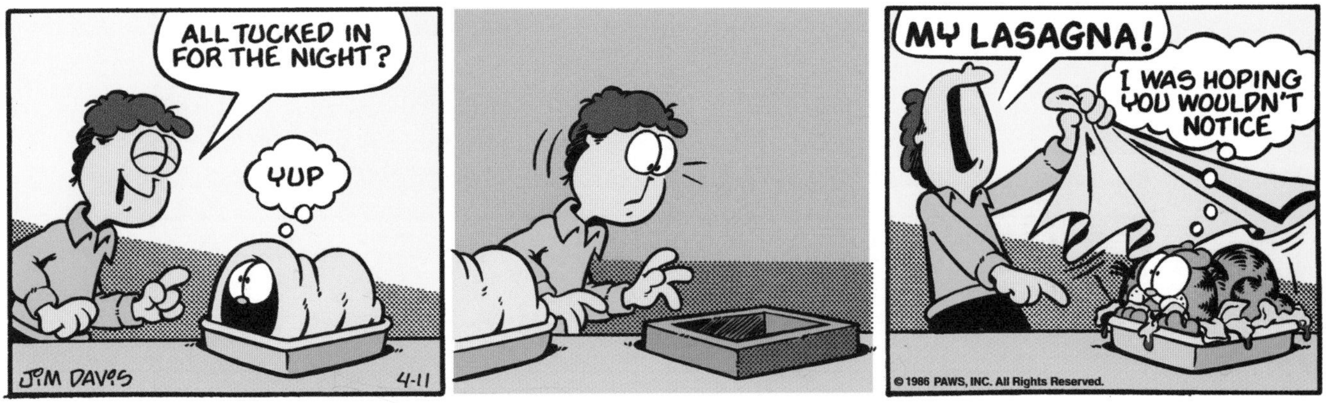
ALL TUCKED IN FOR THE NIGHT?
YUP
JIM DAVIS
4-11
MY LASAGNA!
I WAS HOPING YOU WOULDN'T NOTICE
© 1986 PAWS, INC. All Rights Reserved.

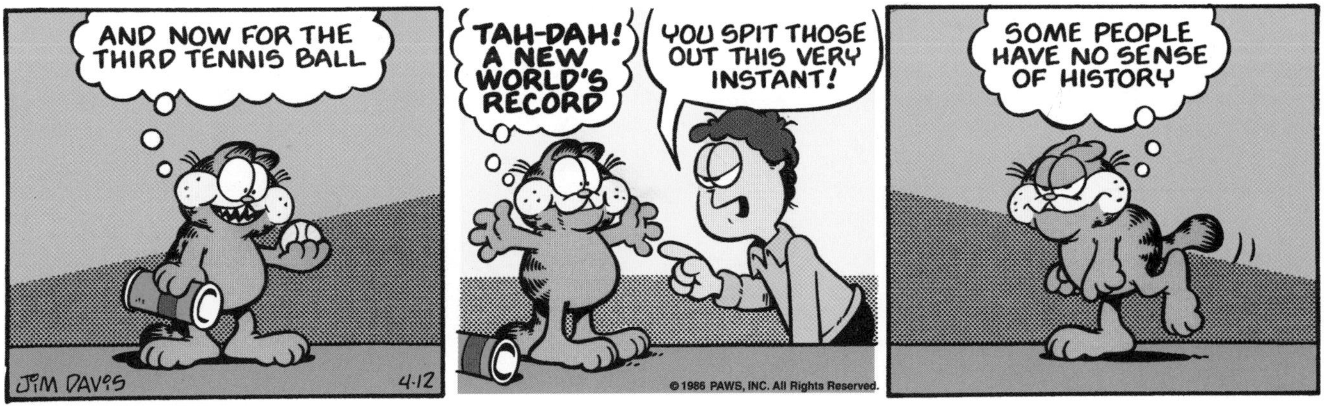
AND NOW FOR THE THIRD TENNIS BALL
JIM DAVIS
4-12
TAH-DAH! A NEW WORLD'S RECORD
YOU SPIT THOSE OUT THIS VERY INSTANT!
© 1986 PAWS, INC. All Rights Reserved.
SOME PEOPLE HAVE NO SENSE OF HISTORY

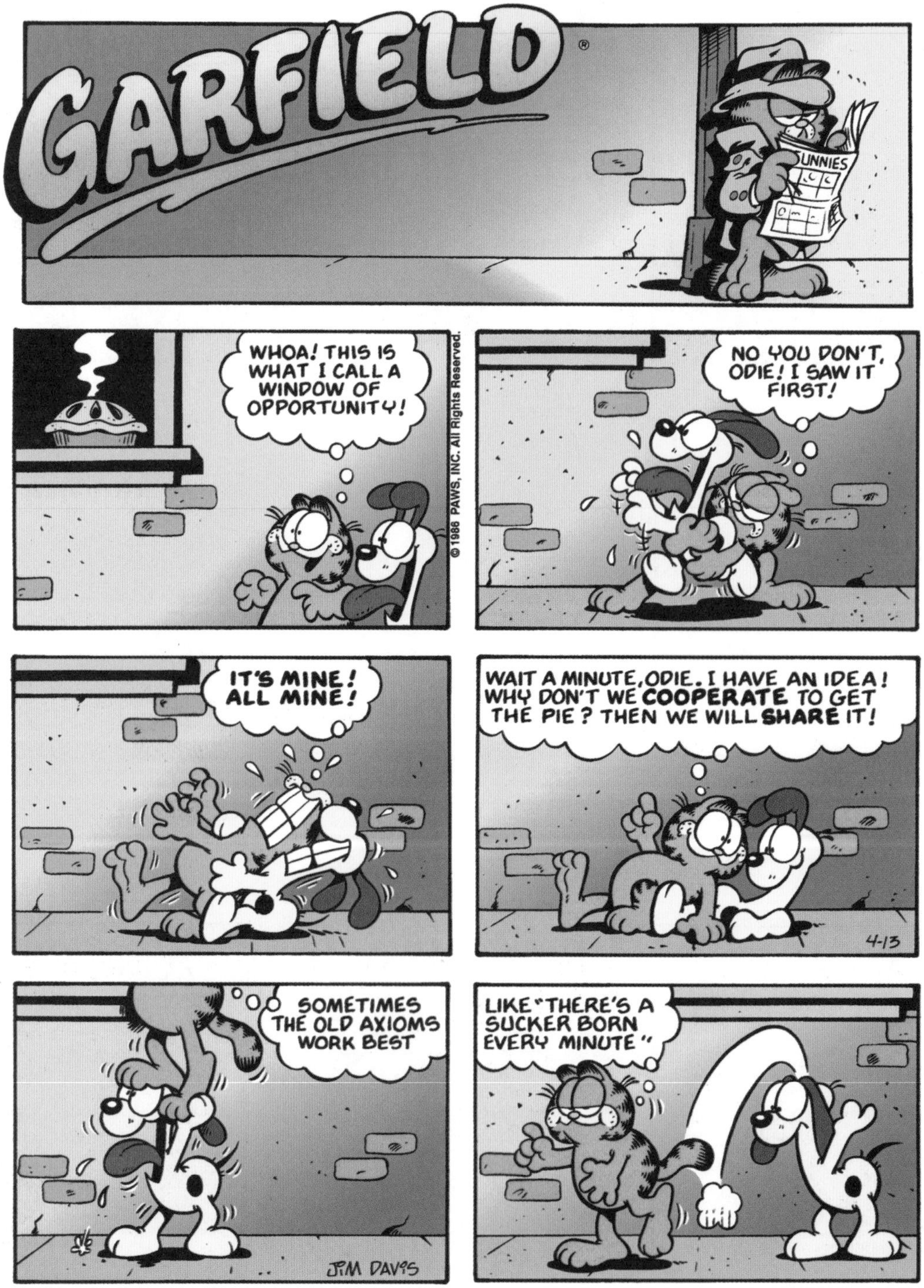
GARFIELD
SUNNIES
WHOA! THIS IS WHAT I CALL A WINDOW OF OPPORTUNITY!
© 1988 PAWS, INC. All Rights Reserved.
NO YOU DON'T, ODIE! I SAW IT FIRST!
IT'S MINE! ALL MINE!
WAIT A MINUTE, ODIE. I HAVE AN IDEA! WHY DON'T WE COOPERATE TO GET THE PIE? THEN WE WILL SHARE IT!
4-13
SOMETIMES THE OLD AXIOMS WORK BEST
JIM DAVIS
LIKE "THERE'S A SUCKER BORN EVERY MINUTE"

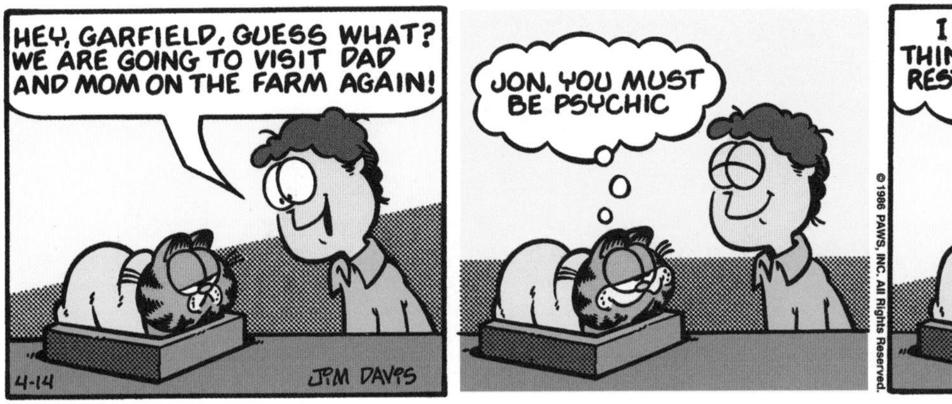
HEY, GARFIELD, GUESS WHAT? WE ARE GOING TO VISIT DAD AND MOM ON THE FARM AGAIN!
4-14
JIM DAVIS
JON, YOU MUST BE PSYCHIC
I WAS JUST LYING HERE THINKING IT WAS TIME TO RESTOCK THE BURRS IN MY FUR
© 1986 PAWS, INC. All Rights Reserved.

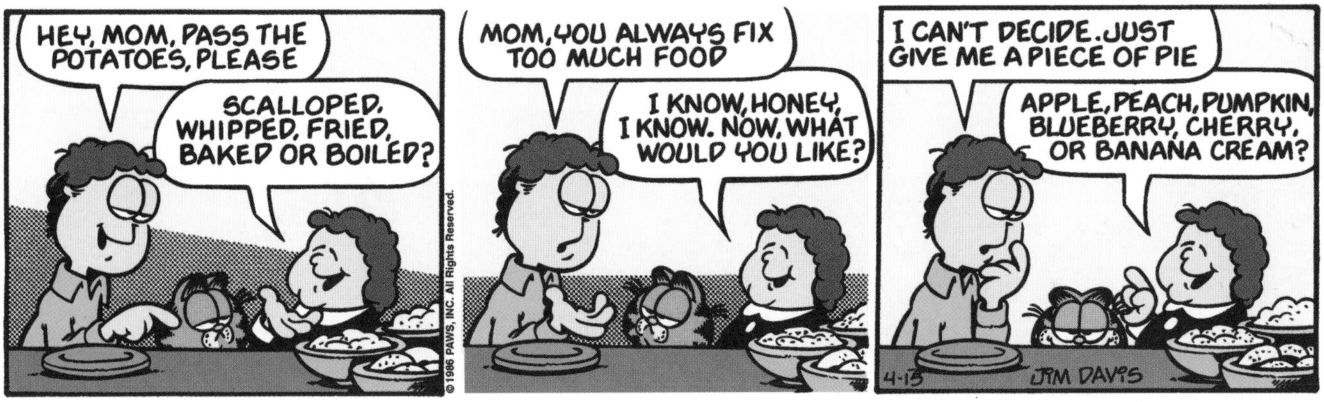
HEY, MOM, PASS THE POTATOES, PLEASE
SCALLOPED, WHIPPED, FRIED, BAKED OR BOILED?
© 1986 PAWS, INC. All Rights Reserved.
MOM, YOU ALWAYS FIX TOO MUCH FOOD
I KNOW, HONEY, I KNOW. NOW, WHAT WOULD YOU LIKE?
I CAN'T DECIDE. JUST GIVE ME A PIECE OF PIE
APPLE, PEACH, PUMPKIN, BLUEBERRY, CHERRY, OR BANANA CREAM?
4-15
JIM DAVIS

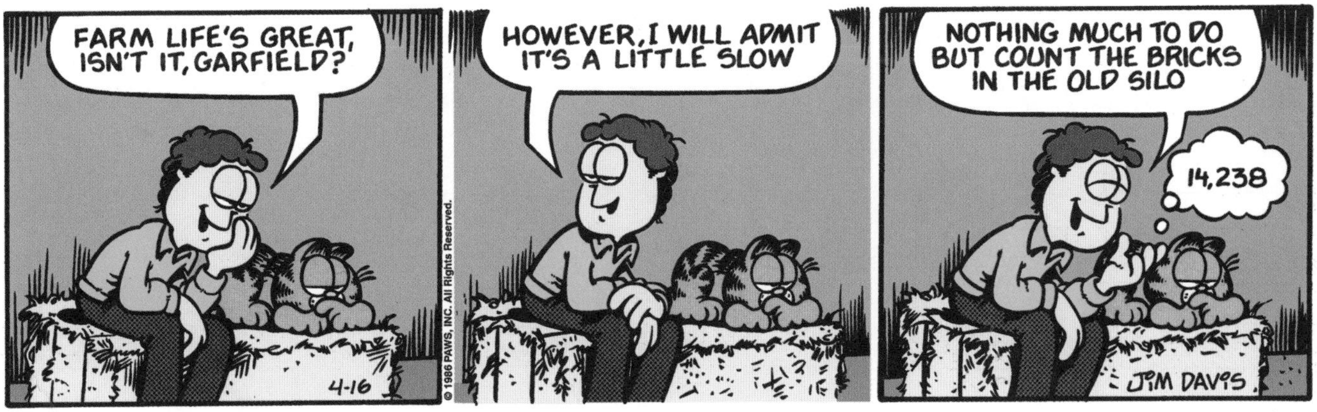
FARM LIFE'S GREAT, ISN'T IT, GARFIELD?
4-16
© 1986 PAWS, INC. All Rights Reserved.
HOWEVER, I WILL ADMIT IT'S A LITTLE SLOW
NOTHING MUCH TO DO BUT COUNT THE BRICKS IN THE OLD SILO
14,238
JIM DAVIS

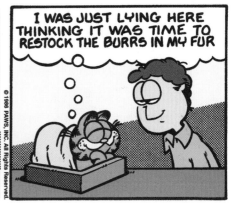

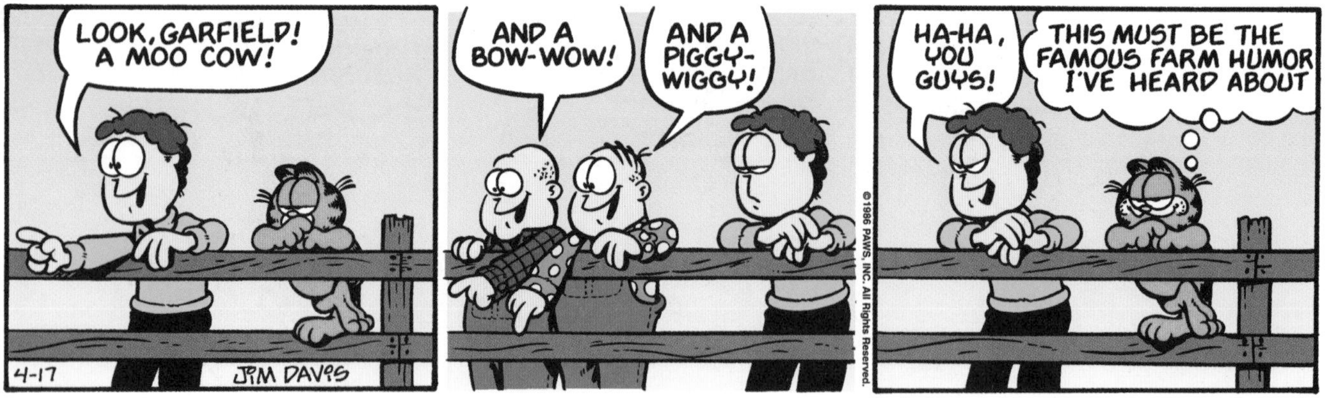
LOOK, GARFIELD! A MOO COW!
4-17
JIM DAVIS
AND A BOW-WOW!
AND A PIGGY-WIGGY!
©1986 PAWS, INC. All Rights Reserved.
HA-HA, YOU GUYS!
THIS MUST BE THE FAMOUS FARM HUMOR I'VE HEARD ABOUT

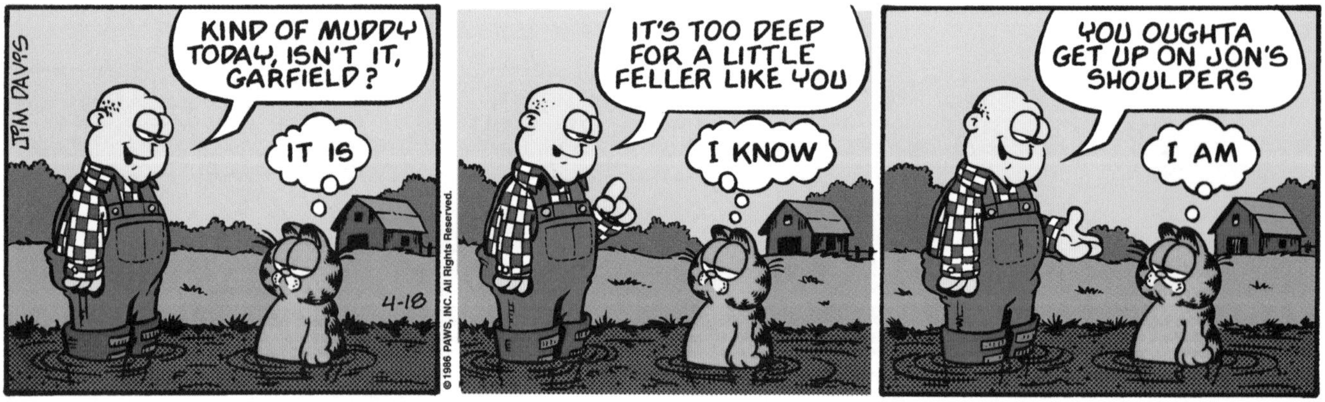
JIM DAVIS
KIND OF MUDDY TODAY, ISN'T IT, GARFIELD?
IT IS
4-18
©1986 PAWS, INC. All Rights Reserved.
IT'S TOO DEEP FOR A LITTLE FELLER LIKE YOU
I KNOW
YOU OUGHTA GET UP ON JON'S SHOULDERS
I AM

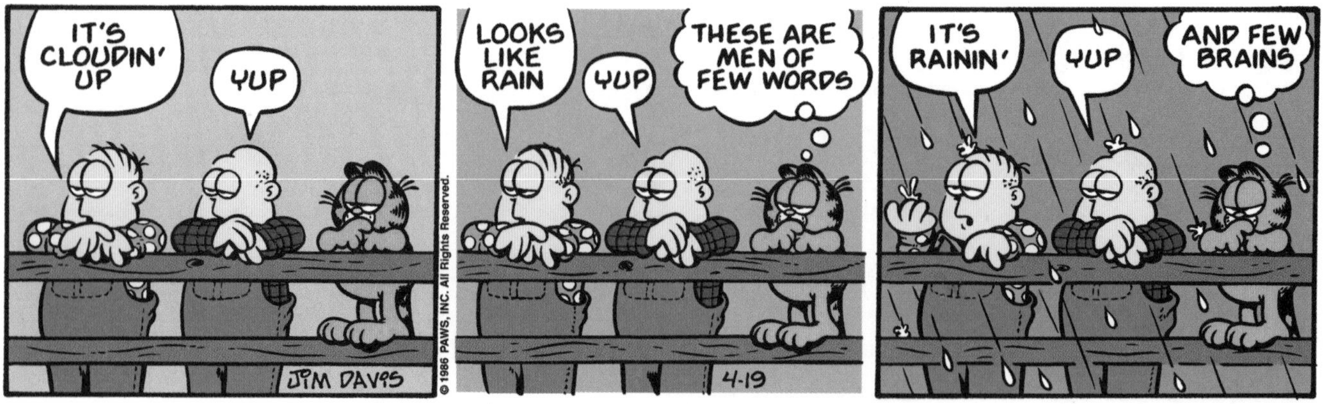
IT'S CLOUDIN' UP
YUP
JIM DAVIS
© 1986 PAWS, INC. All Rights Reserved.
LOOKS LIKE RAIN
YUP
THESE ARE MEN OF FEW WORDS
4-19
IT'S RAININ'
YUP
AND FEW BRAINS

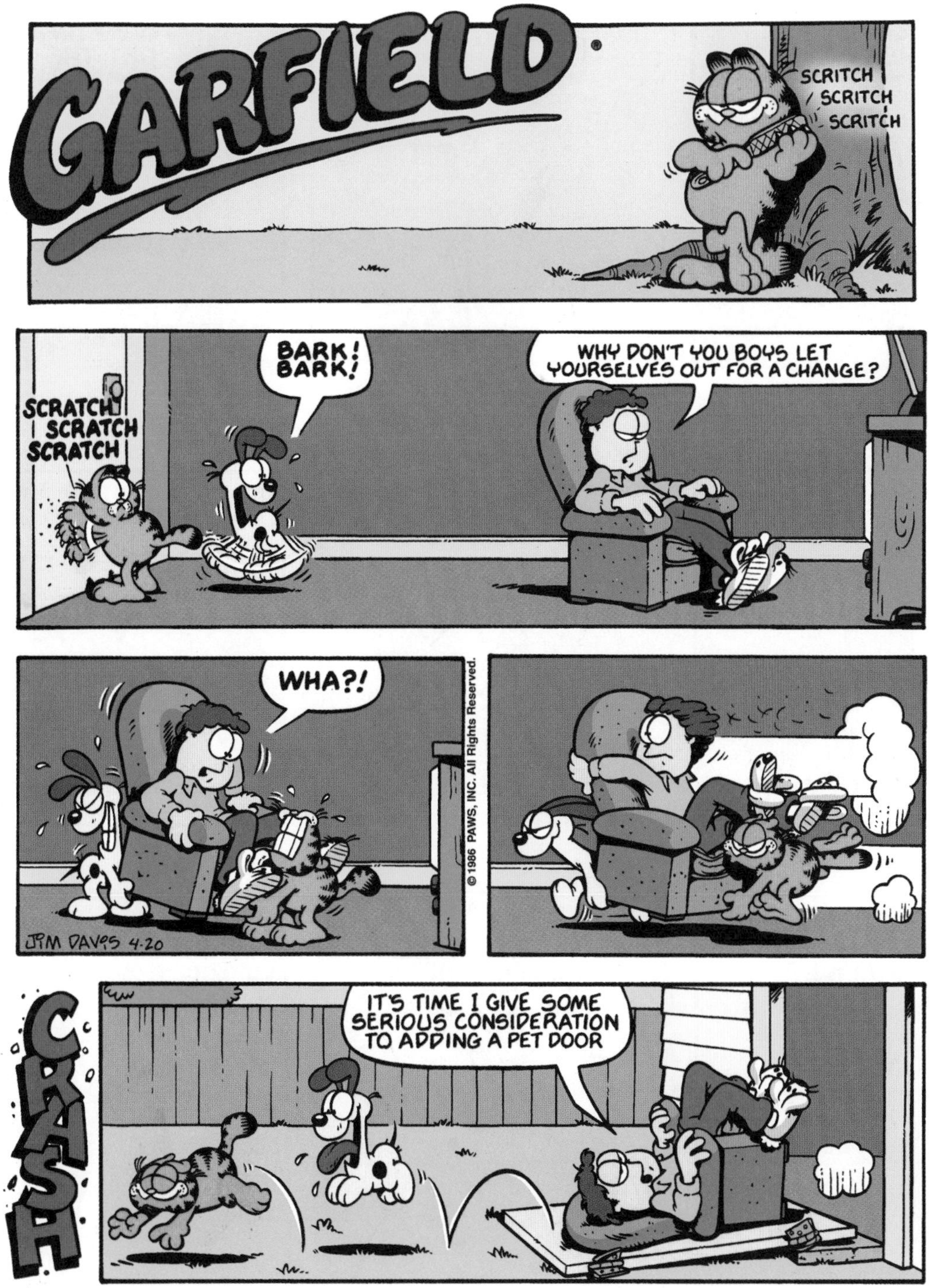
GARFIELD®
SCRITCH SCRITCH SCRITCH
SCRATCH SCRATCH SCRATCH
BARK! BARK!
WHY DON'T YOU BOYS LET YOURSELVES OUT FOR A CHANGE?
WHA?!
JIM DAVIS 4-20
© 1986 PAWS, INC. All Rights Reserved.
CRASH
IT'S TIME I GIVE SOME SERIOUS CONSIDERATION TO ADDING A PET DOOR

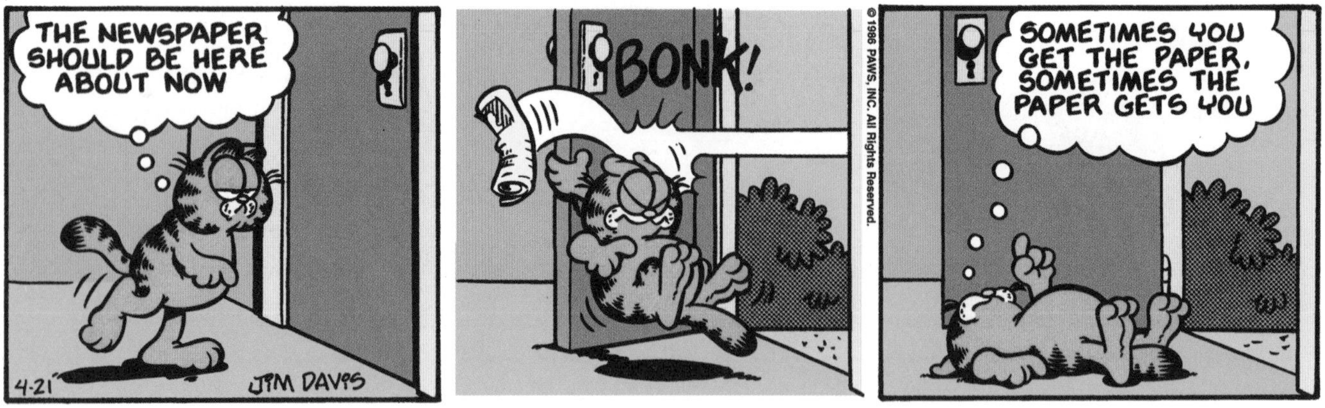
THE NEWSPAPER SHOULD BE HERE ABOUT NOW
4-21
JIM DAVIS
BONK!
© 1986 PAWS, INC. All Rights Reserved.
SOMETIMES YOU GET THE PAPER, SOMETIMES THE PAPER GETS YOU

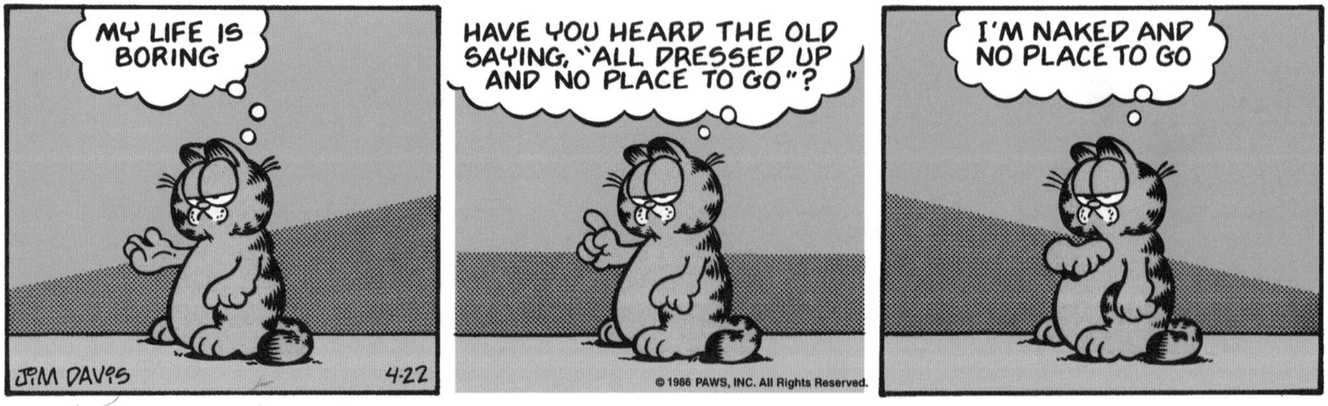
MY LIFE IS BORING
JIM DAVIS
4-22
HAVE YOU HEARD THE OLD SAYING, "ALL DRESSED UP AND NO PLACE TO GO"?
© 1986 PAWS, INC. All Rights Reserved.
I'M NAKED AND NO PLACE TO GO

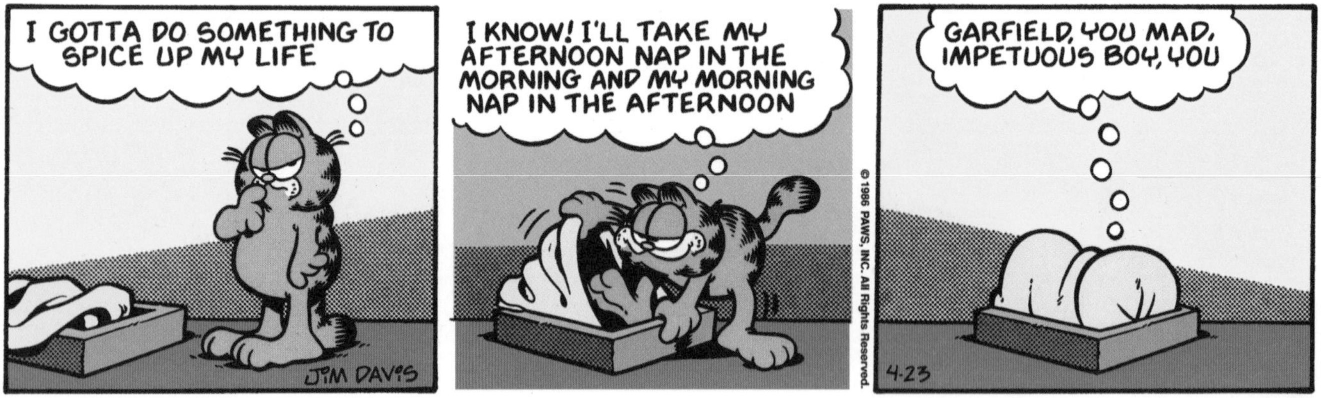
I GOTTA DO SOMETHING TO SPICE UP MY LIFE
JIM DAVIS
I KNOW! I'LL TAKE MY AFTERNOON NAP IN THE MORNING AND MY MORNING NAP IN THE AFTERNOON
© 1986 PAWS, INC. All Rights Reserved.
GARFIELD, YOU MAD, IMPETUOUS BOY, YOU
4-23

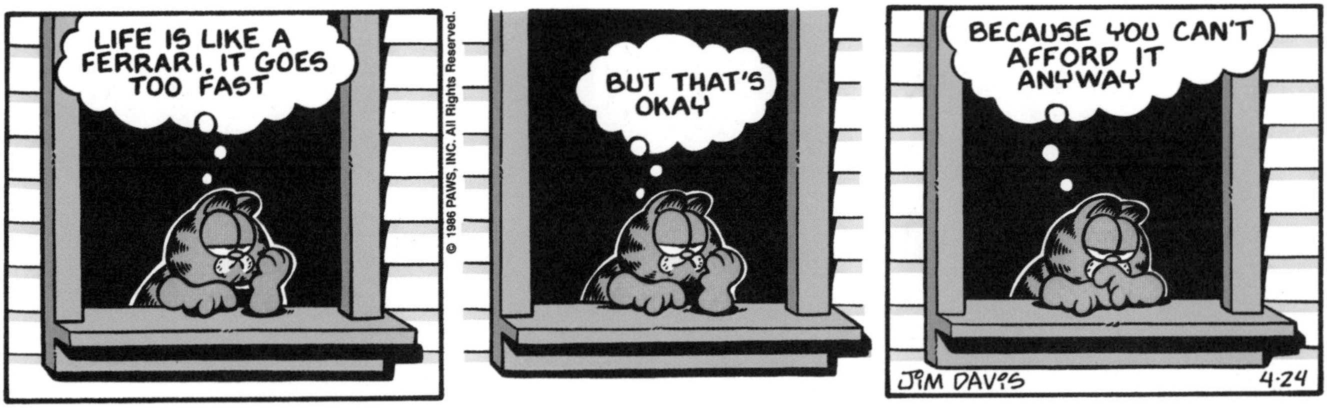
LIFE IS LIKE A FERRARI. IT GOES TOO FAST
© 1986 PAWS, INC. All Rights Reserved.
BUT THAT'S OKAY
BECAUSE YOU CAN'T AFFORD IT ANYWAY
JIM DAVIS
4·24

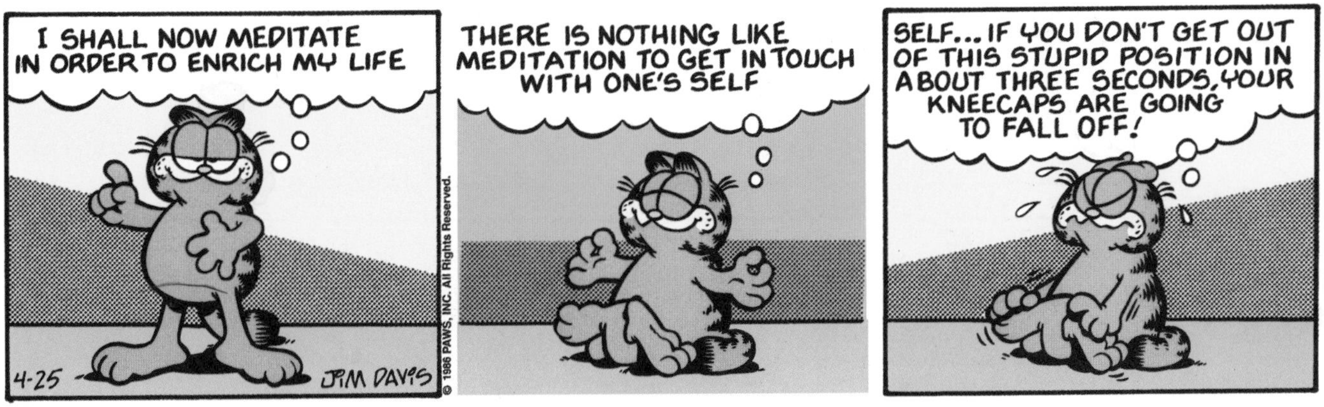
I SHALL NOW MEDITATE IN ORDER TO ENRICH MY LIFE
4-25
JIM DAVIS
© 1986 PAWS, INC. All Rights Reserved.
THERE IS NOTHING LIKE MEDITATION TO GET IN TOUCH WITH ONE'S SELF
SELF... IF YOU DON'T GET OUT OF THIS STUPID POSITION IN ABOUT THREE SECONDS, YOUR KNEECAPS ARE GOING TO FALL OFF!

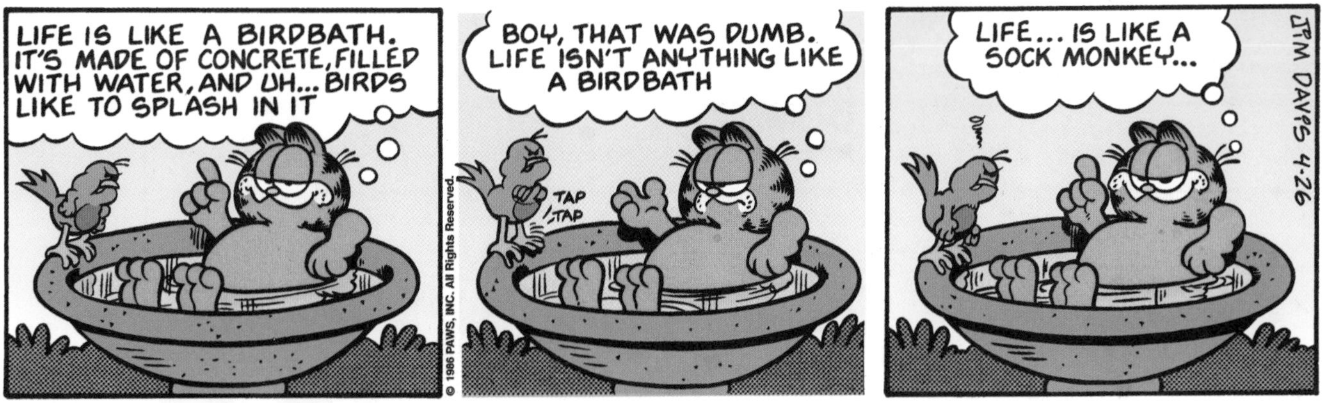
LIFE IS LIKE A BIRDBATH. IT'S MADE OF CONCRETE, FILLED WITH WATER, AND UH... BIRDS LIKE TO SPLASH IN IT
© 1986 PAWS, INC. All Rights Reserved.
BOY, THAT WAS DUMB. LIFE ISN'T ANYTHING LIKE A BIRDBATH
TAP TAP
LIFE... IS LIKE A SOCK MONKEY...
JIM DAVIS 4-26

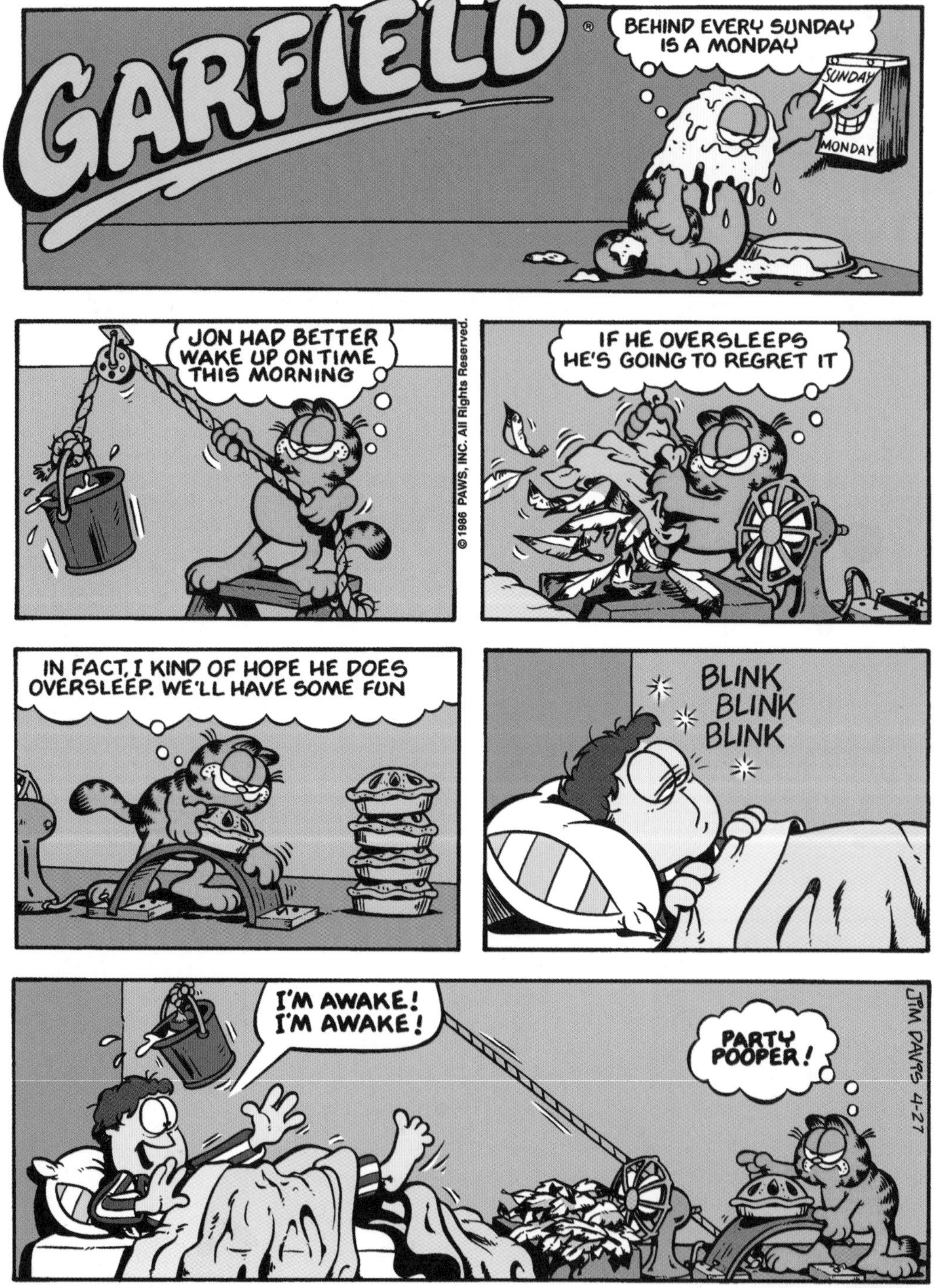
GARFIELD®
BEHIND EVERY SUNDAY IS A MONDAY
SUNDAY
MONDAY
JON HAD BETTER WAKE UP ON TIME THIS MORNING
© 1986 PAWS, INC. All Rights Reserved.
IF HE OVERSLEEPS HE'S GOING TO REGRET IT
IN FACT, I KIND OF HOPE HE DOES OVERSLEEP. WE'LL HAVE SOME FUN
BLINK BLINK BLINK
I'M AWAKE! I'M AWAKE!
PARTY POOPER!
JIM DAVIS 4-27

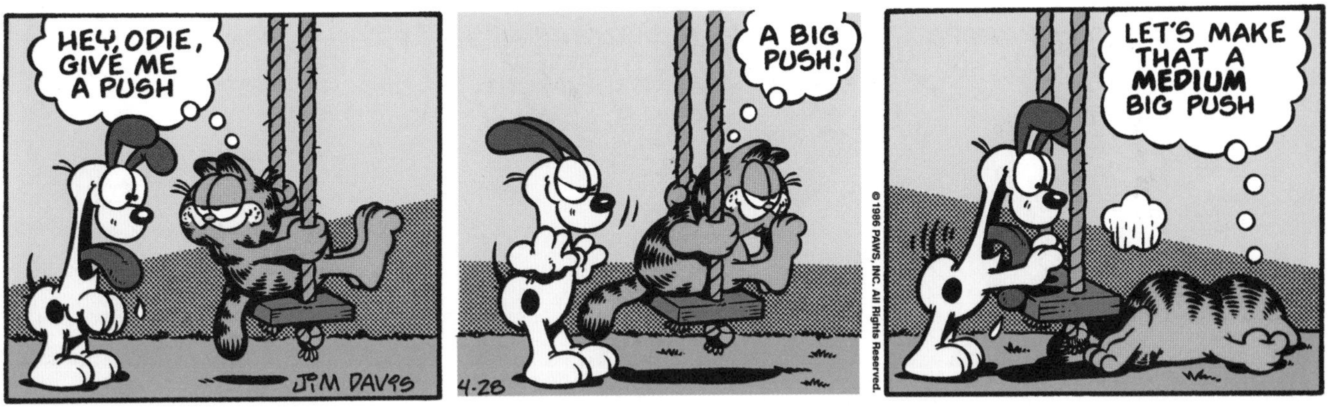
HEY, ODIE, GIVE ME A PUSH
JIM DAVIS
4-28
A BIG PUSH!
© 1986 PAWS, INC. All Rights Reserved.
LET'S MAKE THAT A **MEDIUM** BIG PUSH

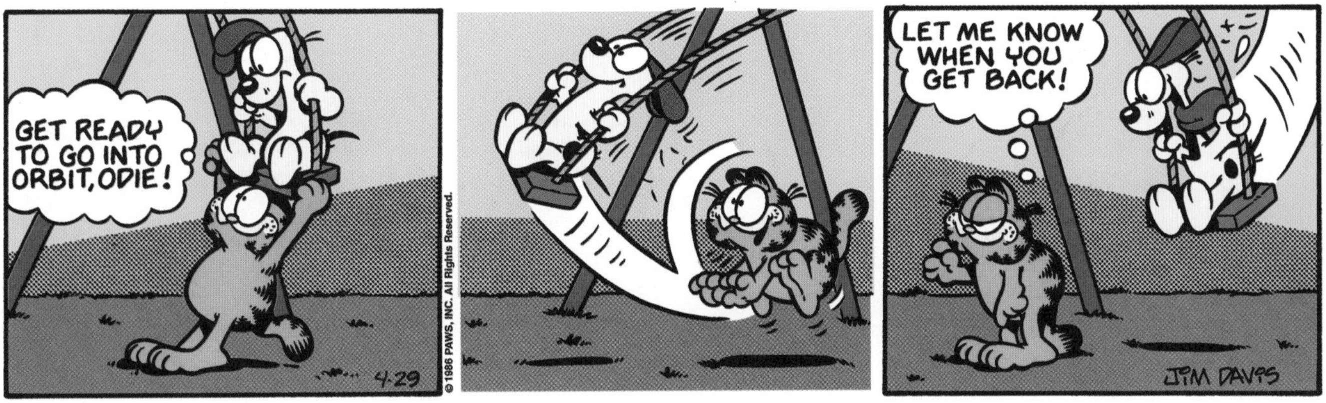
GET READY TO GO INTO ORBIT, ODIE!
4-29
© 1986 PAWS, INC. All Rights Reserved.
LET ME KNOW WHEN YOU GET BACK!
JIM DAVIS

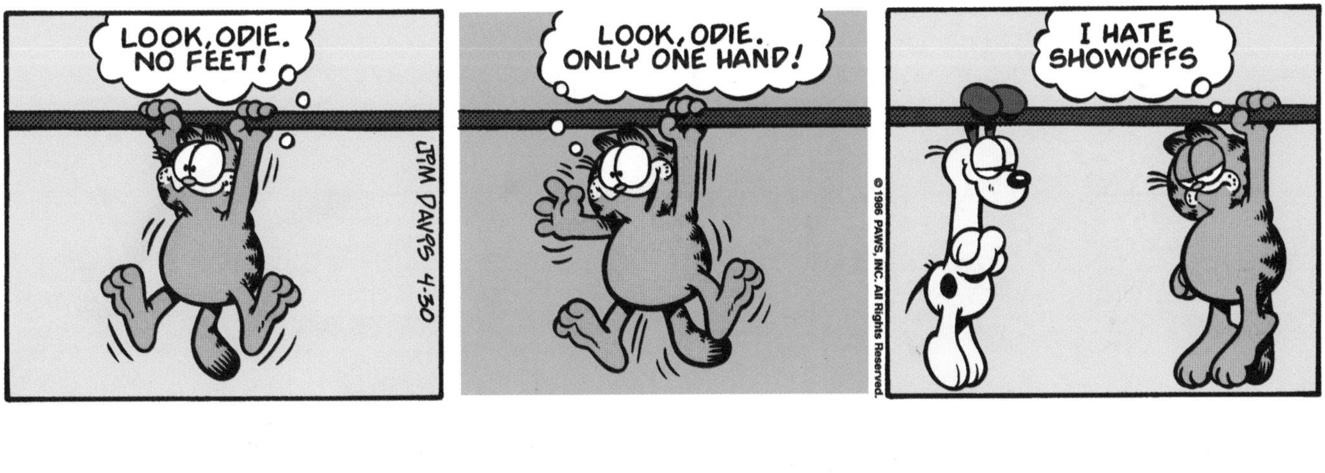
LOOK, ODIE. NO FEET!
JIM DAVIS 4-30
LOOK, ODIE. ONLY ONE HAND!
© 1986 PAWS, INC. All Rights Reserved.
I HATE SHOWOFFS

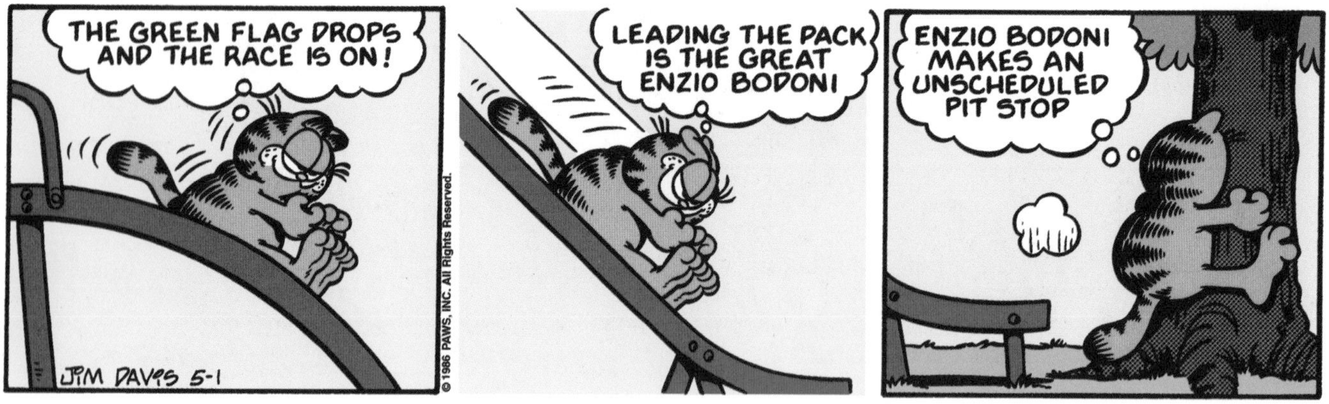
THE GREEN FLAG DROPS AND THE RACE IS ON!
JIM DAVIS 5-1
© 1986 PAWS, INC. All Rights Reserved.
LEADING THE PACK IS THE GREAT ENZIO BODONI
ENZIO BODONI MAKES AN UNSCHEDULED PIT STOP

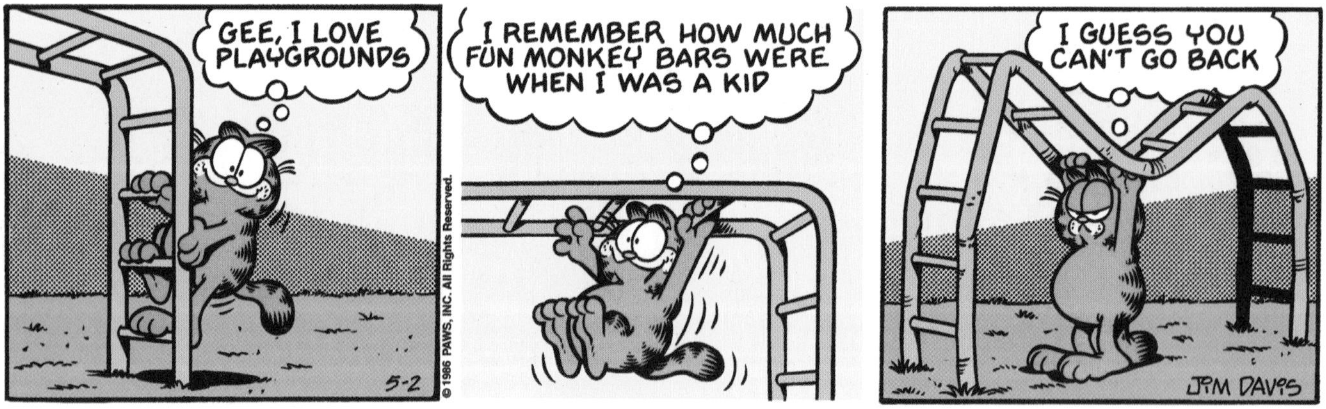
GEE, I LOVE PLAYGROUNDS
5-2
© 1986 PAWS, INC. All Rights Reserved.
I REMEMBER HOW MUCH FUN MONKEY BARS WERE WHEN I WAS A KID
I GUESS YOU CAN'T GO BACK
JIM DAVIS

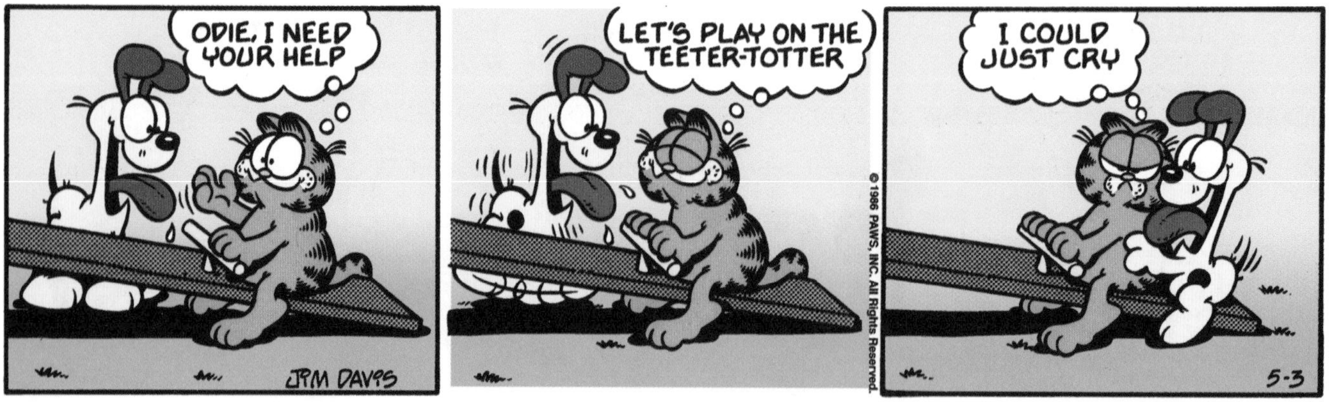
ODIE, I NEED YOUR HELP
JIM DAVIS
LET'S PLAY ON THE TEETER-TOTTER
© 1986 PAWS, INC. All Rights Reserved.
I COULD JUST CRY
5-3

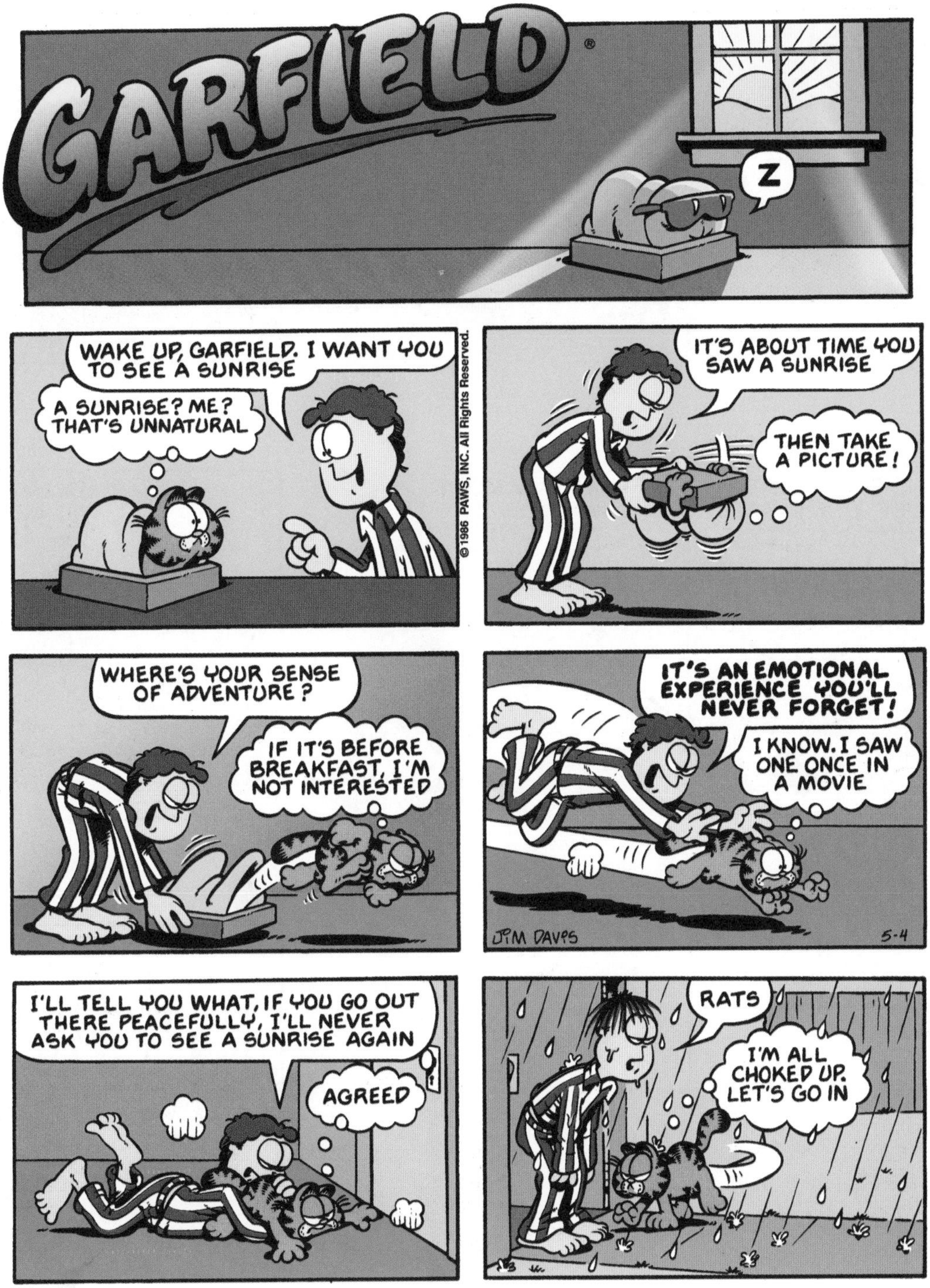
GARFIELD
Z
WAKE UP, GARFIELD. I WANT YOU TO SEE A SUNRISE
A SUNRISE? ME? THAT'S UNNATURAL
IT'S ABOUT TIME YOU SAW A SUNRISE
THEN TAKE A PICTURE!
WHERE'S YOUR SENSE OF ADVENTURE?
IF IT'S BEFORE BREAKFAST, I'M NOT INTERESTED
IT'S AN EMOTIONAL EXPERIENCE YOU'LL NEVER FORGET!
I KNOW. I SAW ONE ONCE IN A MOVIE
JIM DAVIS
5-4
I'LL TELL YOU WHAT, IF YOU GO OUT THERE PEACEFULLY, I'LL NEVER ASK YOU TO SEE A SUNRISE AGAIN
AGREED
RATS
I'M ALL CHOKED UP. LET'S GO IN

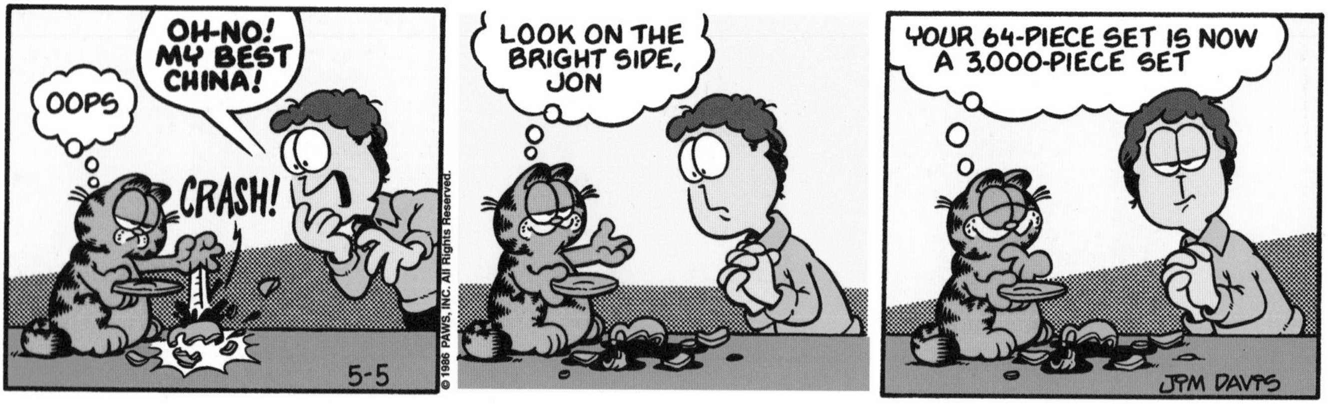
OOPS
OH-NO! MY BEST CHINA!
CRASH!
5-5
© 1986 PAWS, INC. All Rights Reserved.
LOOK ON THE BRIGHT SIDE, JON
YOUR 64-PIECE SET IS NOW A 3,000-PIECE SET
JIM DAVIS

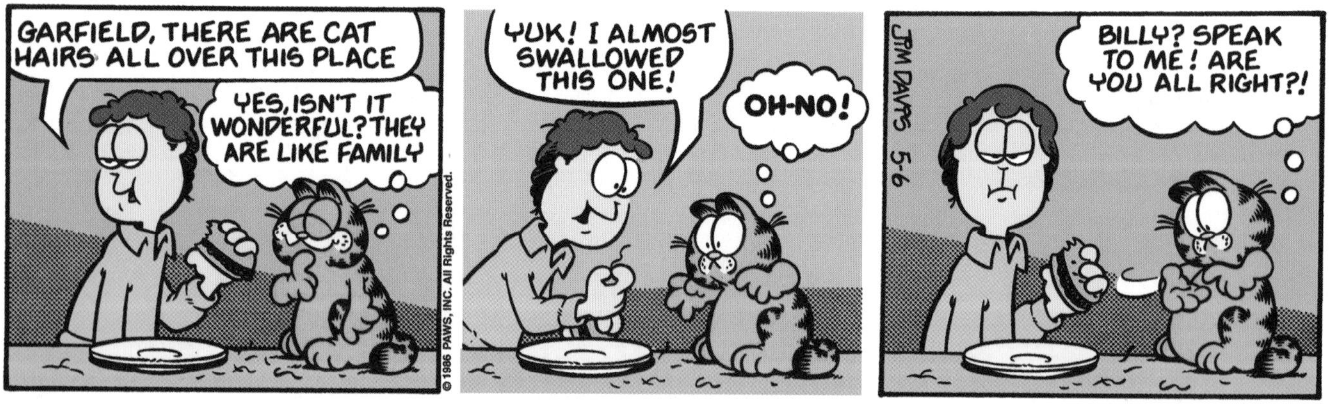
GARFIELD, THERE ARE CAT HAIRS ALL OVER THIS PLACE
YES, ISN'T IT WONDERFUL? THEY ARE LIKE FAMILY
© 1986 PAWS, INC. All Rights Reserved.
YUK! I ALMOST SWALLOWED THIS ONE!
OH-NO!
JIM DAVIS 5-6
BILLY? SPEAK TO ME! ARE YOU ALL RIGHT?!

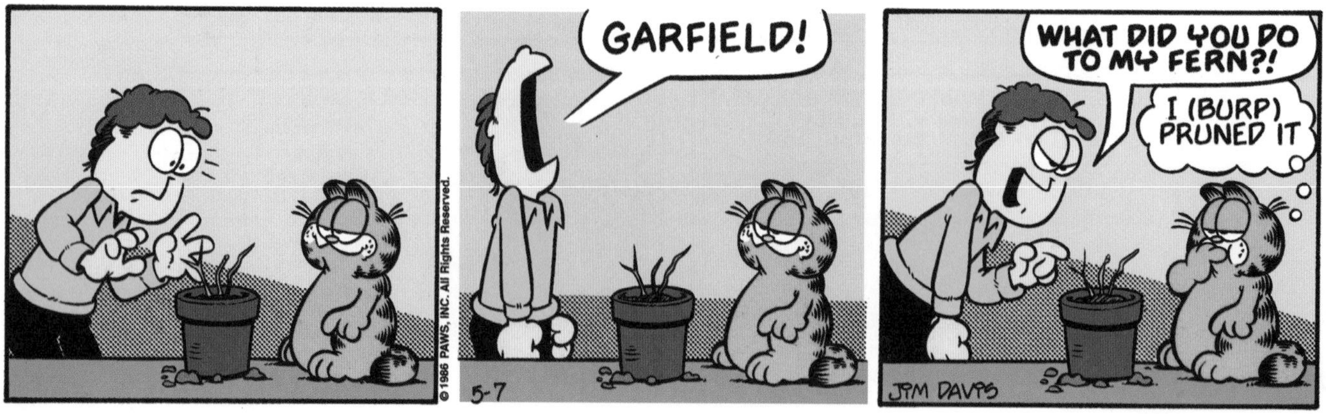
© 1986 PAWS, INC. All Rights Reserved.
GARFIELD!
5-7
WHAT DID YOU DO TO MY FERN?!
I (BURP) PRUNED IT
JIM DAVIS

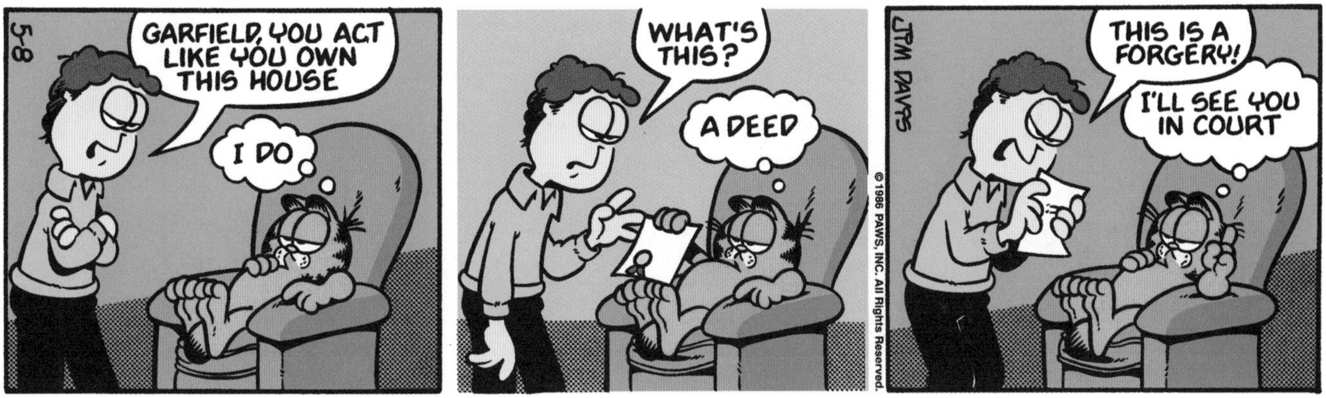
5-8
GARFIELD, YOU ACT LIKE YOU OWN THIS HOUSE
I DO
WHAT'S THIS?
A DEED
JIM DAVIS
© 1986 PAWS, INC. All Rights Reserved.
THIS IS A FORGERY!
I'LL SEE YOU IN COURT

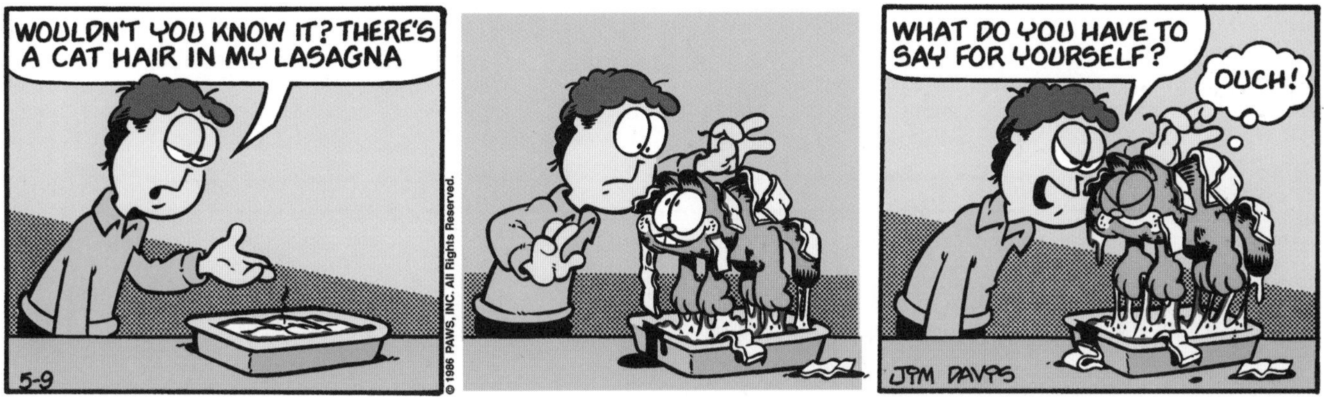
WOULDN'T YOU KNOW IT? THERE'S A CAT HAIR IN MY LASAGNA
5-9
© 1986 PAWS, INC. All Rights Reserved.
WHAT DO YOU HAVE TO SAY FOR YOURSELF?
OUCH!
JIM DAVIS

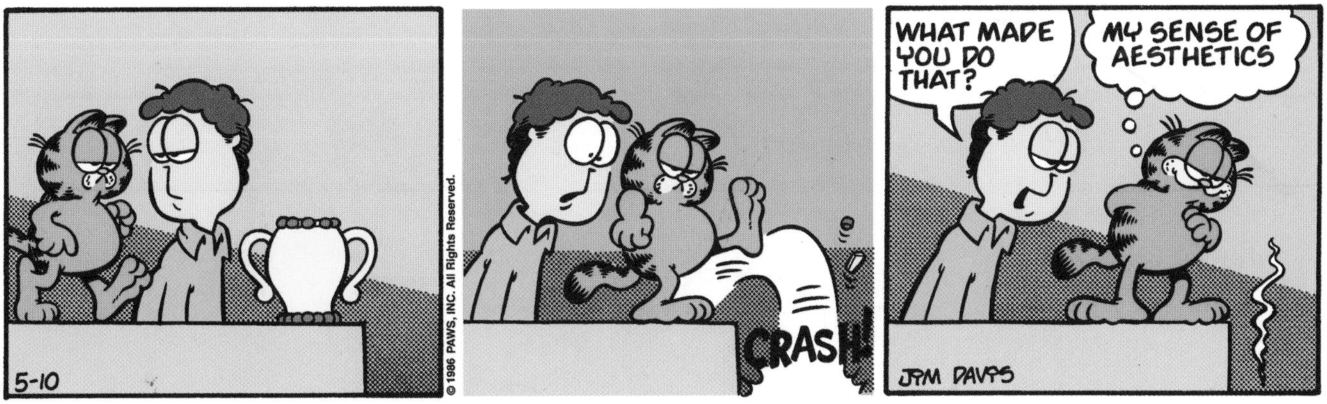
5-10
© 1986 PAWS, INC. All Rights Reserved.
CRASH!
WHAT MADE YOU DO THAT?
MY SENSE OF AESTHETICS
JIM DAVIS

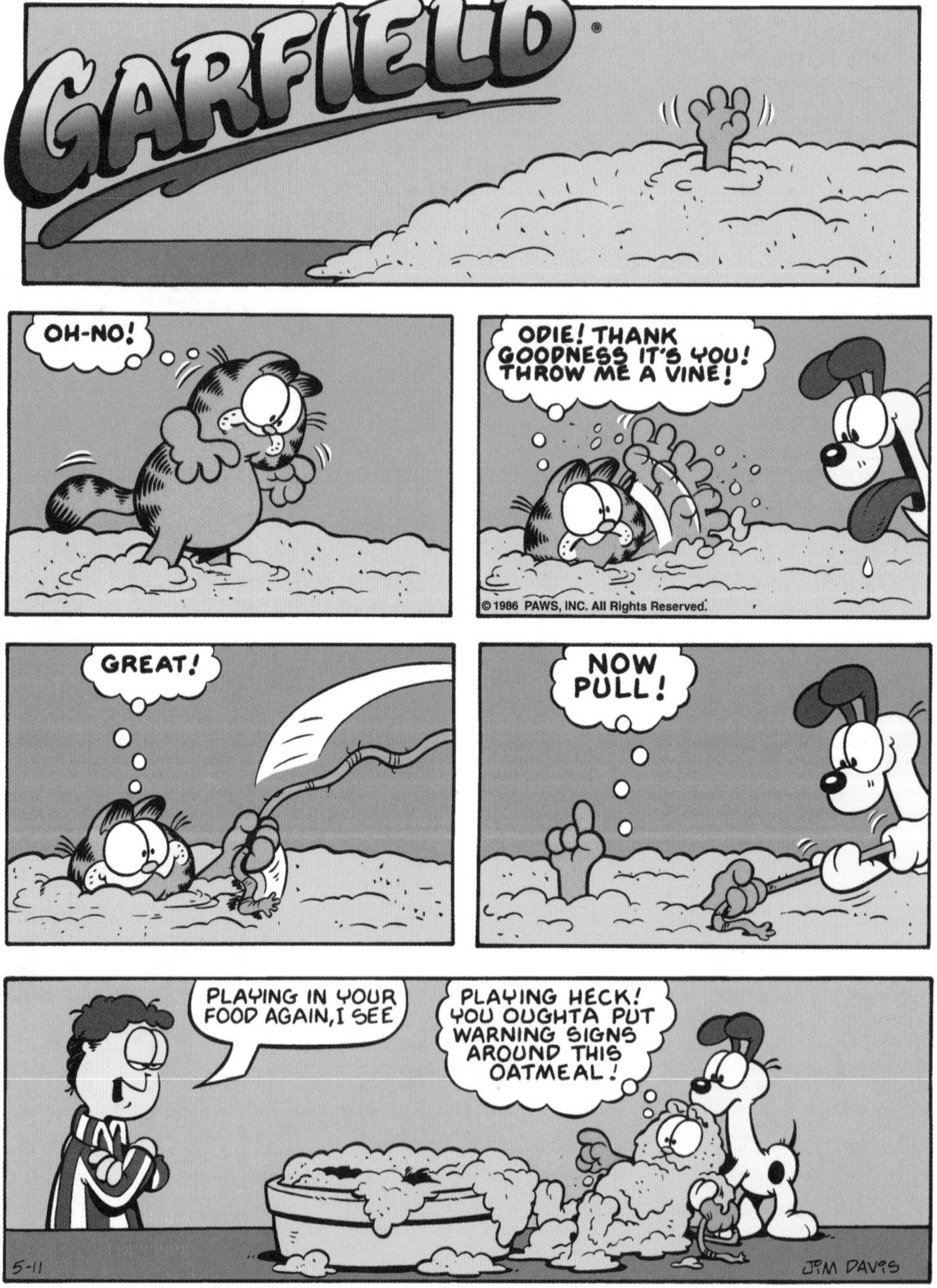
GARFIELD®
OH-NO!
ODIE! THANK GOODNESS IT'S YOU! THROW ME A VINE!
© 1986 PAWS, INC. All Rights Reserved.
GREAT!
NOW PULL!
PLAYING IN YOUR FOOD AGAIN, I SEE
PLAYING HECK! YOU OUGHTA PUT WARNING SIGNS AROUND THIS OATMEAL!
5-11
JIM DAVIS

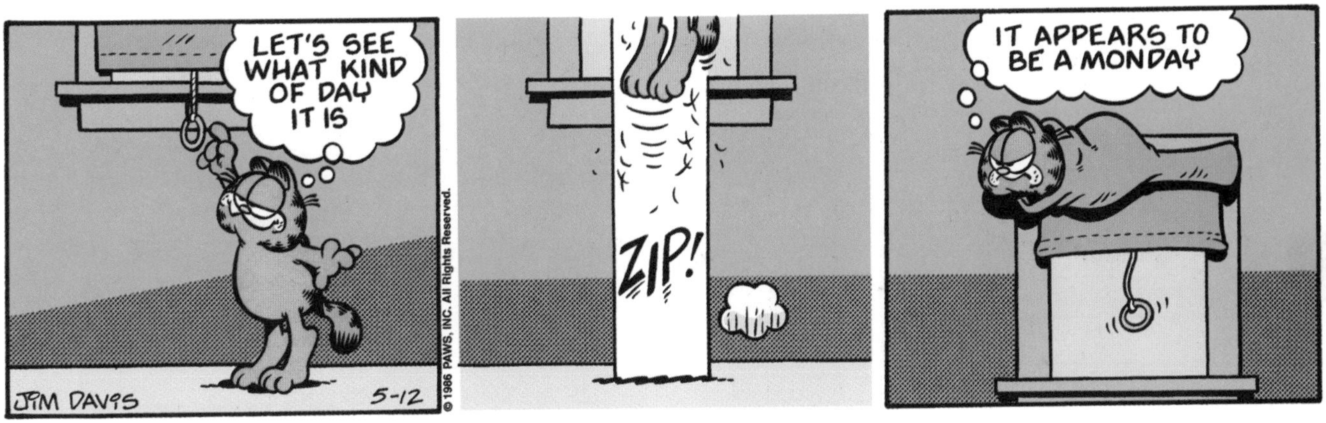
LET'S SEE WHAT KIND OF DAY IT IS
JIM DAVIS
5-12
© 1986 PAWS, INC. All Rights Reserved.
ZIP!
IT APPEARS TO BE A MONDAY

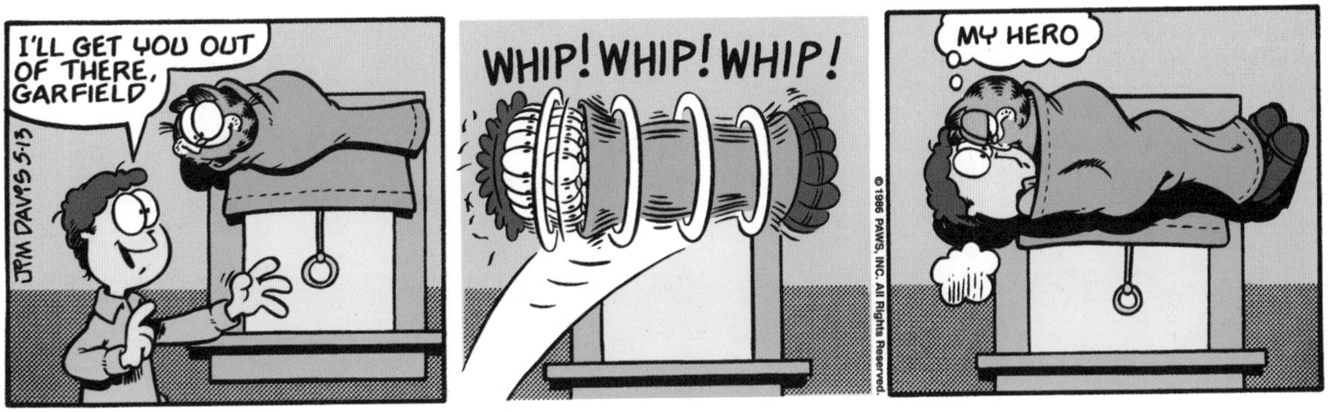
I'LL GET YOU OUT OF THERE, GARFIELD
JIM DAVIS 5-13
WHIP! WHIP! WHIP!
© 1986 PAWS, INC. All Rights Reserved.
MY HERO

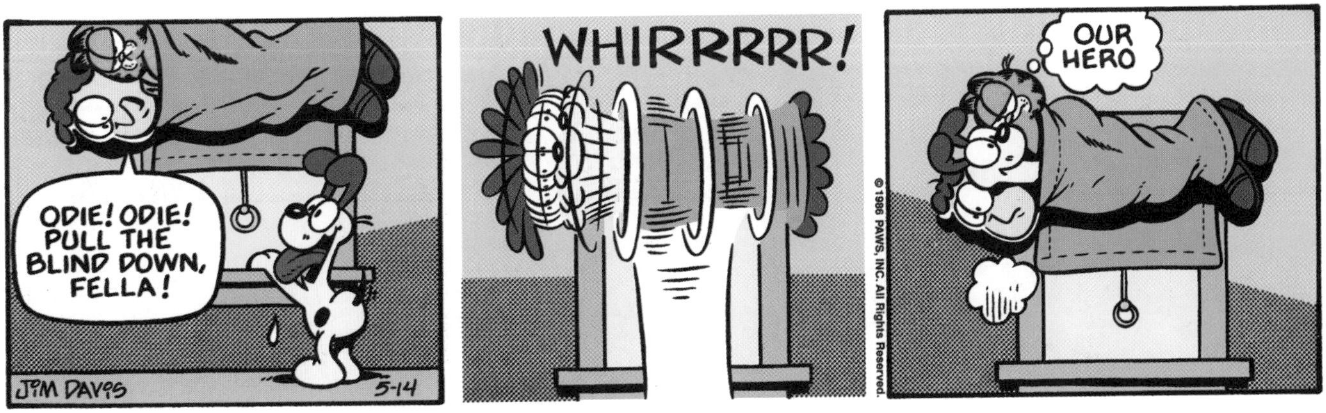
ODIE! ODIE! PULL THE BLIND DOWN, FELLA!
JIM DAVIS
5-14
WHIRRRRR!
© 1986 PAWS, INC. All Rights Reserved.
OUR HERO

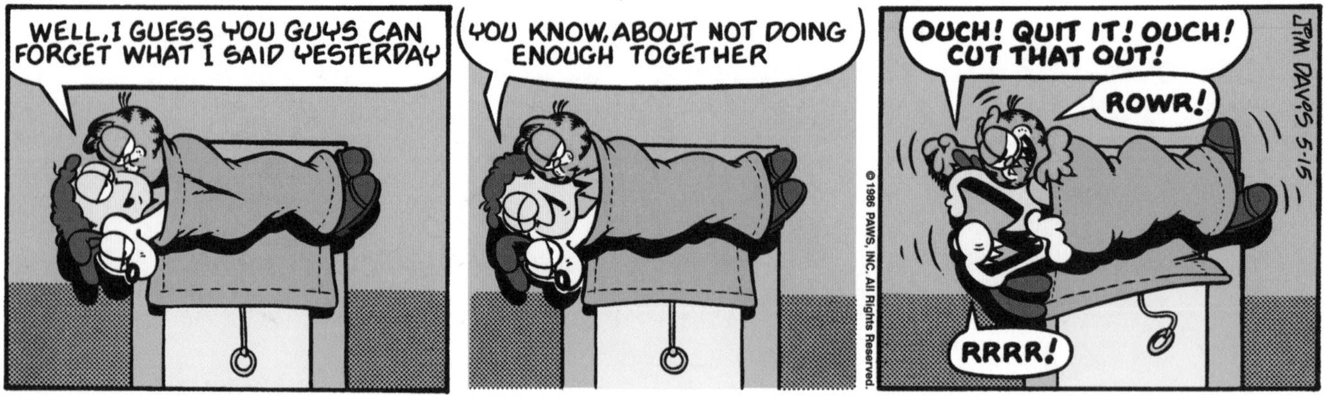
WELL, I GUESS YOU GUYS CAN FORGET WHAT I SAID YESTERDAY
YOU KNOW, ABOUT NOT DOING ENOUGH TOGETHER
OUCH! QUIT IT! OUCH! CUT THAT OUT!
ROWR!
RRRR!
JIM DAVIS 5-15

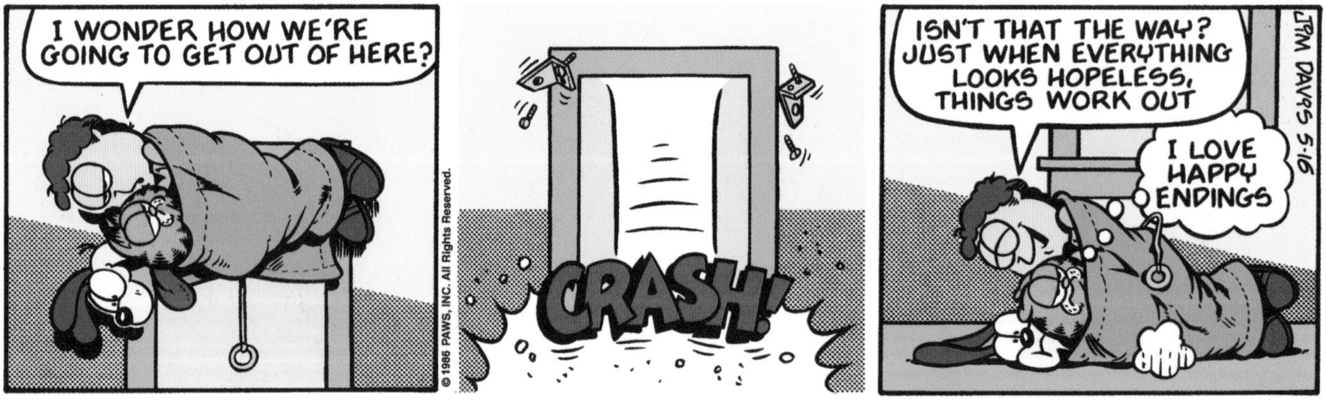
I WONDER HOW WE'RE GOING TO GET OUT OF HERE?
CRASH!
ISN'T THAT THE WAY? JUST WHEN EVERYTHING LOOKS HOPELESS, THINGS WORK OUT
I LOVE HAPPY ENDINGS
JIM DAVIS 5-16

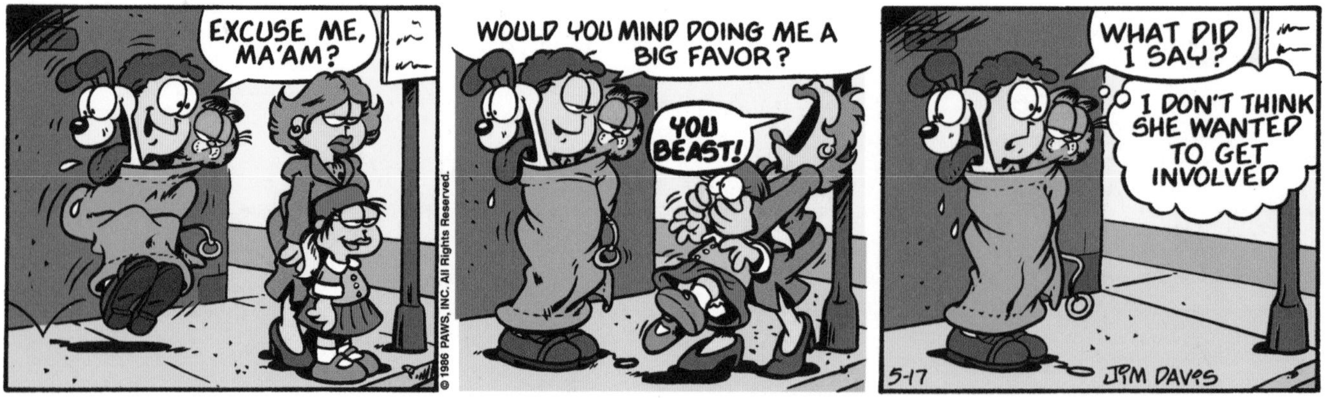
EXCUSE ME, MA'AM?
WOULD YOU MIND DOING ME A BIG FAVOR?
YOU BEAST!
WHAT DID I SAY?
I DON'T THINK SHE WANTED TO GET INVOLVED
5-17
JIM DAVIS

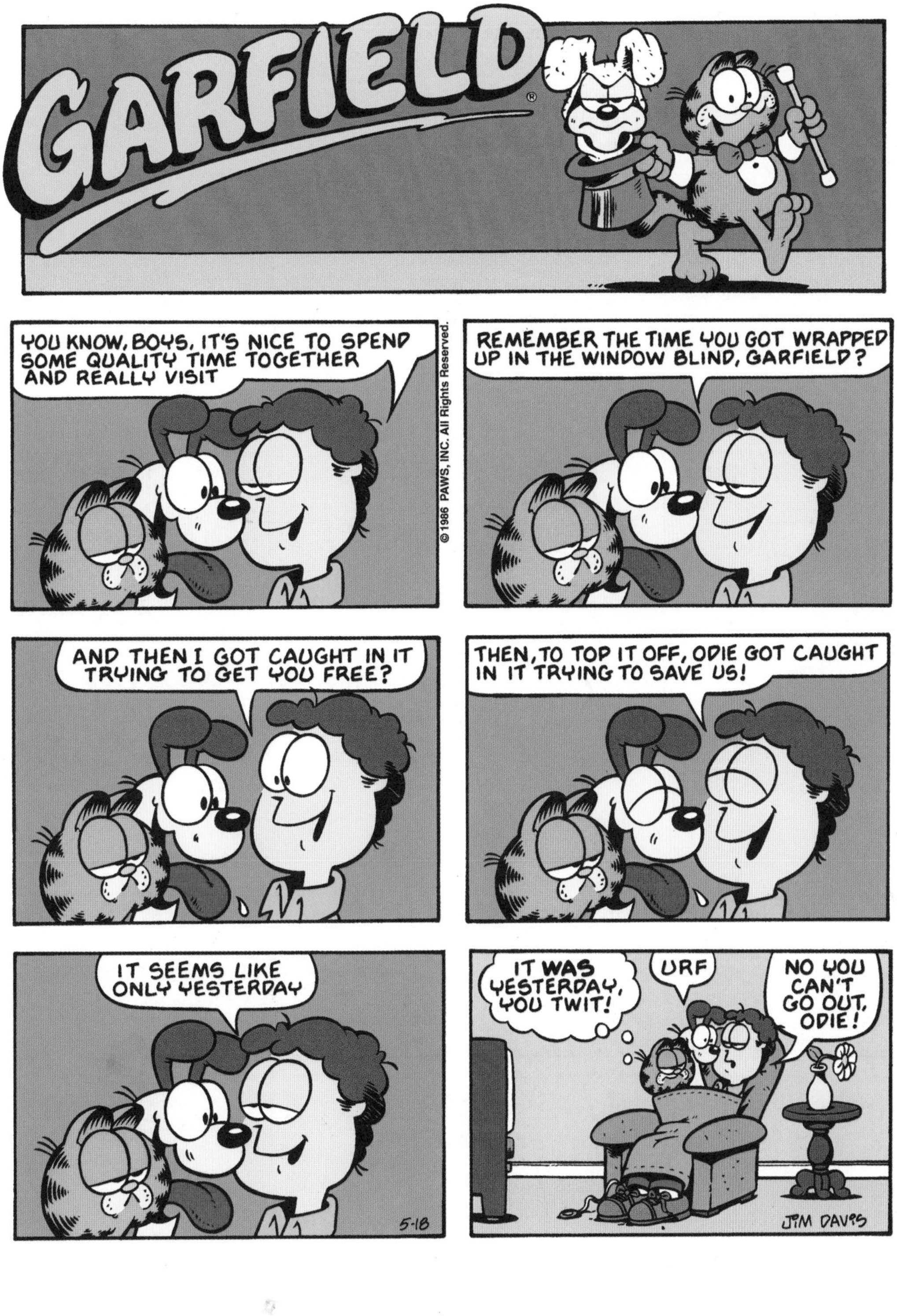
GARFIELD®
©1986 PAWS, INC. All Rights Reserved.
YOU KNOW, BOYS, IT'S NICE TO SPEND SOME QUALITY TIME TOGETHER AND REALLY VISIT
REMEMBER THE TIME YOU GOT WRAPPED UP IN THE WINDOW BLIND, GARFIELD?
AND THEN I GOT CAUGHT IN IT TRYING TO GET YOU FREE?
THEN, TO TOP IT OFF, ODIE GOT CAUGHT IN IT TRYING TO SAVE US!
IT SEEMS LIKE ONLY YESTERDAY
5-18
IT WAS YESTERDAY, YOU TWIT!
URF
NO YOU CAN'T GO OUT, ODIE!
JIM DAVIS

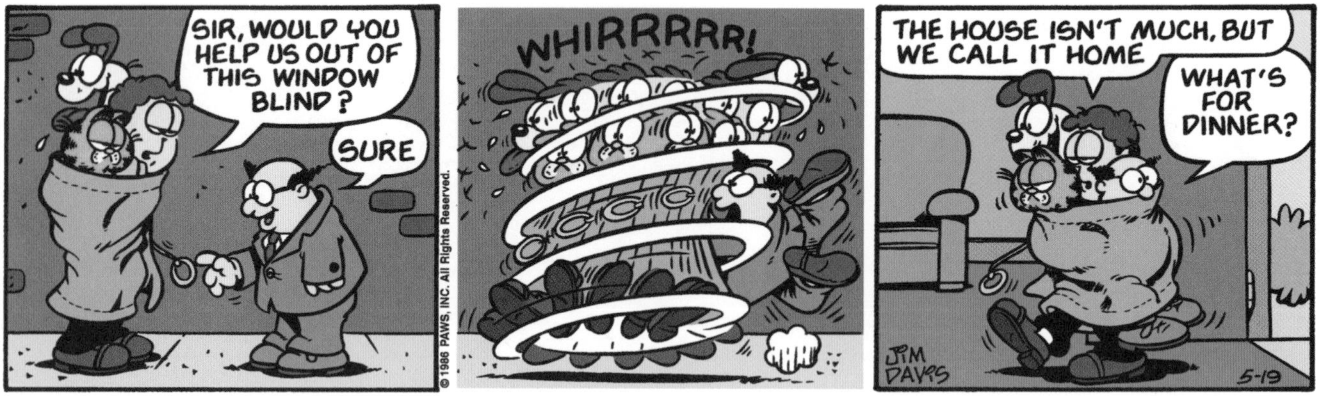
SIR, WOULD YOU HELP US OUT OF THIS WINDOW BLIND?
SURE
© 1986 PAWS, INC. All Rights Reserved.
WHIRRRRRR!
THE HOUSE ISN'T MUCH, BUT WE CALL IT HOME
WHAT'S FOR DINNER?
JIM DAVIS
5-19

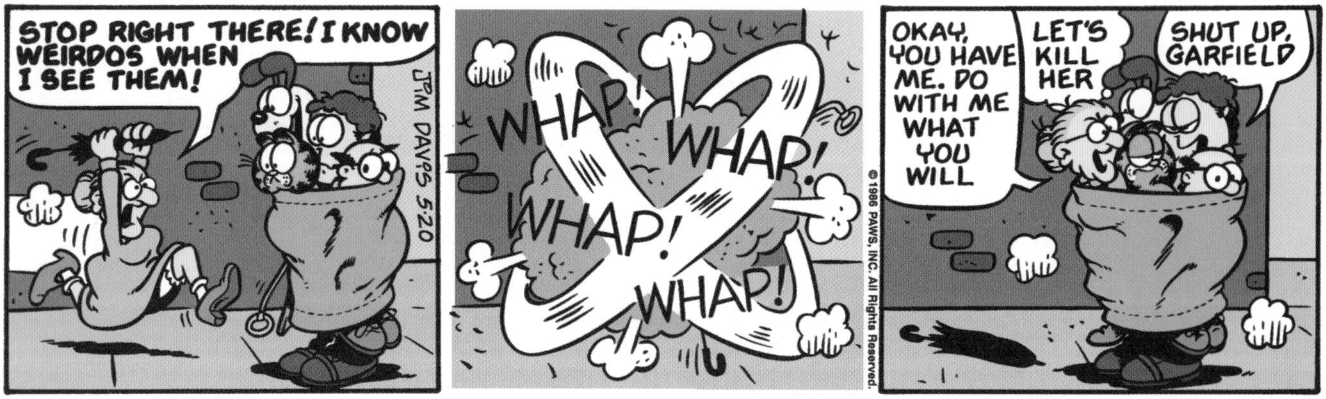
STOP RIGHT THERE! I KNOW WEIRDOS WHEN I SEE THEM!
JIM DAVIS 5-20
WHAP!
WHAP!
WHAP!
WHAP!
© 1986 PAWS, INC. All Rights Reserved.
OKAY, YOU HAVE ME. DO WITH ME WHAT YOU WILL
LET'S KILL HER
SHUT UP, GARFIELD

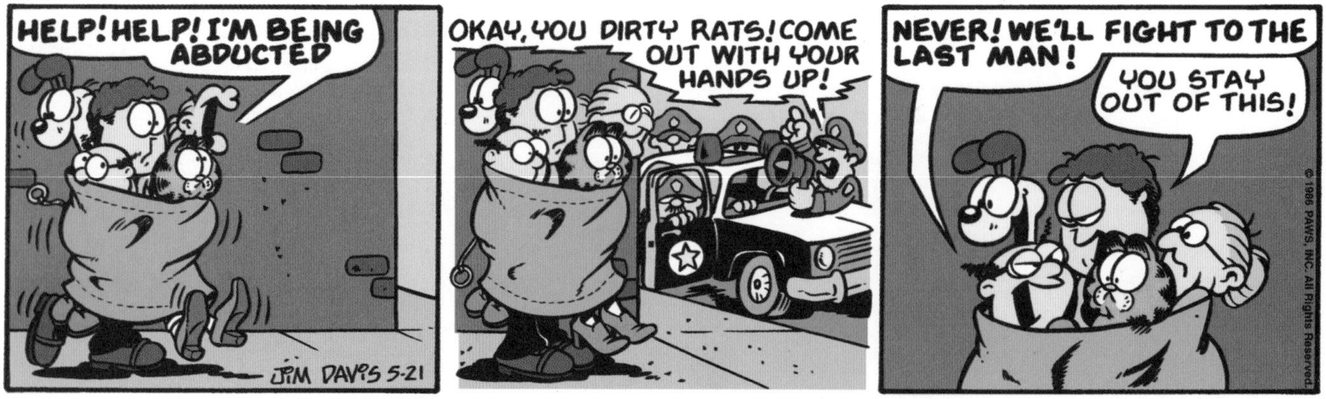
HELP! HELP! I'M BEING ABDUCTED
JIM DAVIS 5-21
OKAY, YOU DIRTY RATS! COME OUT WITH YOUR HANDS UP!
NEVER! WE'LL FIGHT TO THE LAST MAN!
YOU STAY OUT OF THIS!
© 1986 PAWS, INC. All Rights Reserved.

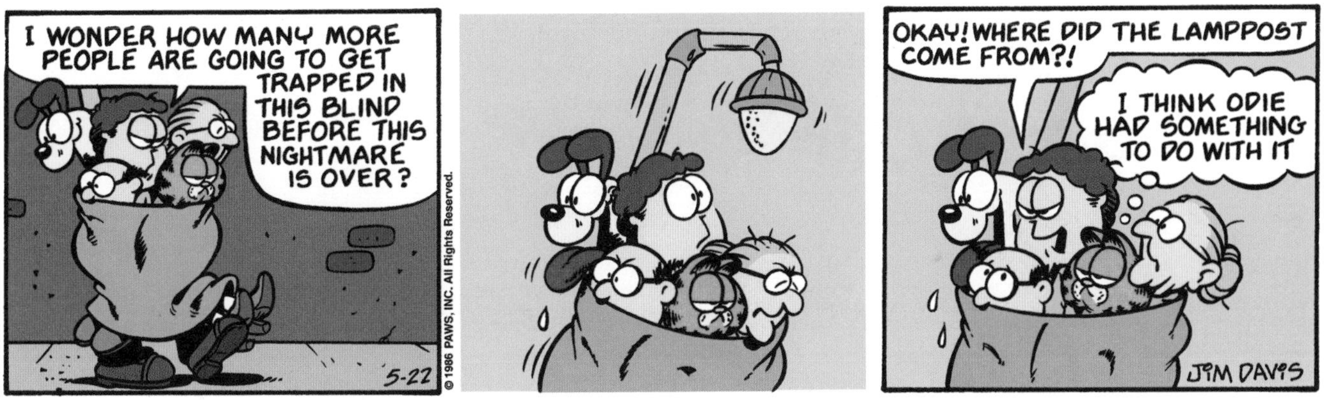
I WONDER HOW MANY MORE PEOPLE ARE GOING TO GET TRAPPED IN THIS BLIND BEFORE THIS NIGHTMARE IS OVER?
5-22
© 1986 PAWS, INC. All Rights Reserved.
OKAY! WHERE DID THE LAMPPOST COME FROM?!
I THINK ODIE HAD SOMETHING TO DO WITH IT
JIM DAVIS

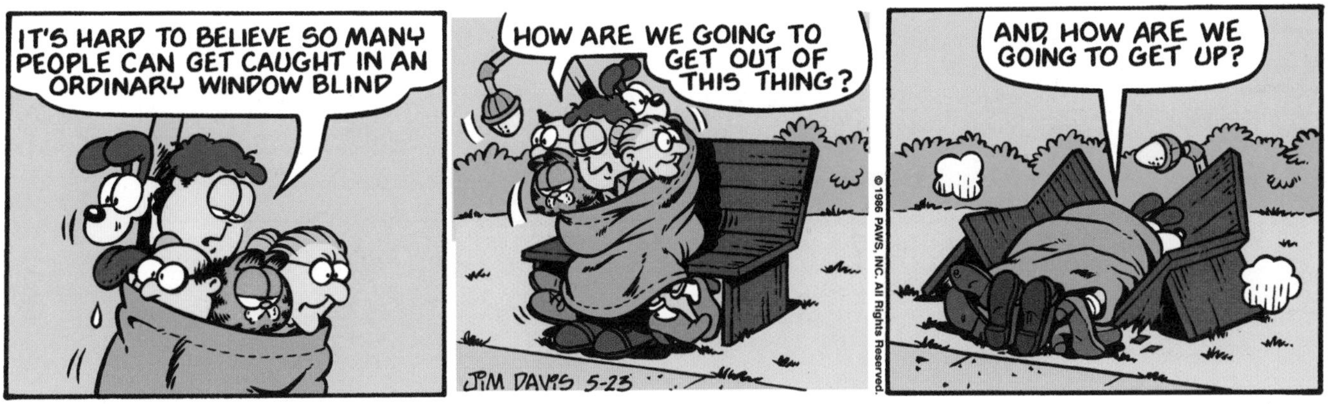
IT'S HARD TO BELIEVE SO MANY PEOPLE CAN GET CAUGHT IN AN ORDINARY WINDOW BLIND
HOW ARE WE GOING TO GET OUT OF THIS THING?
JIM DAVIS 5-23
© 1986 PAWS, INC. All Rights Reserved.
AND, HOW ARE WE GOING TO GET UP?

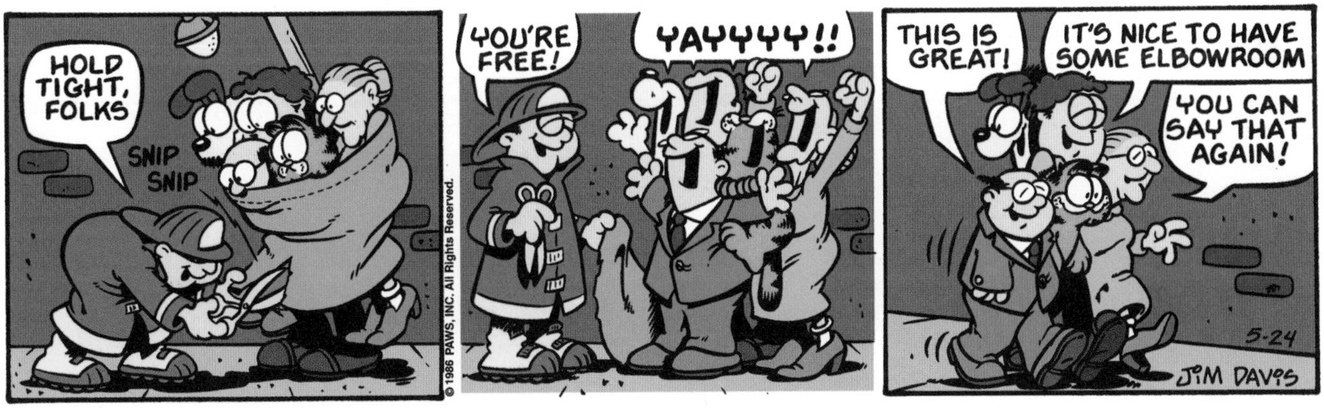
HOLD TIGHT, FOLKS
SNIP SNIP
© 1986 PAWS, INC. All Rights Reserved.
YOU'RE FREE!
YAYYYY!!
THIS IS GREAT!
IT'S NICE TO HAVE SOME ELBOWROOM
YOU CAN SAY THAT AGAIN!
5-24
JIM DAVIS

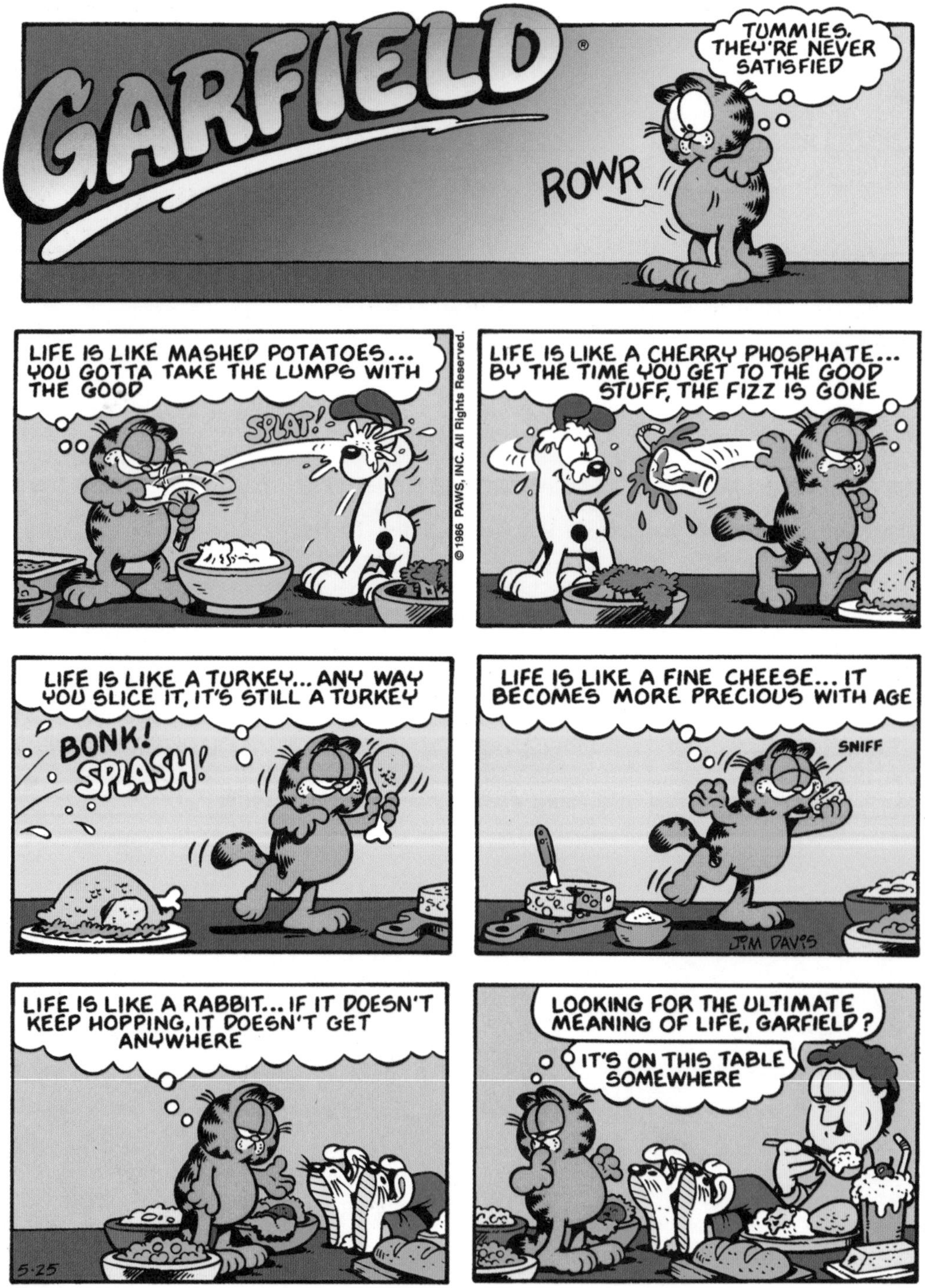

GARFIELD®
TUMMIES. THEY'RE NEVER SATISFIED
ROWR
LIFE IS LIKE MASHED POTATOES... YOU GOTTA TAKE THE LUMPS WITH THE GOOD
SPLAT!
© 1986 PAWS, INC. All Rights Reserved.
LIFE IS LIKE A CHERRY PHOSPHATE... BY THE TIME YOU GET TO THE GOOD STUFF, THE FIZZ IS GONE
LIFE IS LIKE A TURKEY... ANY WAY YOU SLICE IT, IT'S STILL A TURKEY
BONK!
SPLASH!
LIFE IS LIKE A FINE CHEESE... IT BECOMES MORE PRECIOUS WITH AGE
SNIFF
JIM DAVIS
LIFE IS LIKE A RABBIT... IF IT DOESN'T KEEP HOPPING, IT DOESN'T GET ANYWHERE
5-25
LOOKING FOR THE ULTIMATE MEANING OF LIFE, GARFIELD?
IT'S ON THIS TABLE SOMEWHERE

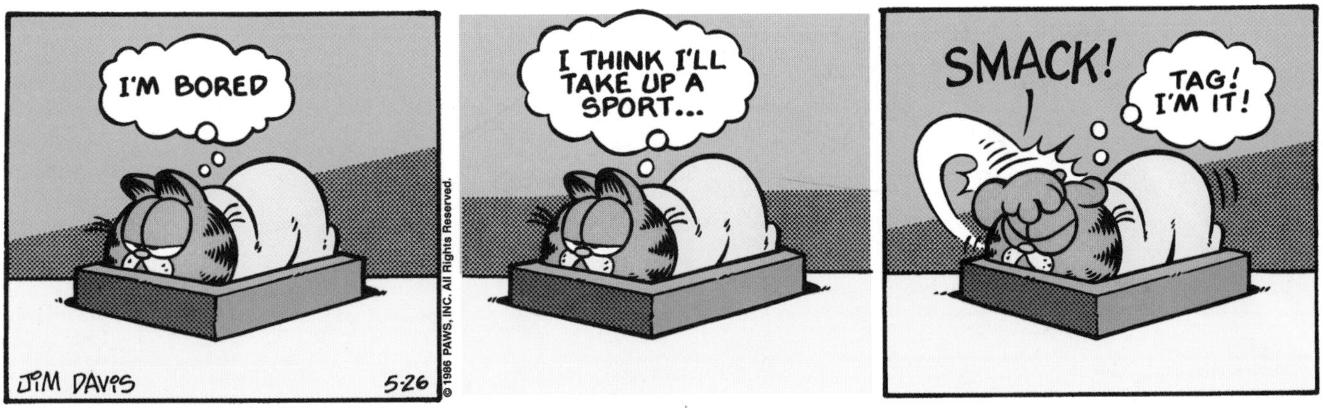
I'M BORED
JIM DAVIS 5-26
© 1986 PAWS, INC. All Rights Reserved.
I THINK I'LL TAKE UP A SPORT...
SMACK!
TAG! I'M IT!

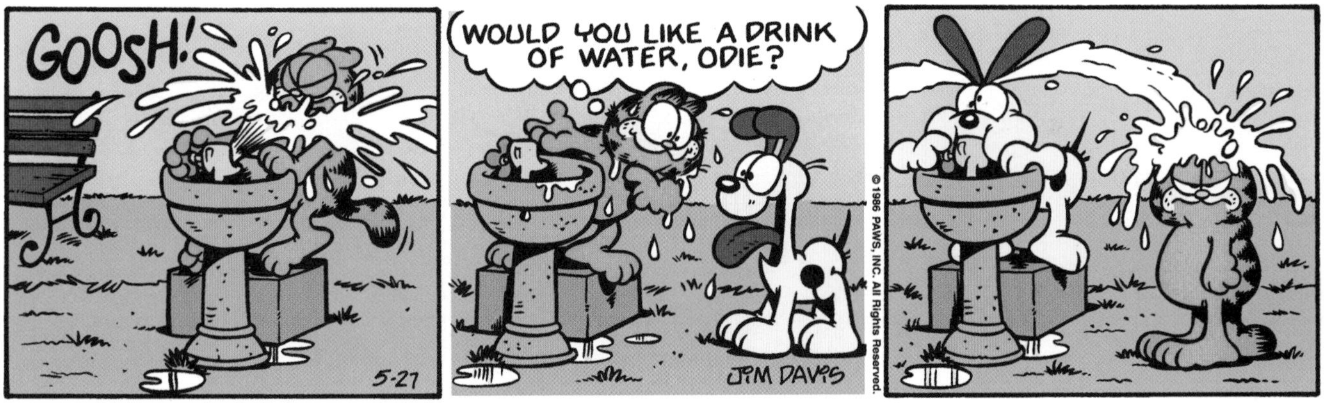
GOOSH!
5-27
WOULD YOU LIKE A DRINK OF WATER, ODIE?
JIM DAVIS
© 1986 PAWS, INC. All Rights Reserved.

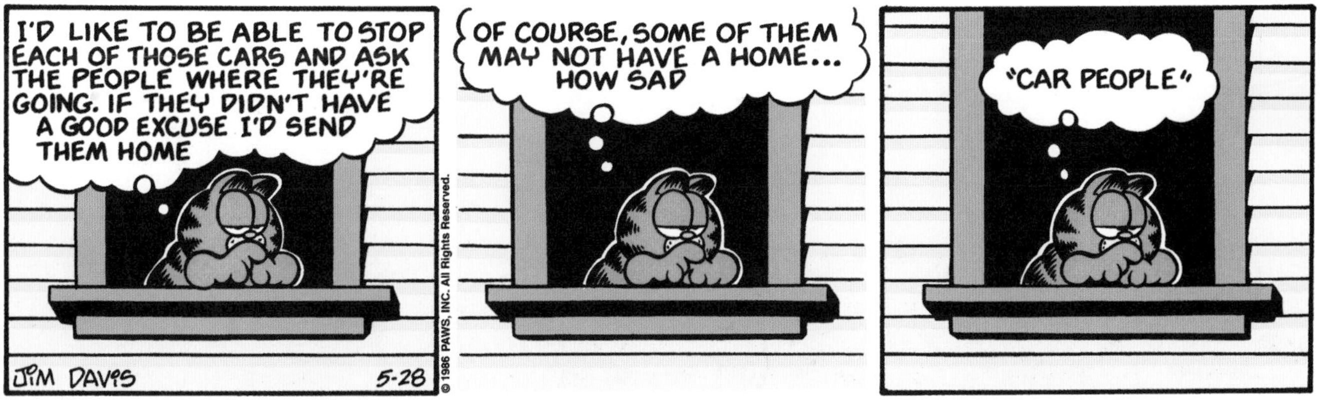
I'D LIKE TO BE ABLE TO STOP EACH OF THOSE CARS AND ASK THE PEOPLE WHERE THEY'RE GOING. IF THEY DIDN'T HAVE A GOOD EXCUSE I'D SEND THEM HOME
JIM DAVIS 5-28
© 1986 PAWS, INC. All Rights Reserved.
OF COURSE, SOME OF THEM MAY NOT HAVE A HOME... HOW SAD
"CAR PEOPLE"

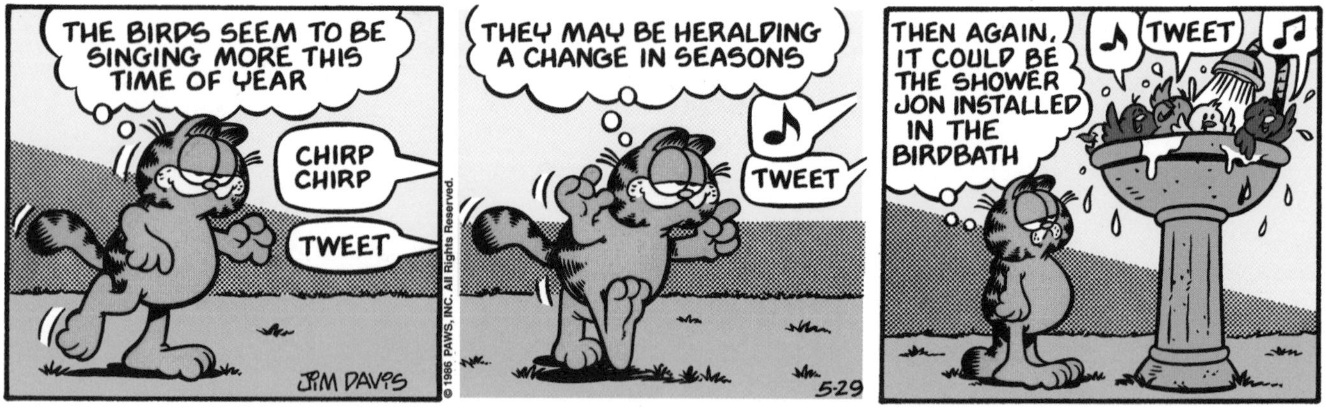
THE BIRDS SEEM TO BE SINGING MORE THIS TIME OF YEAR
CHIRP CHIRP
TWEET
JIM DAVIS
© 1986 PAWS, INC. All Rights Reserved.
THEY MAY BE HERALDING A CHANGE IN SEASONS
TWEET
5-29
THEN AGAIN, IT COULD BE THE SHOWER JON INSTALLED IN THE BIRDBATH
TWEET

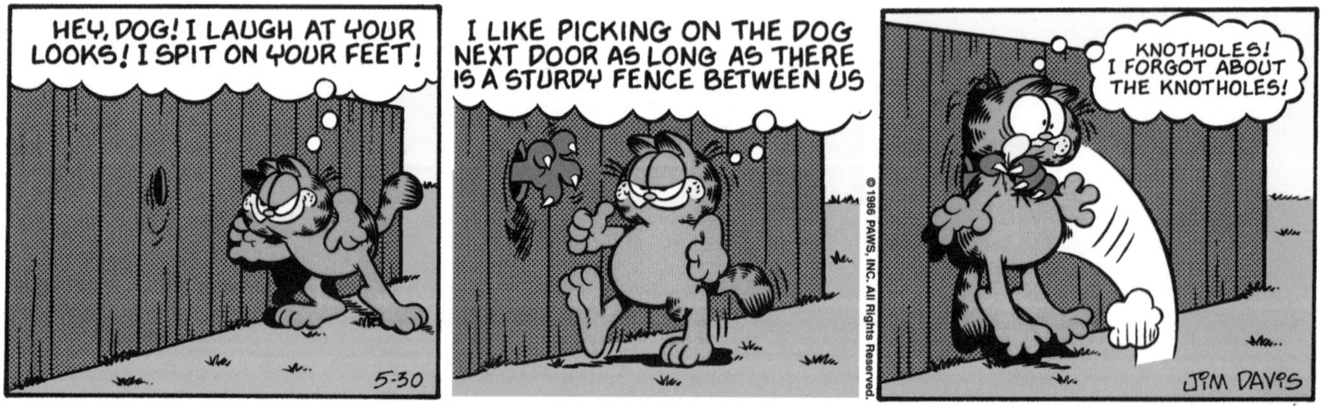
HEY, DOG! I LAUGH AT YOUR LOOKS! I SPIT ON YOUR FEET!
5-30
I LIKE PICKING ON THE DOG NEXT DOOR AS LONG AS THERE IS A STURDY FENCE BETWEEN US
© 1986 PAWS, INC. All Rights Reserved.
KNOTHOLES! I FORGOT ABOUT THE KNOTHOLES!
JIM DAVIS

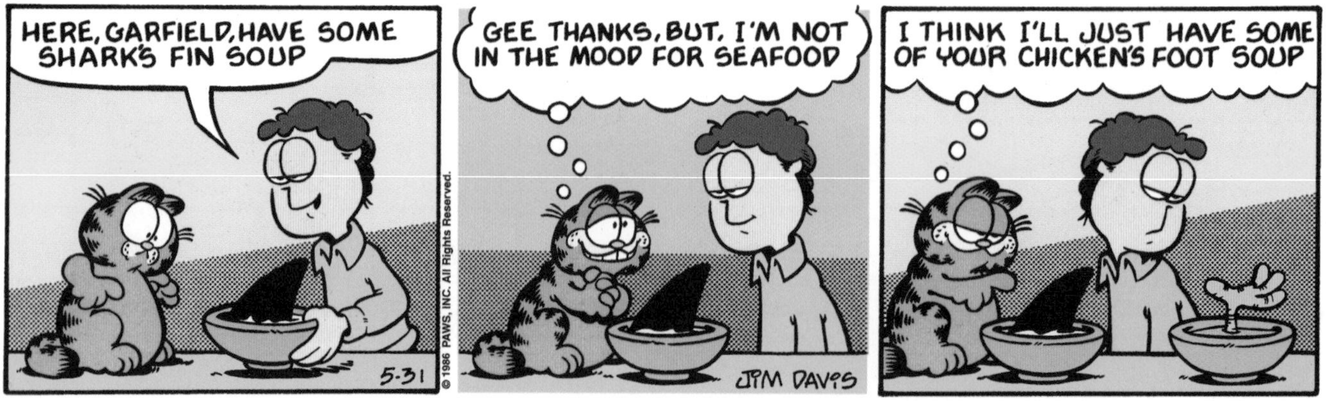
HERE, GARFIELD, HAVE SOME SHARK'S FIN SOUP
5-31
© 1986 PAWS, INC. All Rights Reserved.
GEE THANKS, BUT, I'M NOT IN THE MOOD FOR SEAFOOD
JIM DAVIS
I THINK I'LL JUST HAVE SOME OF YOUR CHICKEN'S FOOT SOUP

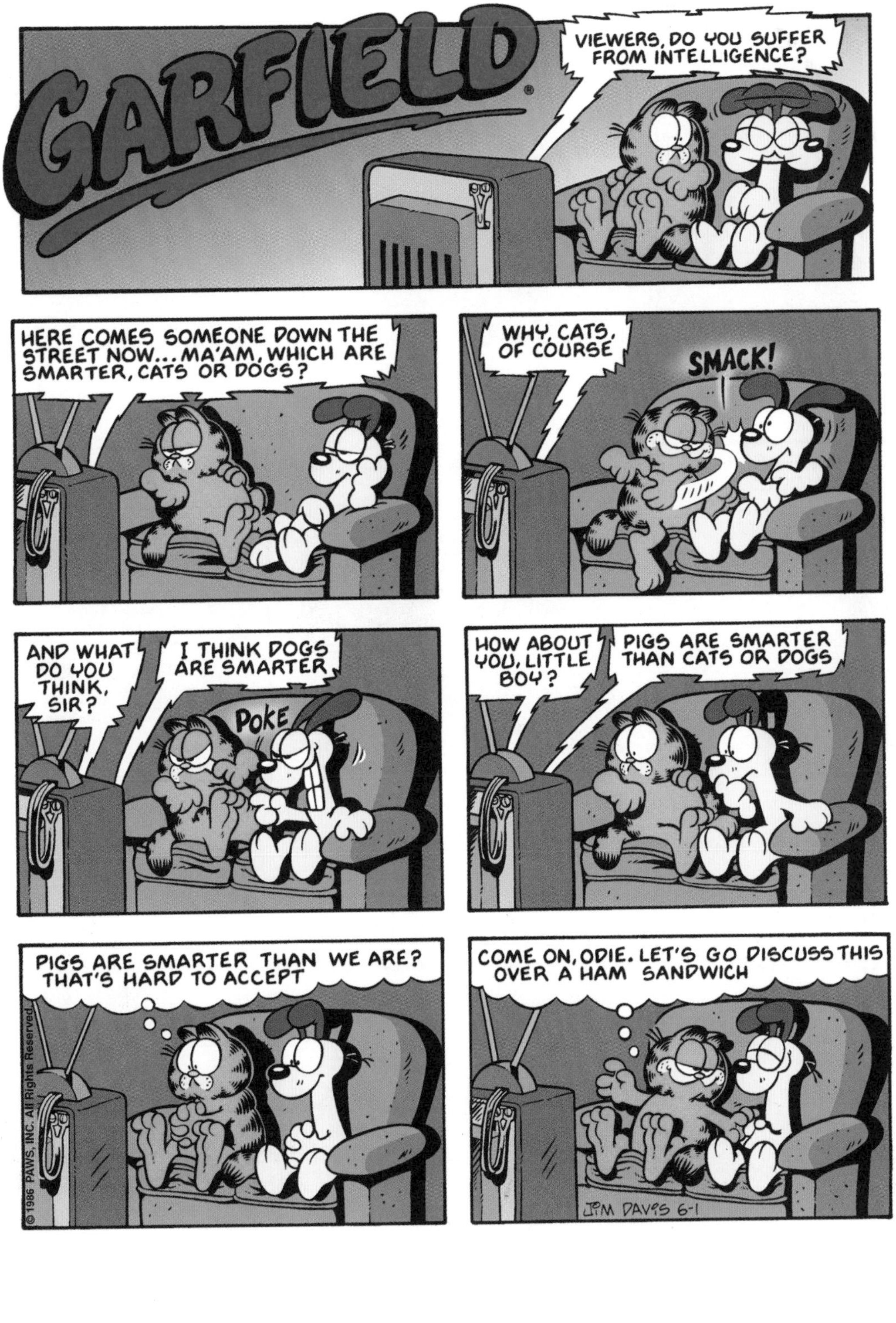
GARFIELD
VIEWERS, DO YOU SUFFER FROM INTELLIGENCE?
HERE COMES SOMEONE DOWN THE STREET NOW... MA'AM, WHICH ARE SMARTER, CATS OR DOGS?
WHY, CATS, OF COURSE
SMACK!
AND WHAT DO YOU THINK, SIR?
I THINK DOGS ARE SMARTER
POKE
HOW ABOUT YOU, LITTLE BOY?
PIGS ARE SMARTER THAN CATS OR DOGS
PIGS ARE SMARTER THAN WE ARE? THAT'S HARD TO ACCEPT
© 1986 PAWS, INC. All Rights Reserved.
COME ON, ODIE. LET'S GO DISCUSS THIS OVER A HAM SANDWICH
JIM DAVIS 6-1

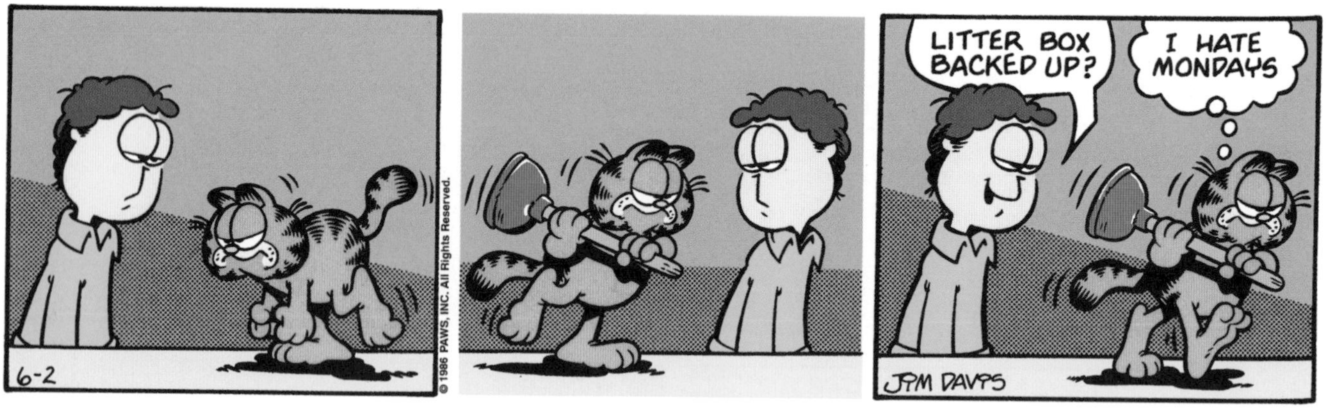
6-2
© 1986 PAWS, INC. All Rights Reserved.
LITTER BOX BACKED UP?
I HATE MONDAYS
JIM DAVIS

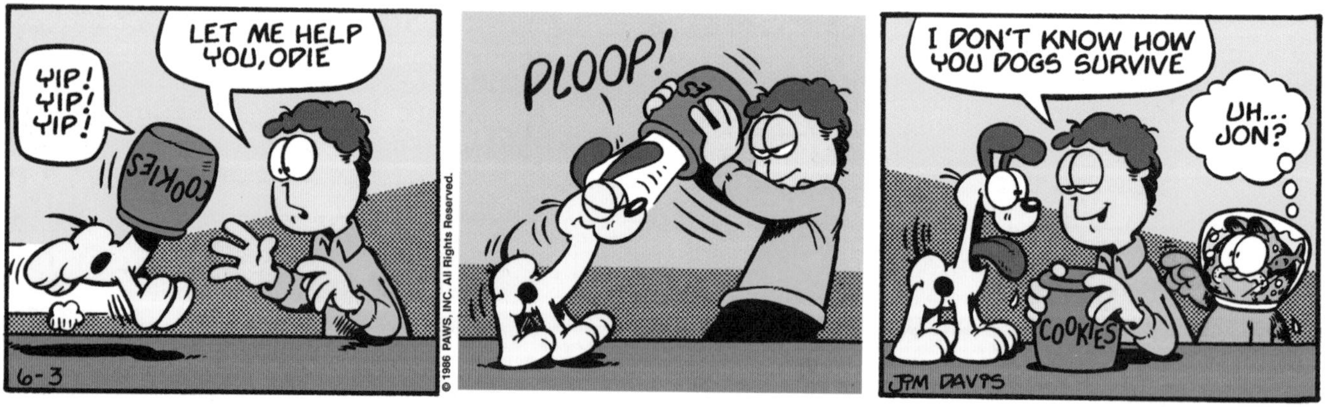
YIP! YIP! YIP!
LET ME HELP YOU, ODIE
COOKIES
6-3
© 1986 PAWS, INC. All Rights Reserved.
PLOOP!
I DON'T KNOW HOW YOU DOGS SURVIVE
UH... JON?
COOKIES
JIM DAVIS

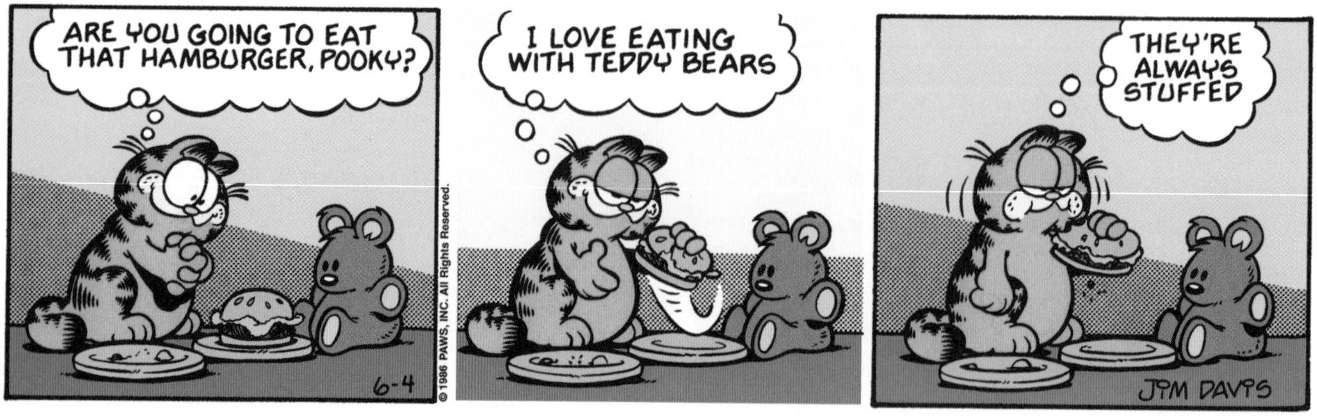
ARE YOU GOING TO EAT THAT HAMBURGER, POOKY?
6-4
© 1986 PAWS, INC. All Rights Reserved.
I LOVE EATING WITH TEDDY BEARS
THEY'RE ALWAYS STUFFED
JIM DAVIS

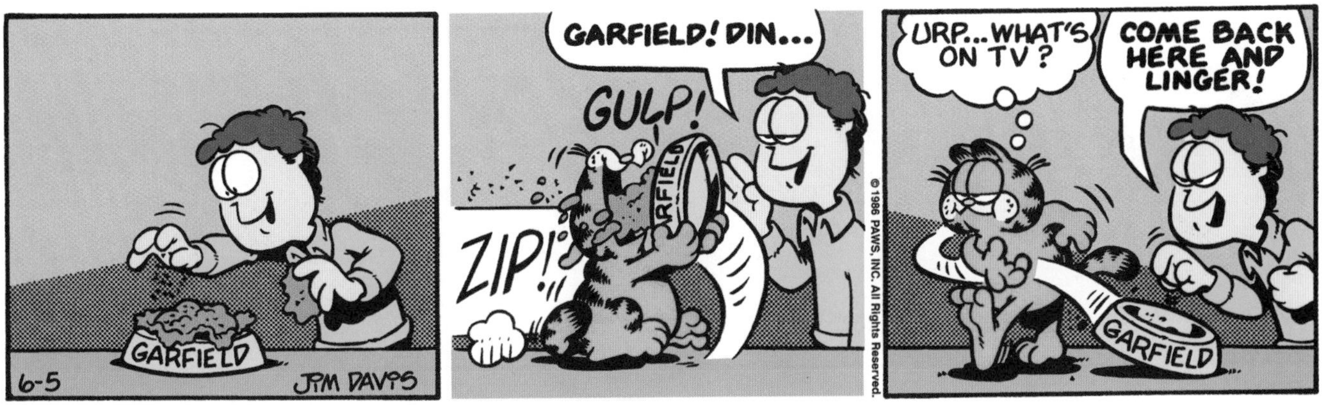
6-5
JIM DAVIS
ZIP!
GULP!
GARFIELD! DIN...
© 1986 PAWS, INC. All Rights Reserved.
URP... WHAT'S ON TV?
COME BACK HERE AND LINGER!
GARFIELD

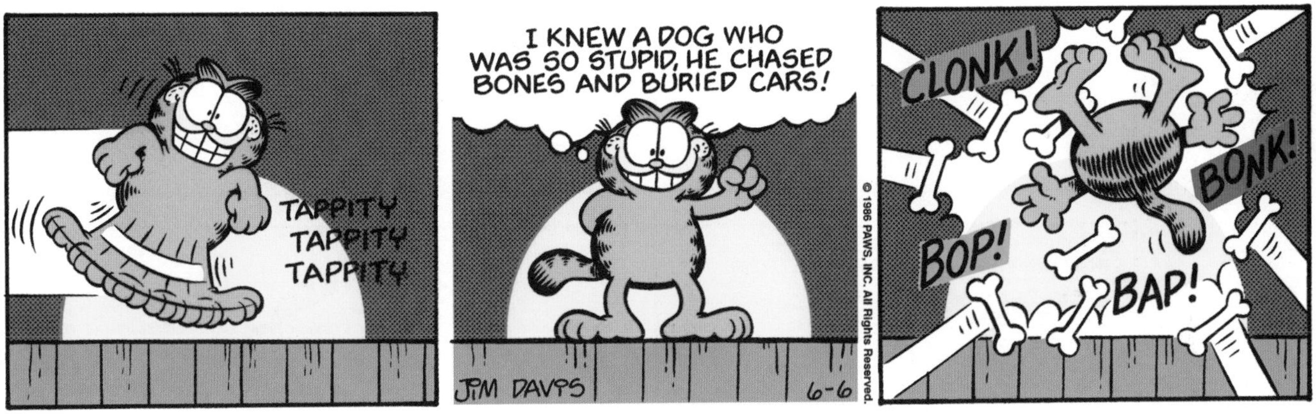
TAPPITY
TAPPITY
TAPPITY
I KNEW A DOG WHO WAS SO STUPID, HE CHASED BONES AND BURIED CARS!
JIM DAVIS
6-6
© 1986 PAWS, INC. All Rights Reserved.
CLONK!
BONK!
BOP!
BAP!

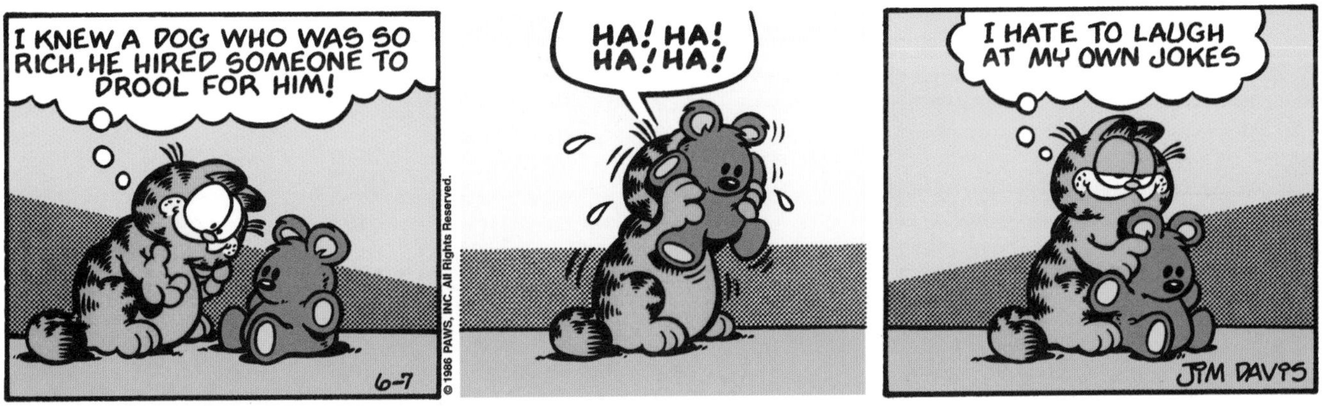
I KNEW A DOG WHO WAS SO RICH, HE HIRED SOMEONE TO DROOL FOR HIM!
6-7
© 1986 PAWS, INC. All Rights Reserved.
HA! HA! HA! HA!
I HATE TO LAUGH AT MY OWN JOKES
JIM DAVIS

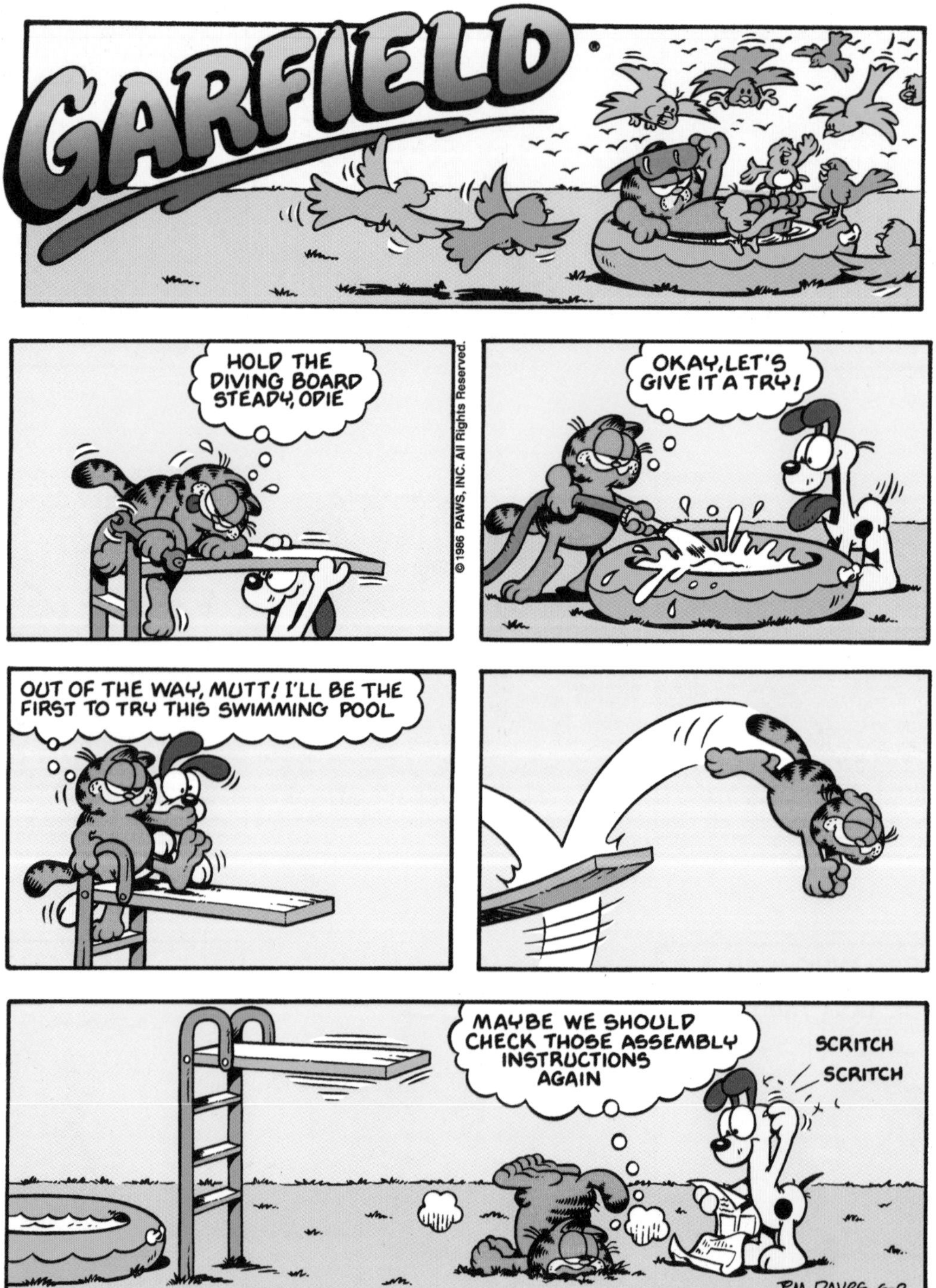
GARFIELD
HOLD THE DIVING BOARD STEADY, ODIE
© 1986 PAWS, INC. All Rights Reserved.
OKAY, LET'S GIVE IT A TRY!
OUT OF THE WAY, MUTT! I'LL BE THE FIRST TO TRY THIS SWIMMING POOL
MAYBE WE SHOULD CHECK THOSE ASSEMBLY INSTRUCTIONS AGAIN
SCRITCH
SCRITCH
JIM DAVIS 6-8

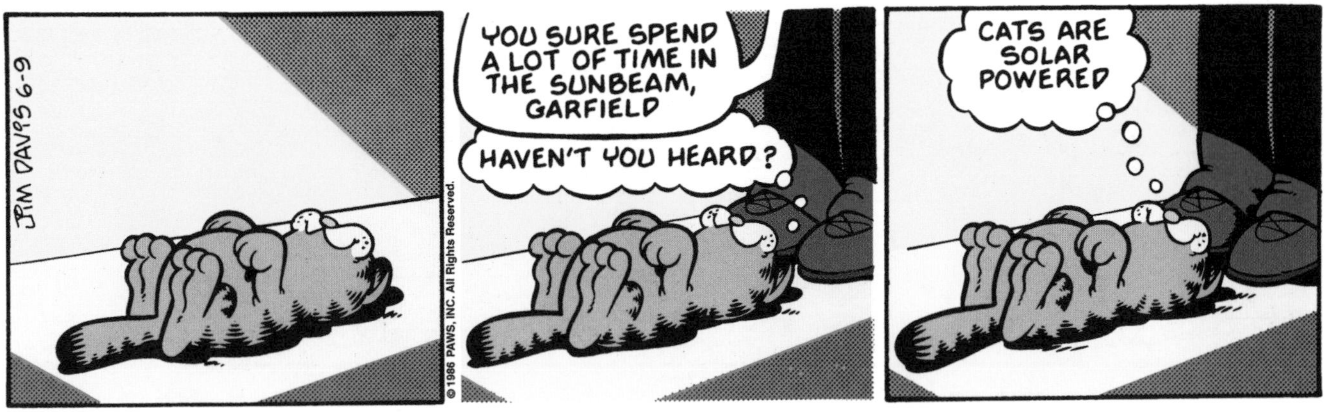
JIM DAVIS 6-9
© 1986 PAWS, INC. All Rights Reserved.
YOU SURE SPEND A LOT OF TIME IN THE SUNBEAM, GARFIELD
HAVEN'T YOU HEARD?
CATS ARE SOLAR POWERED

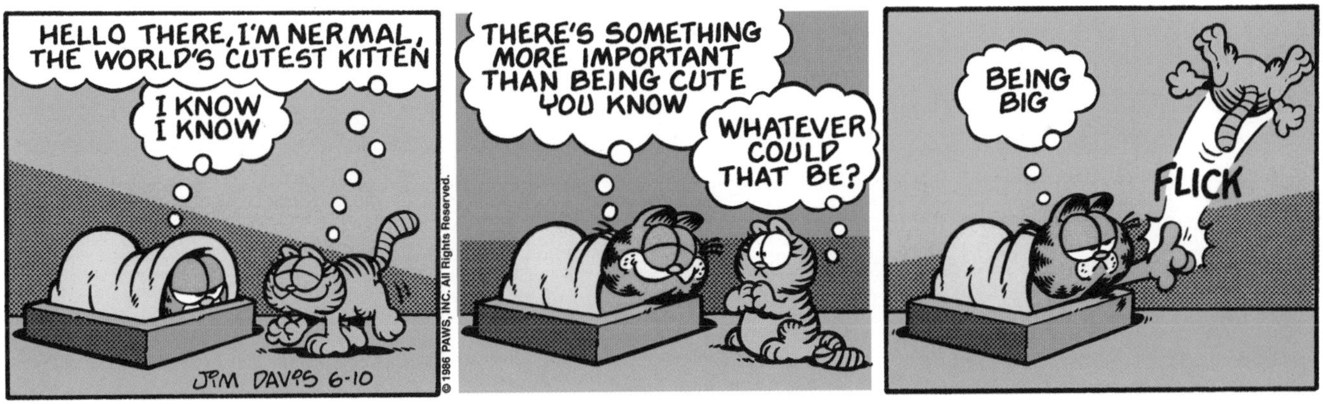
HELLO THERE, I'M NERMAL, THE WORLD'S CUTEST KITTEN
I KNOW I KNOW
JIM DAVIS 6-10
© 1986 PAWS, INC. All Rights Reserved.
THERE'S SOMETHING MORE IMPORTANT THAN BEING CUTE YOU KNOW
WHATEVER COULD THAT BE?
BEING BIG
FLICK

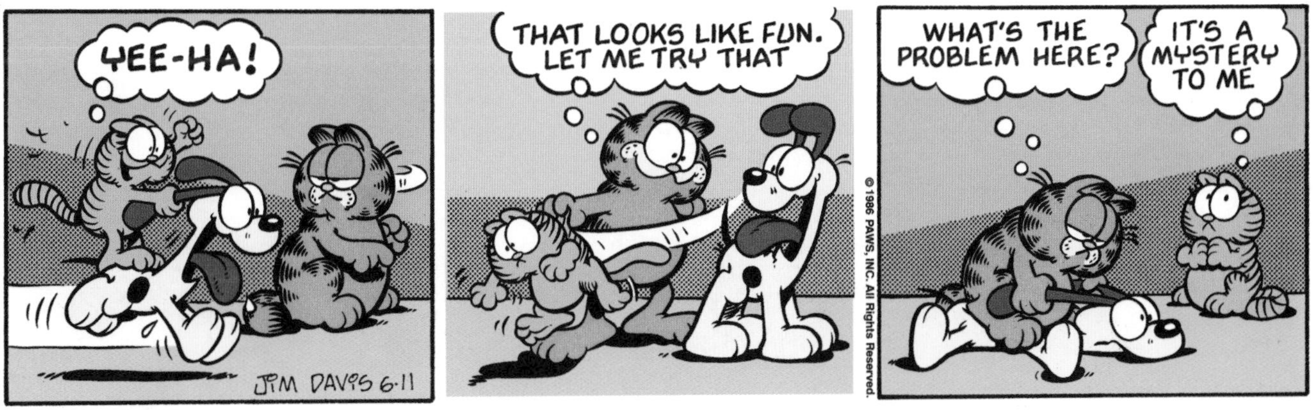
YEE-HA!
JIM DAVIS 6-11
THAT LOOKS LIKE FUN. LET ME TRY THAT
© 1986 PAWS, INC. All Rights Reserved.
WHAT'S THE PROBLEM HERE?
IT'S A MYSTERY TO ME

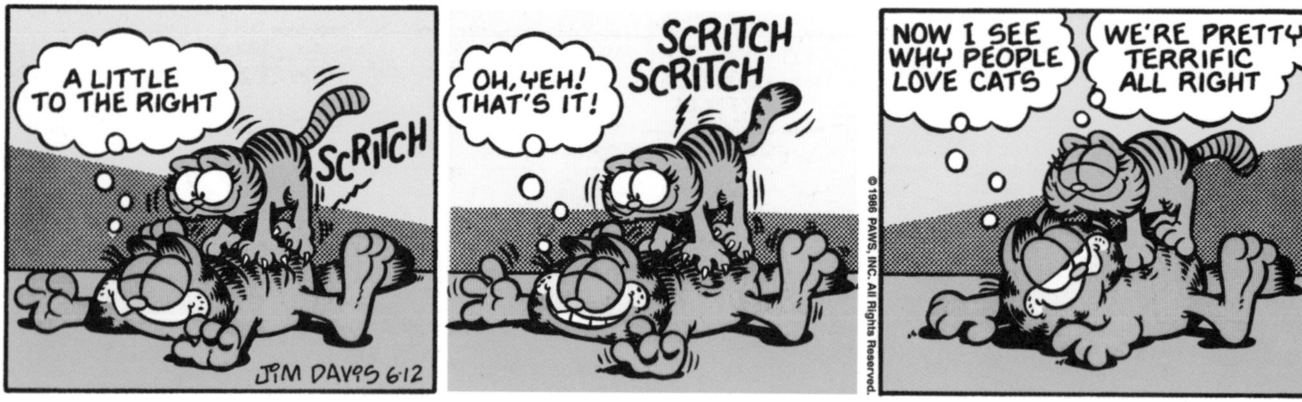
A LITTLE TO THE RIGHT
SCRITCH
JIM DAVIS 6-12
OH, YEH! THAT'S IT!
SCRITCH SCRITCH
© 1986 PAWS, INC. All Rights Reserved.
NOW I SEE WHY PEOPLE LOVE CATS
WE'RE PRETTY TERRIFIC ALL RIGHT

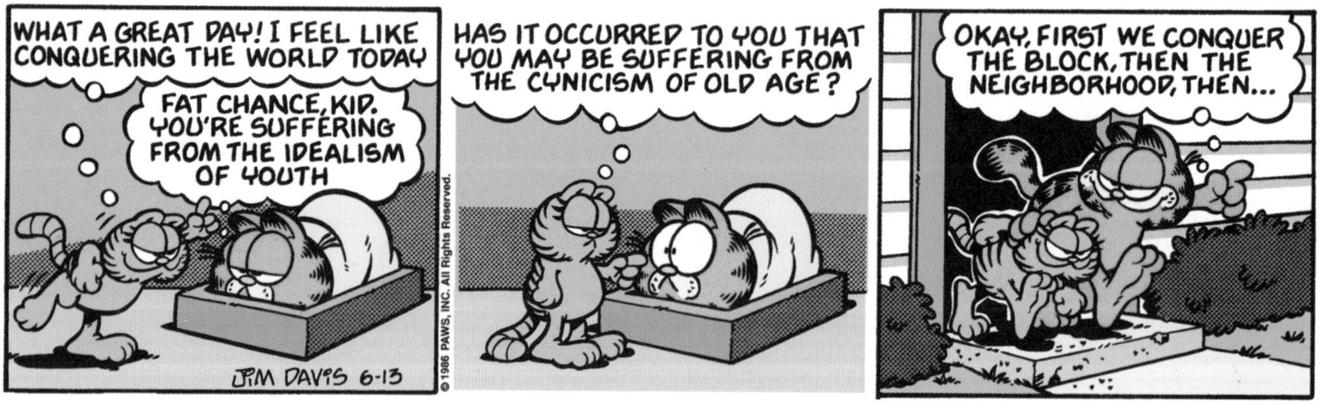
WHAT A GREAT DAY! I FEEL LIKE CONQUERING THE WORLD TODAY
FAT CHANCE, KID. YOU'RE SUFFERING FROM THE IDEALISM OF YOUTH
JIM DAVIS 6-13
© 1986 PAWS, INC. All Rights Reserved.
HAS IT OCCURRED TO YOU THAT YOU MAY BE SUFFERING FROM THE CYNICISM OF OLD AGE?
OKAY, FIRST WE CONQUER THE BLOCK, THEN THE NEIGHBORHOOD, THEN...

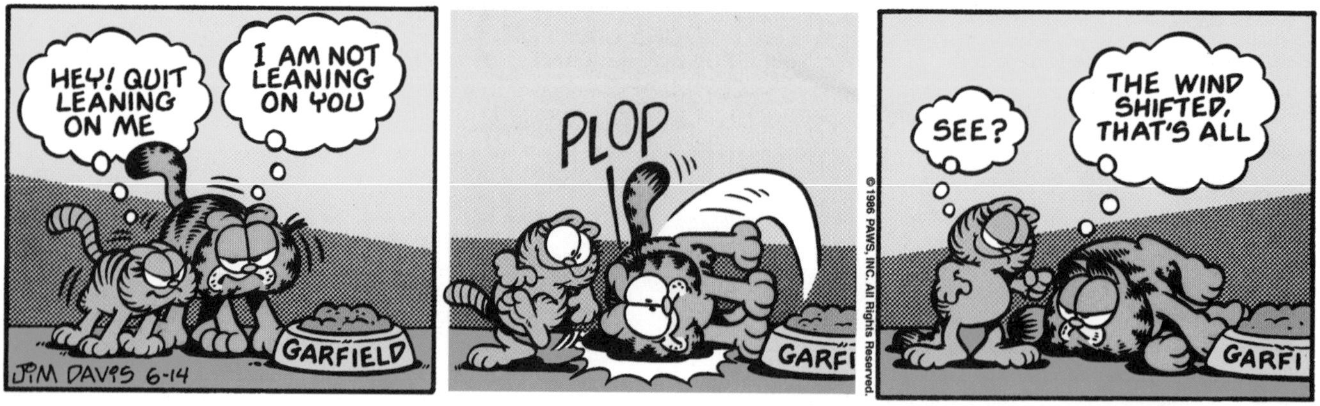
HEY! QUIT LEANING ON ME
I AM NOT LEANING ON YOU
GARFIELD
JIM DAVIS 6-14
PLOP
GARFI
© 1986 PAWS, INC. All Rights Reserved.
SEE?
THE WIND SHIFTED, THAT'S ALL
GARFI

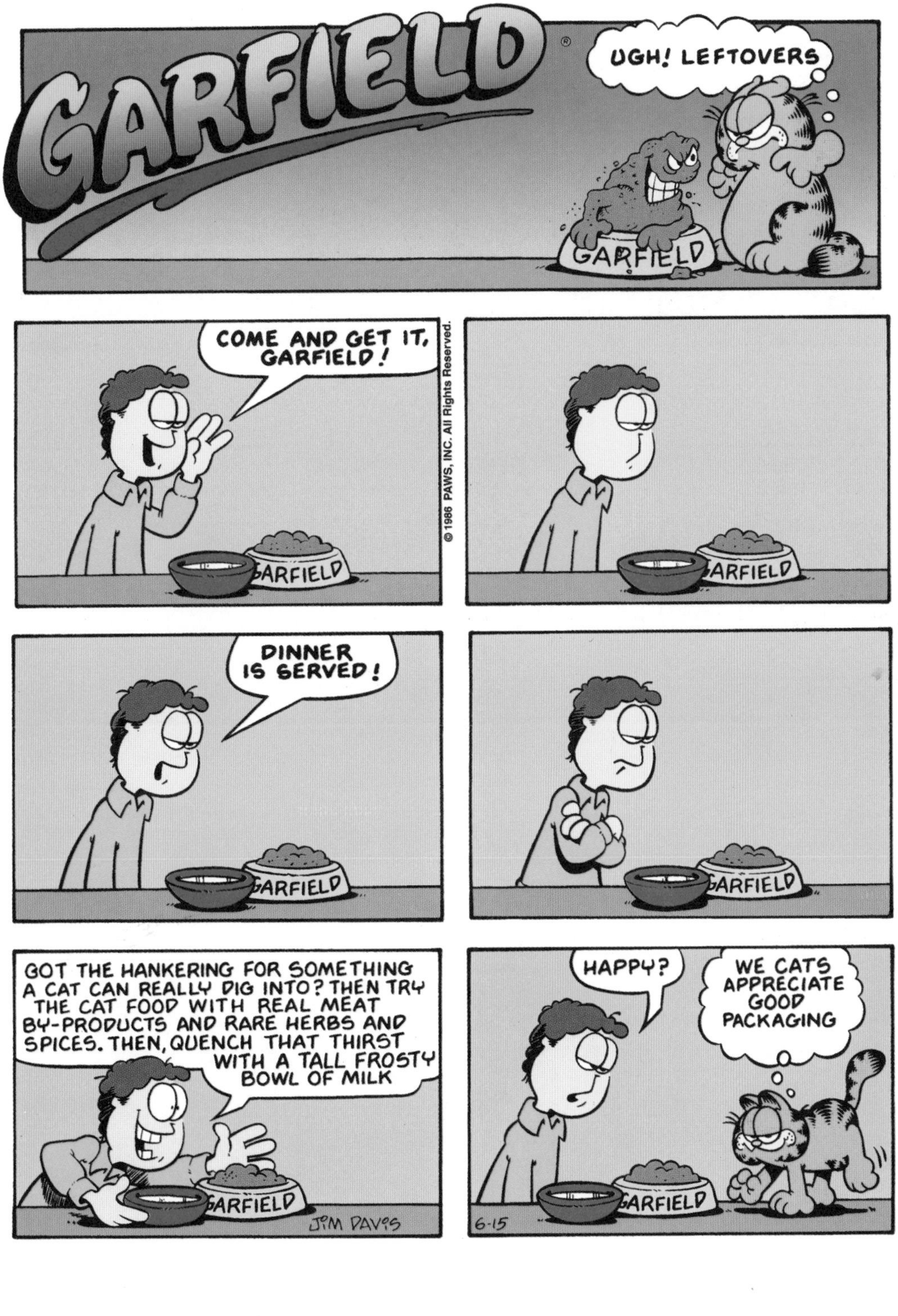
GARFIELD
UGH! LEFTOVERS
GARFIELD
COME AND GET IT, GARFIELD!
GARFIELD
GARFIELD
DINNER IS SERVED!
GARFIELD
GARFIELD
GOT THE HANKERING FOR SOMETHING A CAT CAN REALLY DIG INTO? THEN TRY THE CAT FOOD WITH REAL MEAT BY-PRODUCTS AND RARE HERBS AND SPICES. THEN, QUENCH THAT THIRST WITH A TALL FROSTY BOWL OF MILK
GARFIELD
JIM DAVIS
HAPPY?
WE CATS APPRECIATE GOOD PACKAGING
GARFIELD
6-15

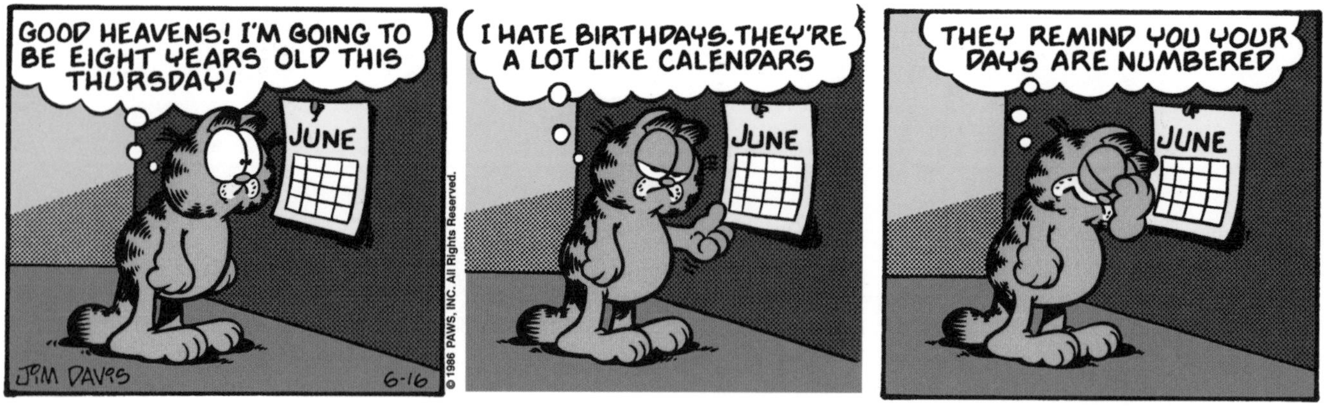
GOOD HEAVENS! I'M GOING TO BE EIGHT YEARS OLD THIS THURSDAY!
JUNE
JIM DAVIS 6-16
© 1986 PAWS, INC. All Rights Reserved.
I HATE BIRTHDAYS. THEY'RE A LOT LIKE CALENDARS
JUNE
THEY REMIND YOU YOUR DAYS ARE NUMBERED
JUNE

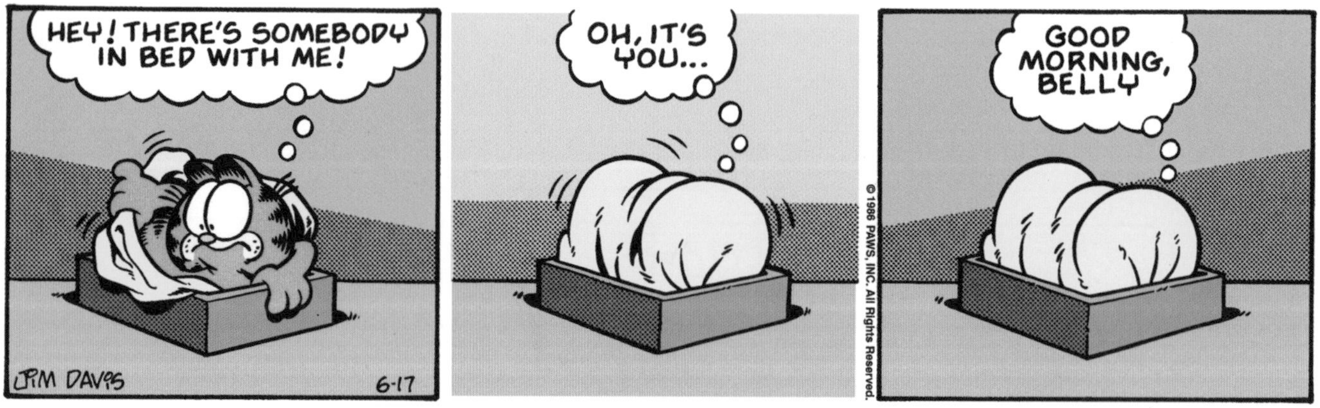
HEY! THERE'S SOMEBODY IN BED WITH ME!
JIM DAVIS 6-17
OH, IT'S YOU...
© 1986 PAWS, INC. All Rights Reserved.
GOOD MORNING, BELLY

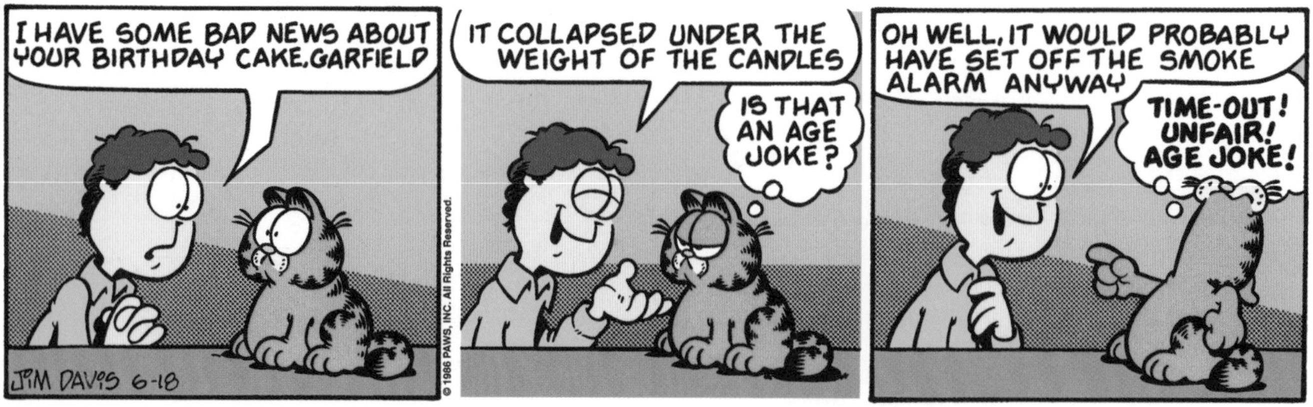
I HAVE SOME BAD NEWS ABOUT YOUR BIRTHDAY CAKE, GARFIELD
JIM DAVIS 6-18
© 1986 PAWS, INC. All Rights Reserved.
IT COLLAPSED UNDER THE WEIGHT OF THE CANDLES
IS THAT AN AGE JOKE?
OH WELL, IT WOULD PROBABLY HAVE SET OFF THE SMOKE ALARM ANYWAY
TIME-OUT! UNFAIR! AGE JOKE!

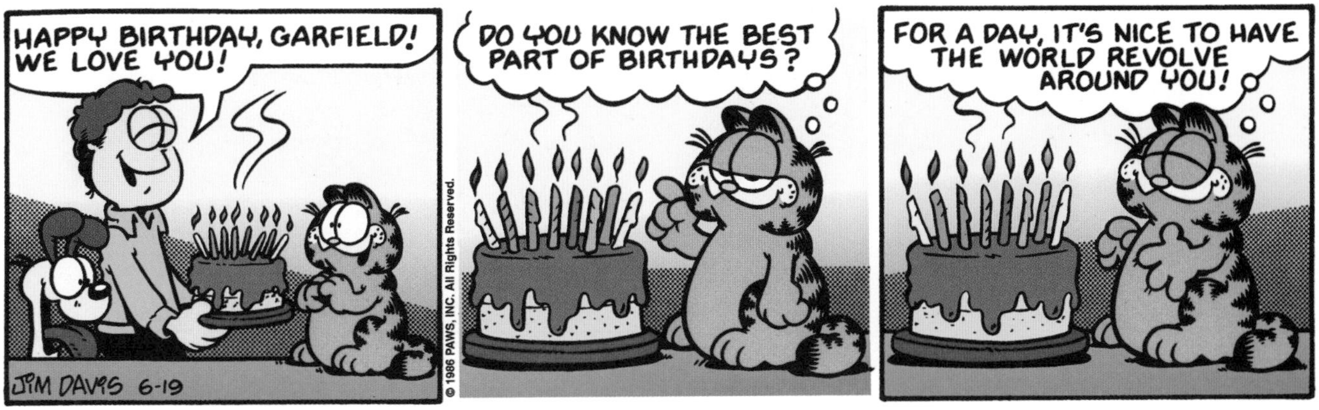
HAPPY BIRTHDAY, GARFIELD! WE LOVE YOU!
JIM DAVIS 6-19
© 1986 PAWS, INC. All Rights Reserved.
DO YOU KNOW THE BEST PART OF BIRTHDAYS?
FOR A DAY, IT'S NICE TO HAVE THE WORLD REVOLVE AROUND YOU!

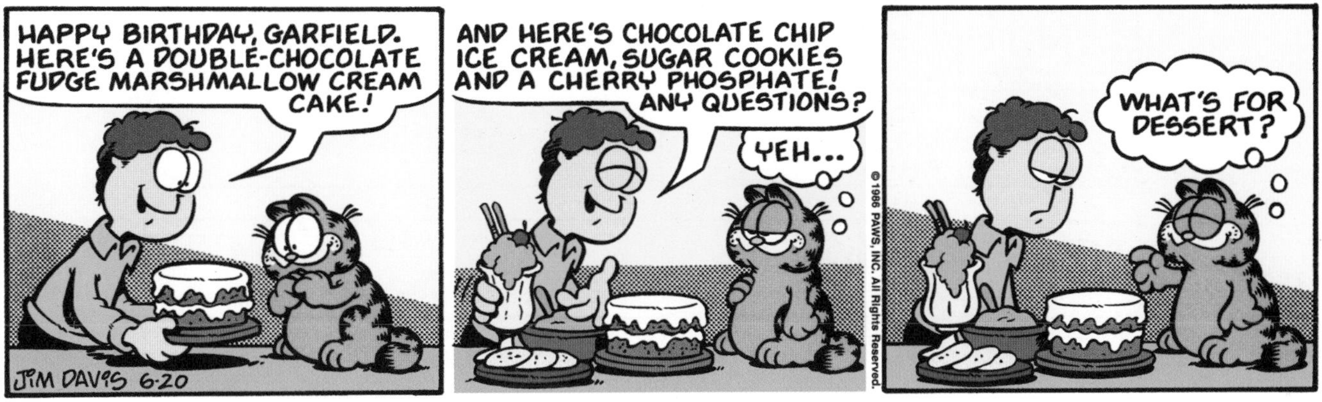
HAPPY BIRTHDAY, GARFIELD. HERE'S A DOUBLE-CHOCOLATE FUDGE MARSHMALLOW CREAM CAKE!
JIM DAVIS 6-20
AND HERE'S CHOCOLATE CHIP ICE CREAM, SUGAR COOKIES AND A CHERRY PHOSPHATE! ANY QUESTIONS?
YEH...
© 1986 PAWS, INC. All Rights Reserved.
WHAT'S FOR DESSERT?

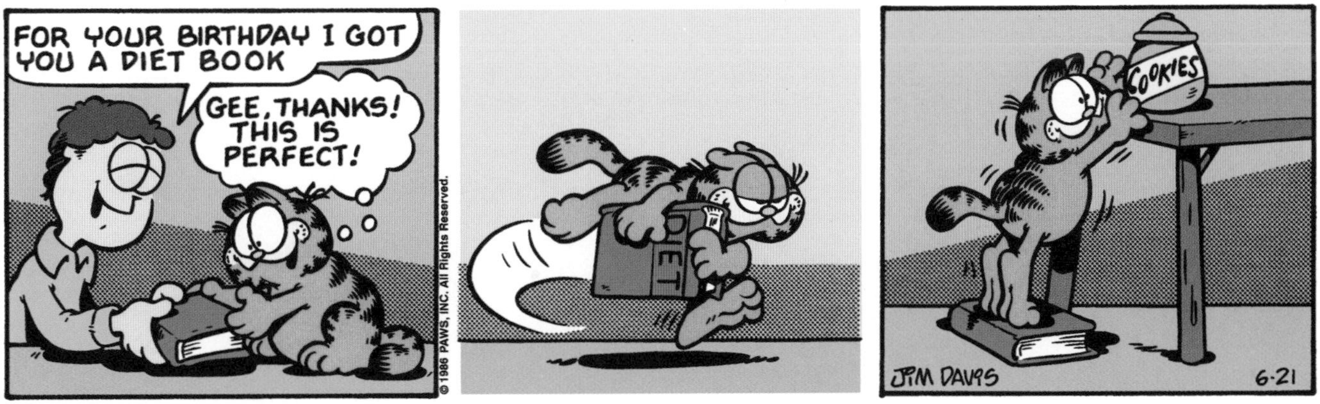
FOR YOUR BIRTHDAY I GOT YOU A DIET BOOK
GEE, THANKS! THIS IS PERFECT!
© 1986 PAWS, INC. All Rights Reserved.
DIET
COOKIES
JIM DAVIS
6-21

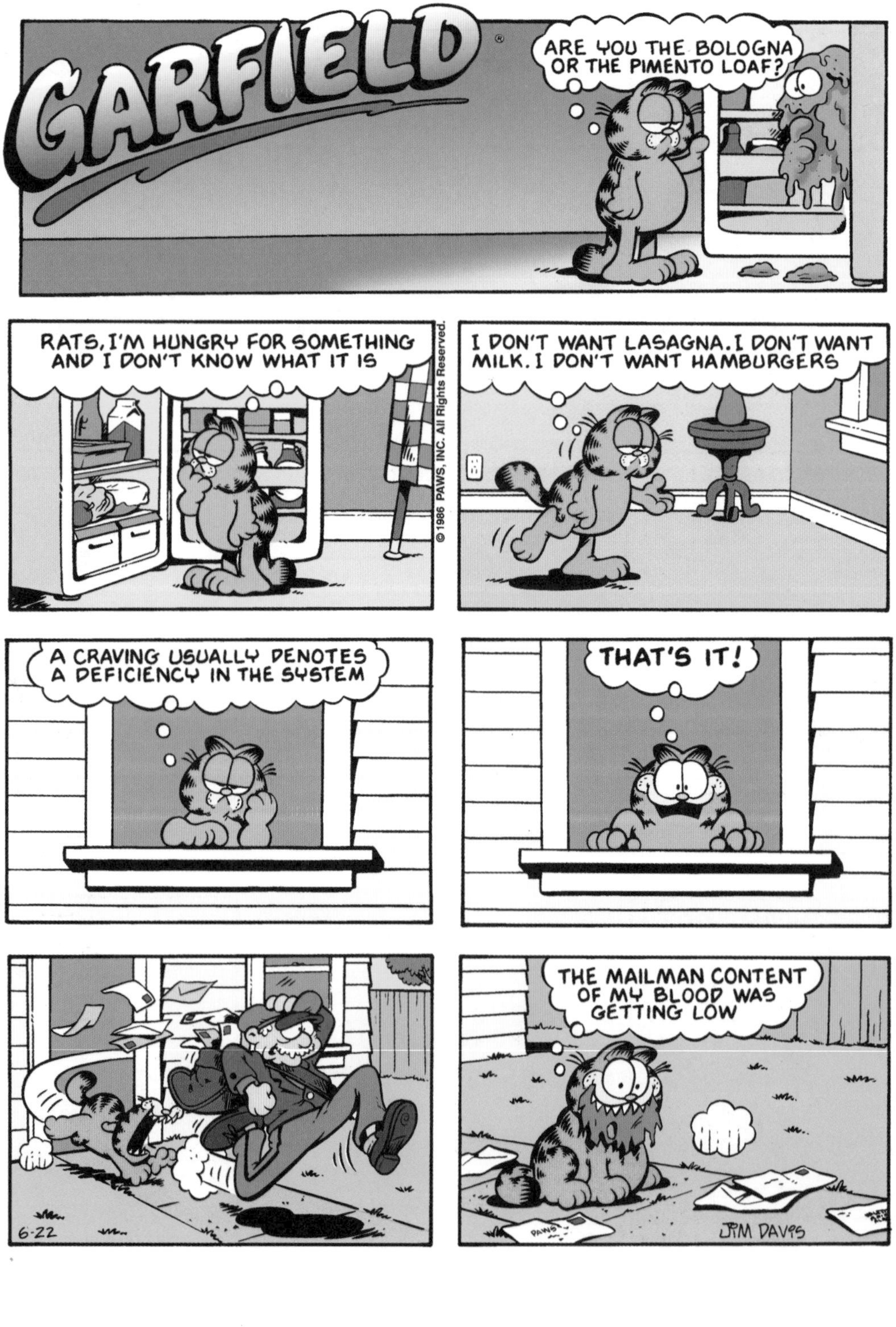
GARFIELD
ARE YOU THE BOLOGNA OR THE PIMENTO LOAF?
RATS, I'M HUNGRY FOR SOMETHING AND I DON'T KNOW WHAT IT IS
© 1986 PAWS, INC. All Rights Reserved.
I DON'T WANT LASAGNA. I DON'T WANT MILK. I DON'T WANT HAMBURGERS
A CRAVING USUALLY DENOTES A DEFICIENCY IN THE SYSTEM
THAT'S IT!
6-22
THE MAILMAN CONTENT OF MY BLOOD WAS GETTING LOW
JIM DAVIS

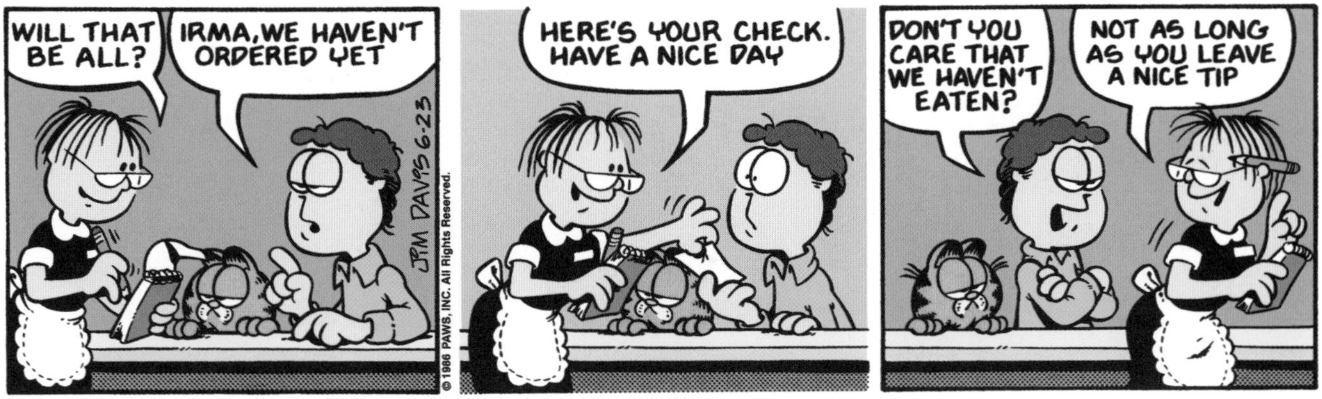
WILL THAT BE ALL?
IRMA, WE HAVEN'T ORDERED YET
JIM DAVIS 6-23
© 1986 PAWS, INC. All Rights Reserved.
HERE'S YOUR CHECK. HAVE A NICE DAY
DON'T YOU CARE THAT WE HAVEN'T EATEN?
NOT AS LONG AS YOU LEAVE A NICE TIP

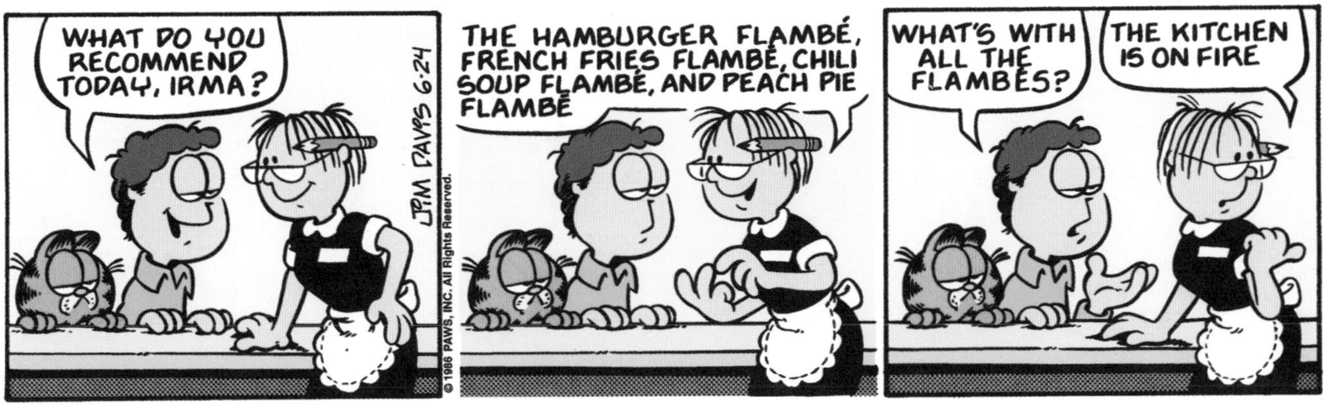
WHAT DO YOU RECOMMEND TODAY, IRMA?
JIM DAVIS 6-24
© 1986 PAWS, INC. All Rights Reserved.
THE HAMBURGER FLAMBÉ, FRENCH FRIES FLAMBÉ, CHILI SOUP FLAMBÉ, AND PEACH PIE FLAMBÉ
WHAT'S WITH ALL THE FLAMBÉS?
THE KITCHEN IS ON FIRE

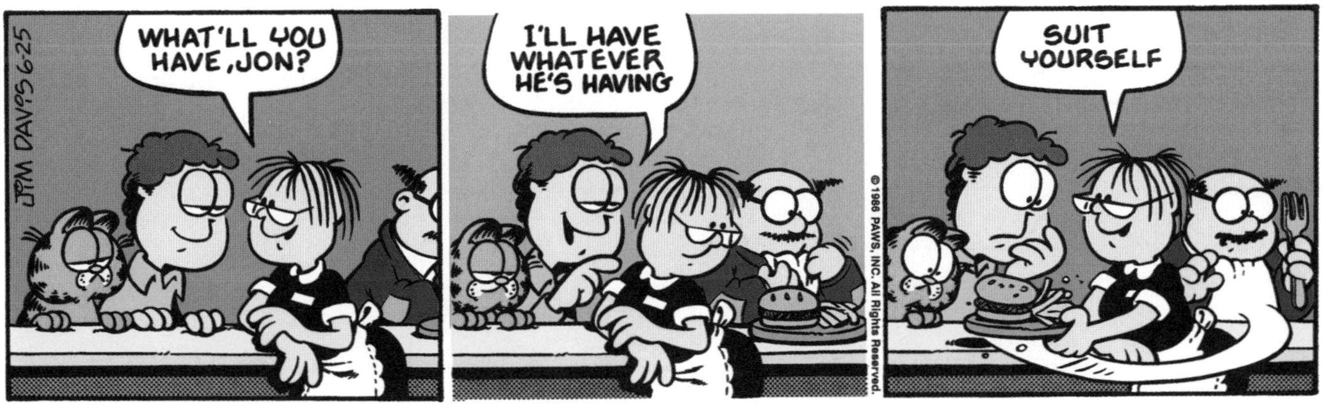
JIM DAVIS 6-25
WHAT'LL YOU HAVE, JON?
I'LL HAVE WHATEVER HE'S HAVING
© 1986 PAWS, INC. All Rights Reserved.
SUIT YOURSELF

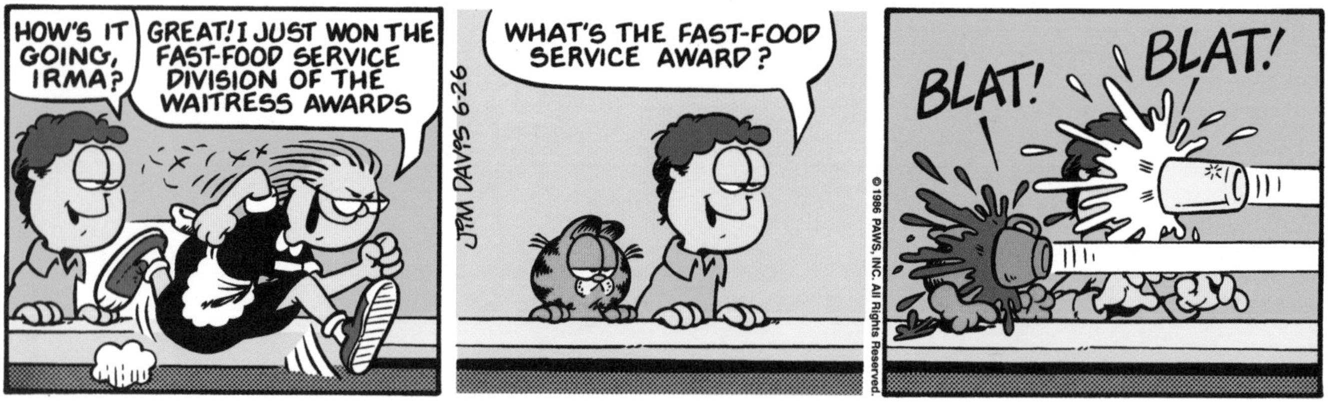
HOW'S IT GOING, IRMA?
GREAT! I JUST WON THE FAST-FOOD SERVICE DIVISION OF THE WAITRESS AWARDS
JIM DAVIS 6-26
WHAT'S THE FAST-FOOD SERVICE AWARD?
© 1986 PAWS, INC. All Rights Reserved.
BLAT!
BLAT!

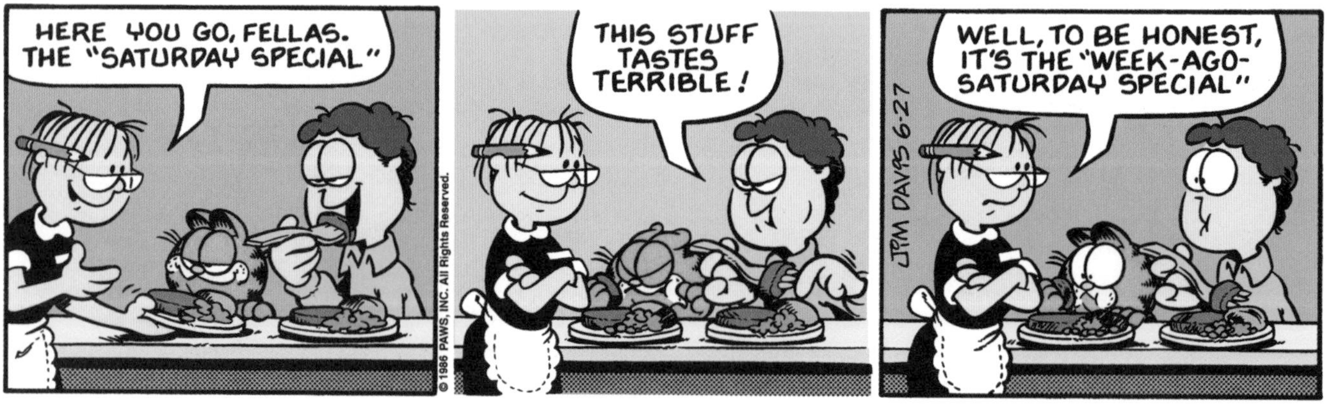
HERE YOU GO, FELLAS. THE "SATURDAY SPECIAL"
© 1986 PAWS, INC. All Rights Reserved.
THIS STUFF TASTES TERRIBLE!
JIM DAVIS 6-27
WELL, TO BE HONEST, IT'S THE "WEEK-AGO-SATURDAY SPECIAL"

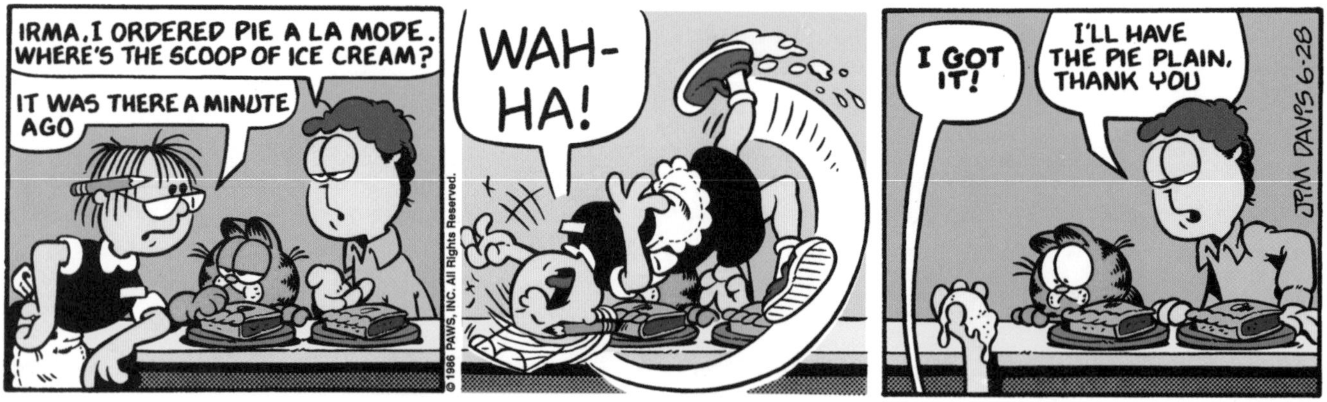
IRMA, I ORDERED PIE A LA MODE. WHERE'S THE SCOOP OF ICE CREAM?
IT WAS THERE A MINUTE AGO
© 1986 PAWS, INC. All Rights Reserved.
WAH-HA!
I GOT IT!
I'LL HAVE THE PIE PLAIN, THANK YOU
JIM DAVIS 6-28

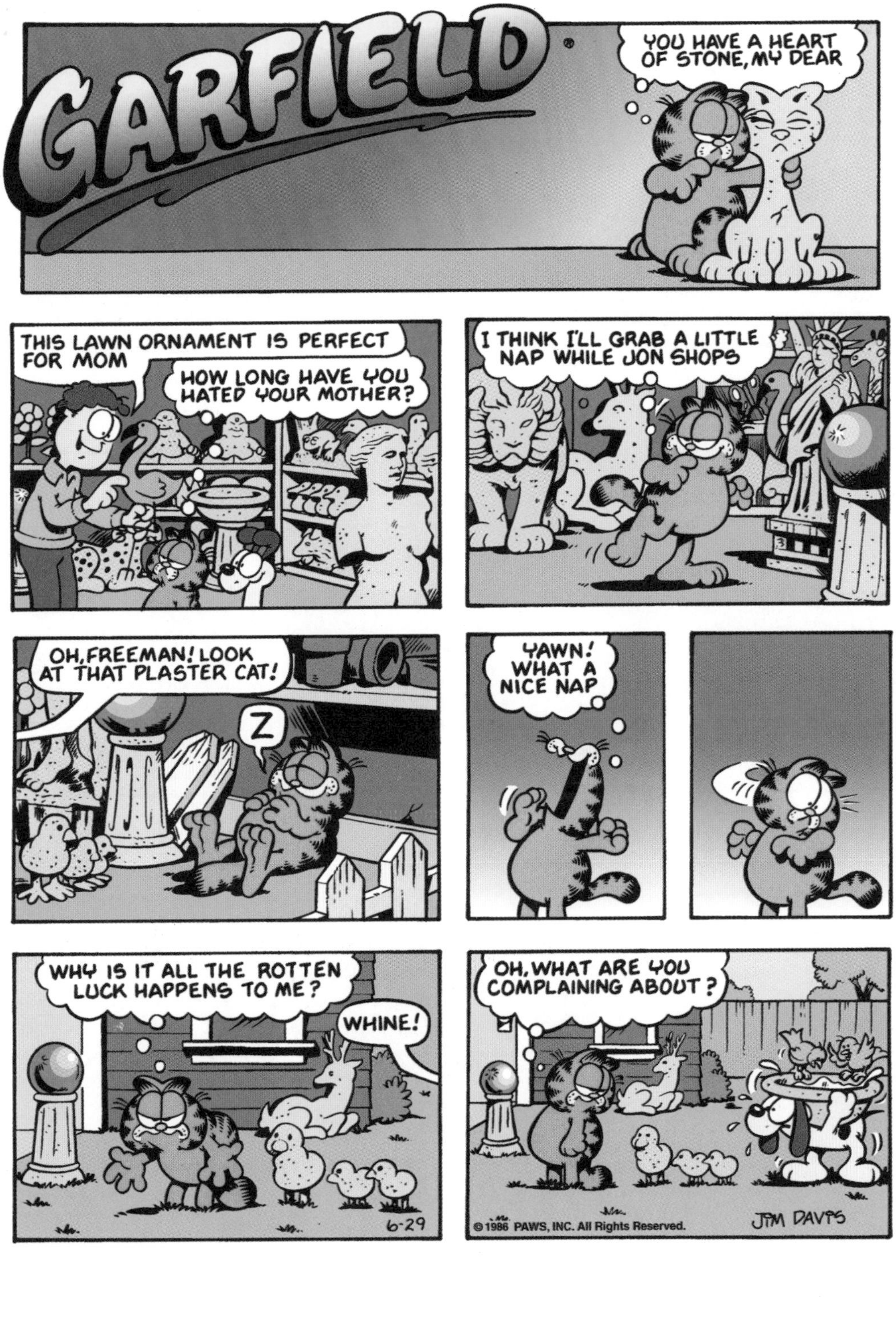
GARFIELD
YOU HAVE A HEART OF STONE, MY DEAR
THIS LAWN ORNAMENT IS PERFECT FOR MOM
HOW LONG HAVE YOU HATED YOUR MOTHER?
I THINK I'LL GRAB A LITTLE NAP WHILE JON SHOPS
OH, FREEMAN! LOOK AT THAT PLASTER CAT!
Z
YAWN! WHAT A NICE NAP
WHY IS IT ALL THE ROTTEN LUCK HAPPENS TO ME?
WHINE!
6-29
OH, WHAT ARE YOU COMPLAINING ABOUT?
© 1986 PAWS, INC. All Rights Reserved.
JIM DAVIS

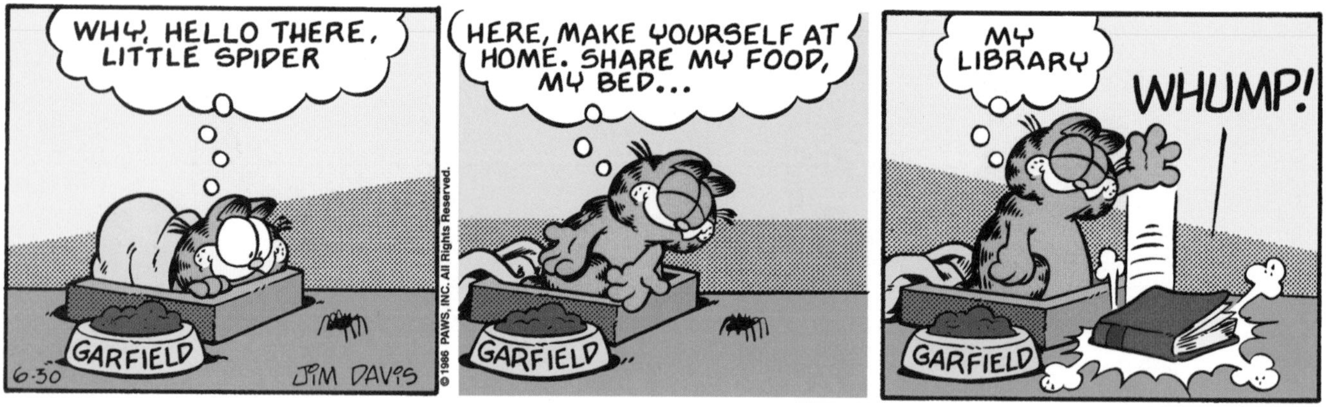
WHY, HELLO THERE, LITTLE SPIDER
GARFIELD
6-30
JIM DAVIS
© 1986 PAWS, INC. All Rights Reserved.
HERE, MAKE YOURSELF AT HOME. SHARE MY FOOD, MY BED...
GARFIELD
MY LIBRARY
WHUMP!
GARFIELD

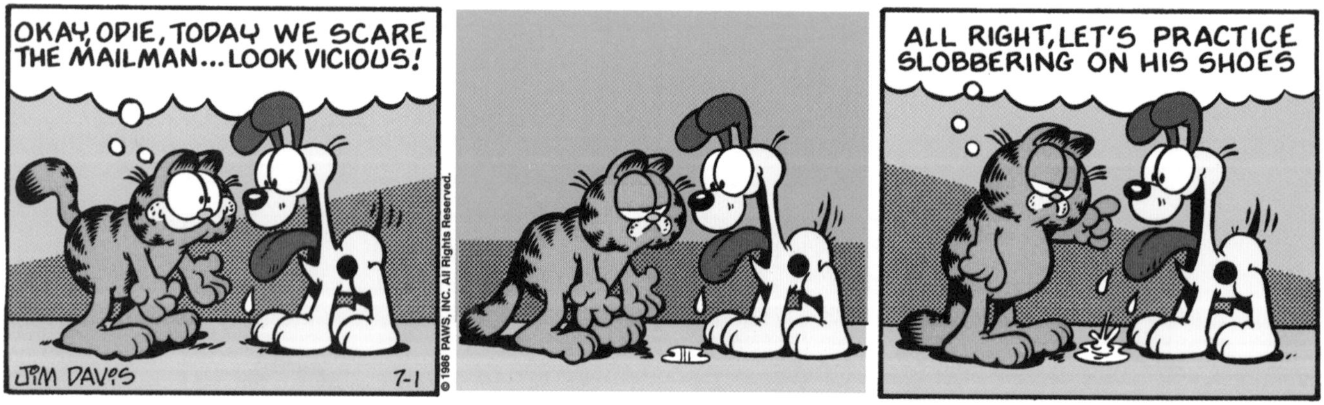
OKAY, ODIE, TODAY WE SCARE THE MAILMAN... LOOK VICIOUS!
JIM DAVIS
7-1
© 1986 PAWS, INC. All Rights Reserved.
ALL RIGHT, LET'S PRACTICE SLOBBERING ON HIS SHOES

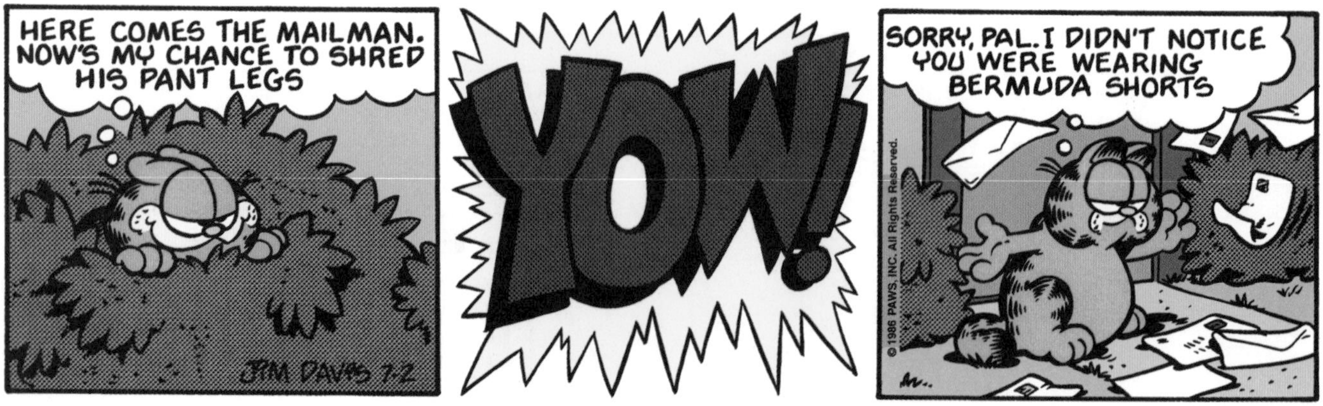
HERE COMES THE MAILMAN. NOW'S MY CHANCE TO SHRED HIS PANT LEGS
JIM DAVIS 7-2
YOW!
SORRY, PAL. I DIDN'T NOTICE YOU WERE WEARING BERMUDA SHORTS
© 1986 PAWS, INC. All Rights Reserved.

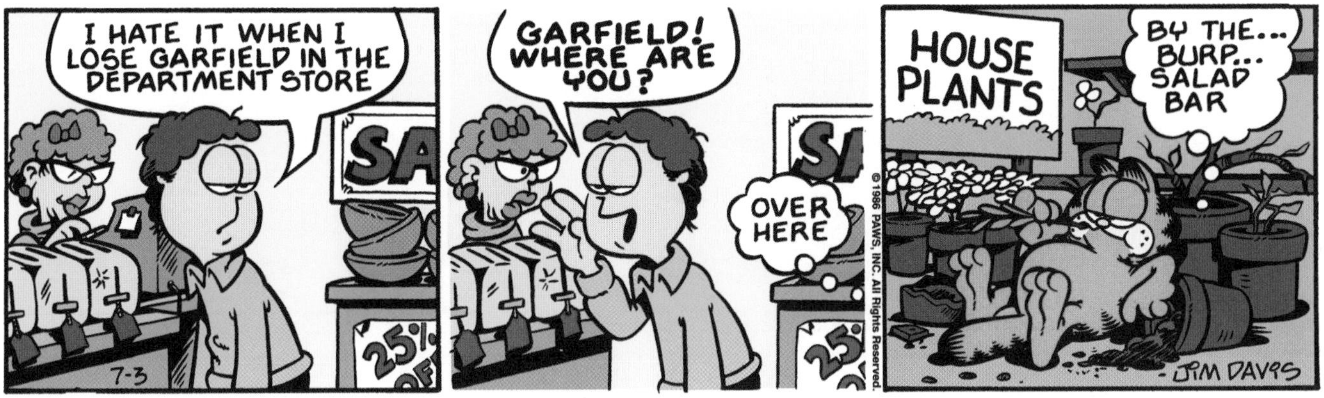
I HATE IT WHEN I LOSE GARFIELD IN THE DEPARTMENT STORE
7-3
GARFIELD! WHERE ARE YOU?
OVER HERE
© 1986 PAWS, INC. All Rights Reserved.
HOUSE PLANTS
BY THE... BURP... SALAD BAR
JIM DAVIS

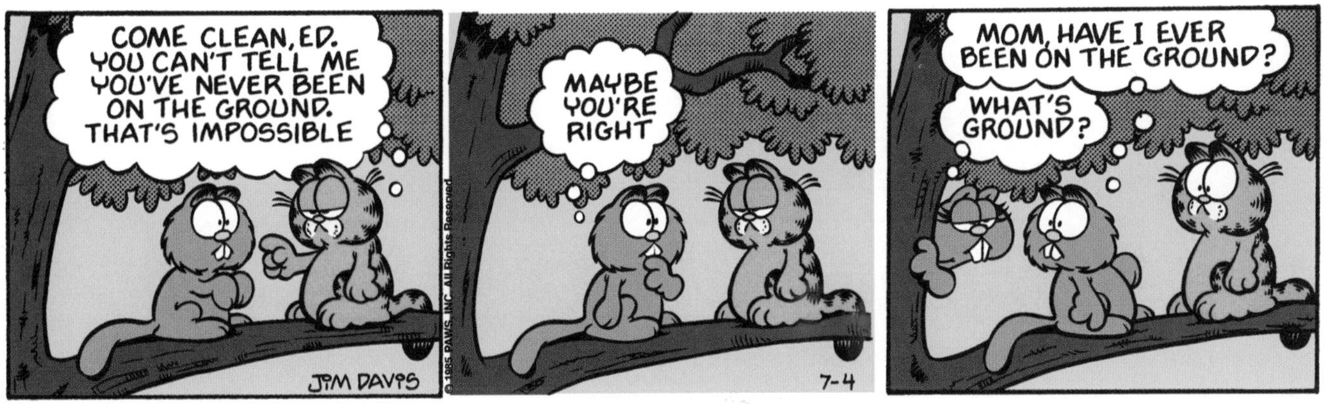
COME CLEAN, ED. YOU CAN'T TELL ME YOU'VE NEVER BEEN ON THE GROUND. THAT'S IMPOSSIBLE
JIM DAVIS
© 1985 PAWS, INC. All Rights Reserved.
MAYBE YOU'RE RIGHT
7-4
MOM, HAVE I EVER BEEN ON THE GROUND?
WHAT'S GROUND?

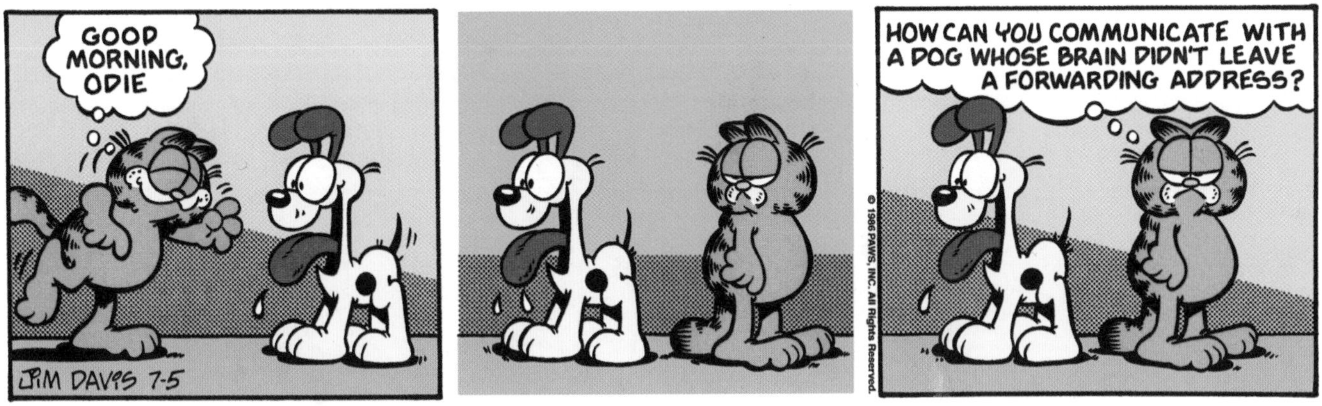
GOOD MORNING, ODIE
JIM DAVIS 7-5
© 1986 PAWS, INC. All Rights Reserved.
HOW CAN YOU COMMUNICATE WITH A DOG WHOSE BRAIN DIDN'T LEAVE A FORWARDING ADDRESS?

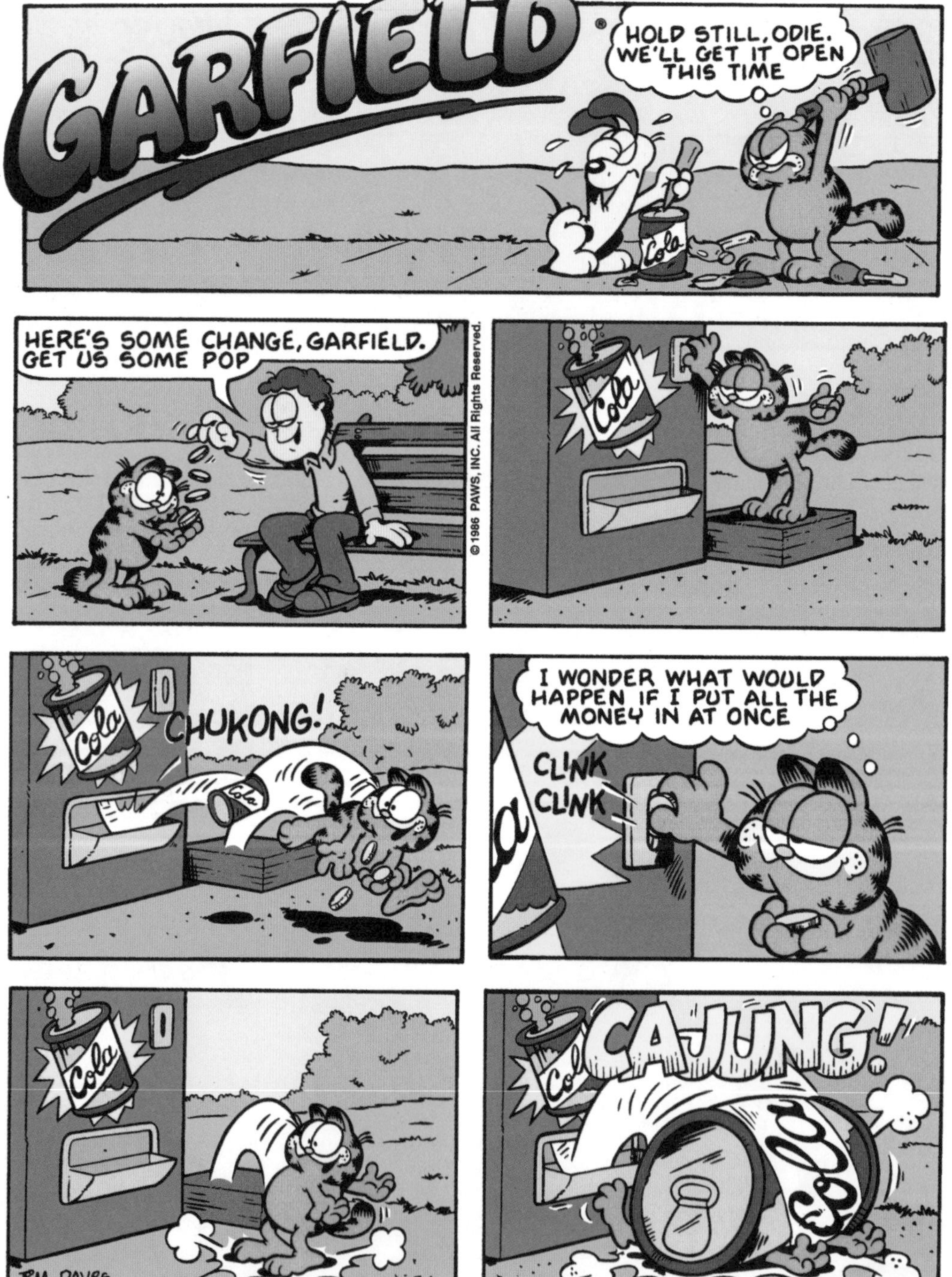
GARFIELD
HOLD STILL, ODIE. WE'LL GET IT OPEN THIS TIME
Cola
HERE'S SOME CHANGE, GARFIELD. GET US SOME POP
© 1986 PAWS, INC. All Rights Reserved.
Cola
Cola
CHUKONG!
I WONDER WHAT WOULD HAPPEN IF I PUT ALL THE MONEY IN AT ONCE
CLINK
CLINK
Cola
JIM DAVIS
7-6
CAJUNG!
Cola

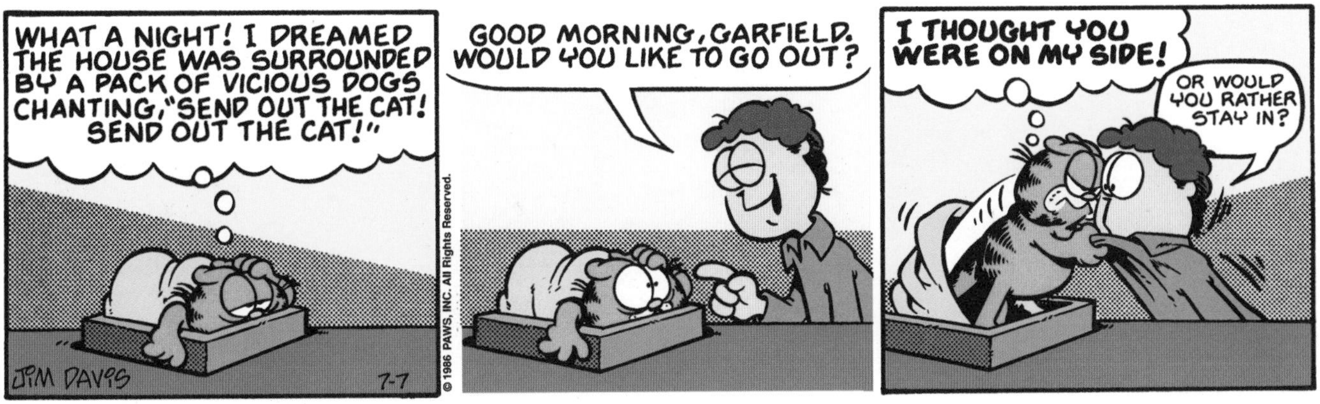
WHAT A NIGHT! I DREAMED THE HOUSE WAS SURROUNDED BY A PACK OF VICIOUS DOGS CHANTING, "SEND OUT THE CAT! SEND OUT THE CAT!"
JIM DAVIS 7-7
© 1986 PAWS, INC. All Rights Reserved.
GOOD MORNING, GARFIELD. WOULD YOU LIKE TO GO OUT?
I THOUGHT YOU WERE ON MY SIDE!
OR WOULD YOU RATHER STAY IN?

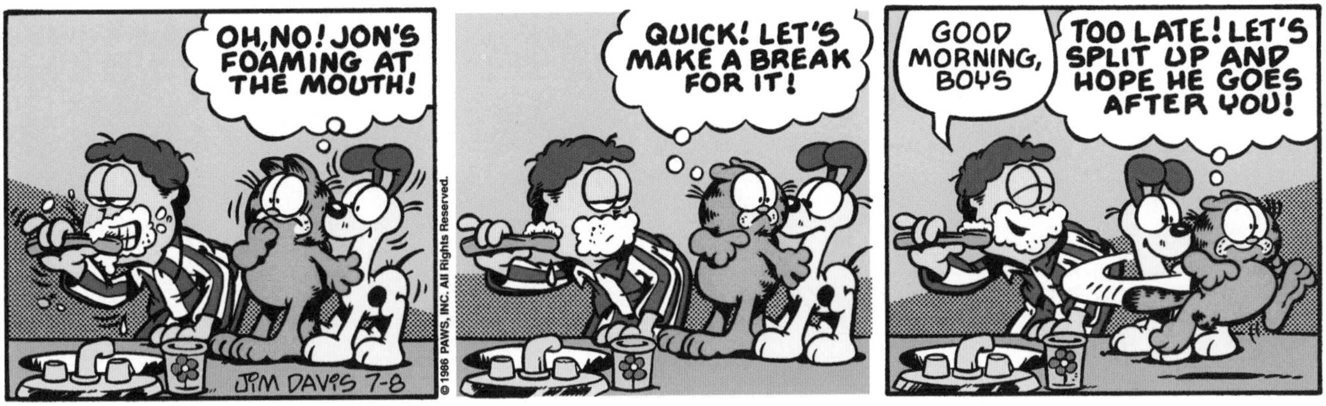
OH, NO! JON'S FOAMING AT THE MOUTH!
JIM DAVIS 7-8
© 1986 PAWS, INC. All Rights Reserved.
QUICK! LET'S MAKE A BREAK FOR IT!
GOOD MORNING, BOYS
TOO LATE! LET'S SPLIT UP AND HOPE HE GOES AFTER YOU!

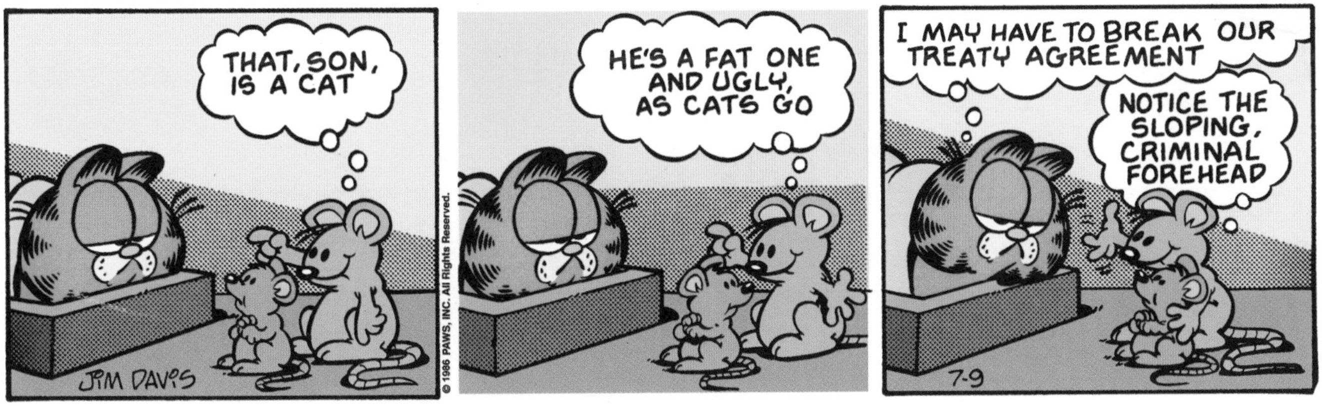
THAT, SON, IS A CAT
JIM DAVIS
© 1986 PAWS, INC. All Rights Reserved.
HE'S A FAT ONE AND UGLY, AS CATS GO
I MAY HAVE TO BREAK OUR TREATY AGREEMENT
NOTICE THE SLOPING, CRIMINAL FOREHEAD
7-9

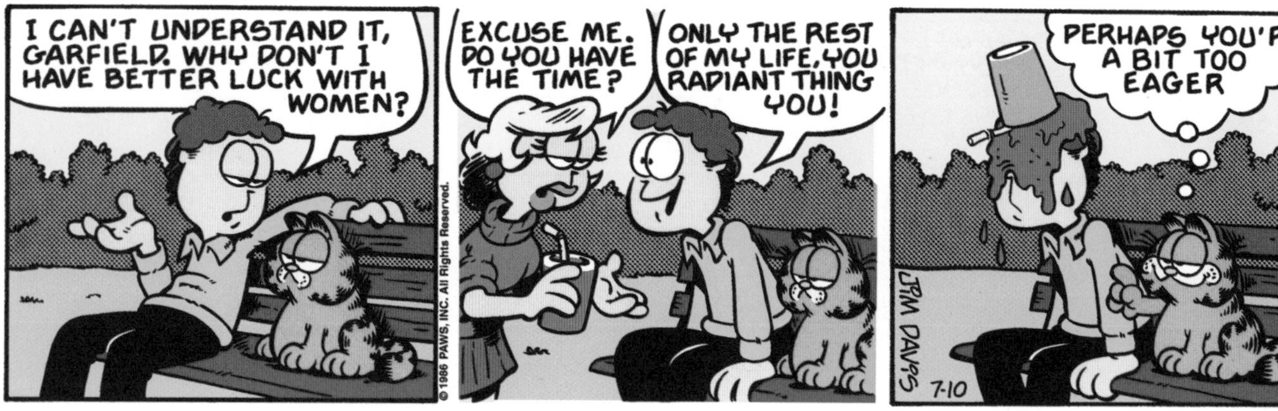
I CAN'T UNDERSTAND IT, GARFIELD. WHY DON'T I HAVE BETTER LUCK WITH WOMEN?
EXCUSE ME. DO YOU HAVE THE TIME?
ONLY THE REST OF MY LIFE, YOU RADIANT THING YOU!
PERHAPS YOU'RE A BIT TOO EAGER
JIM DAVIS 7-10

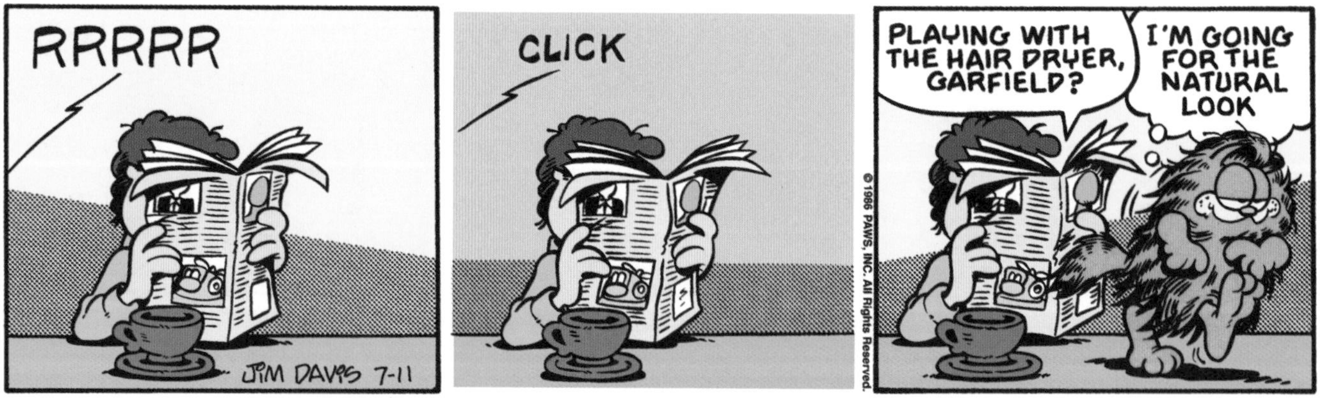
RRRRR
JIM DAVIS 7-11
CLICK
PLAYING WITH THE HAIR DRYER, GARFIELD?
I'M GOING FOR THE NATURAL LOOK

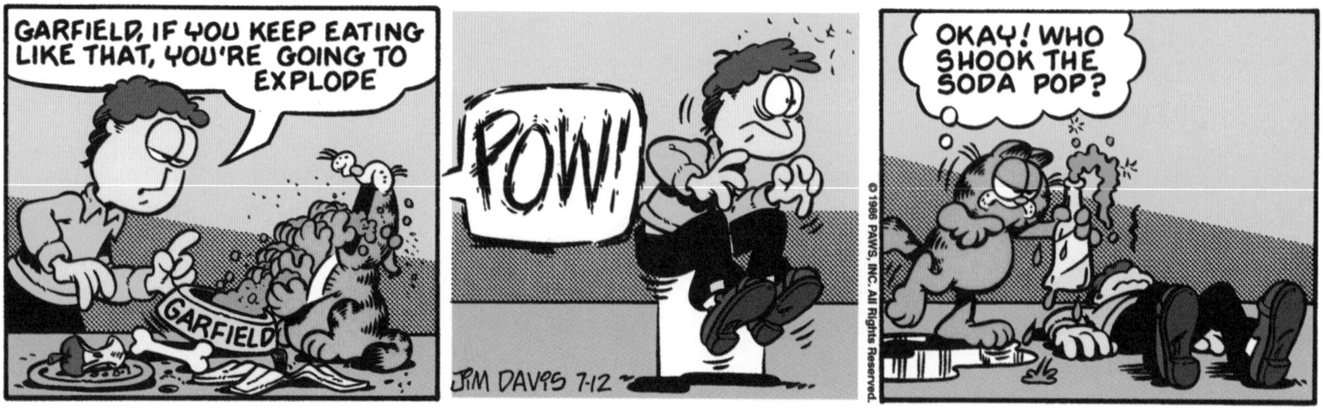
GARFIELD, IF YOU KEEP EATING LIKE THAT, YOU'RE GOING TO EXPLODE
GARFIELD
POW!
JIM DAVIS 7-12
OKAY! WHO SHOOK THE SODA POP?

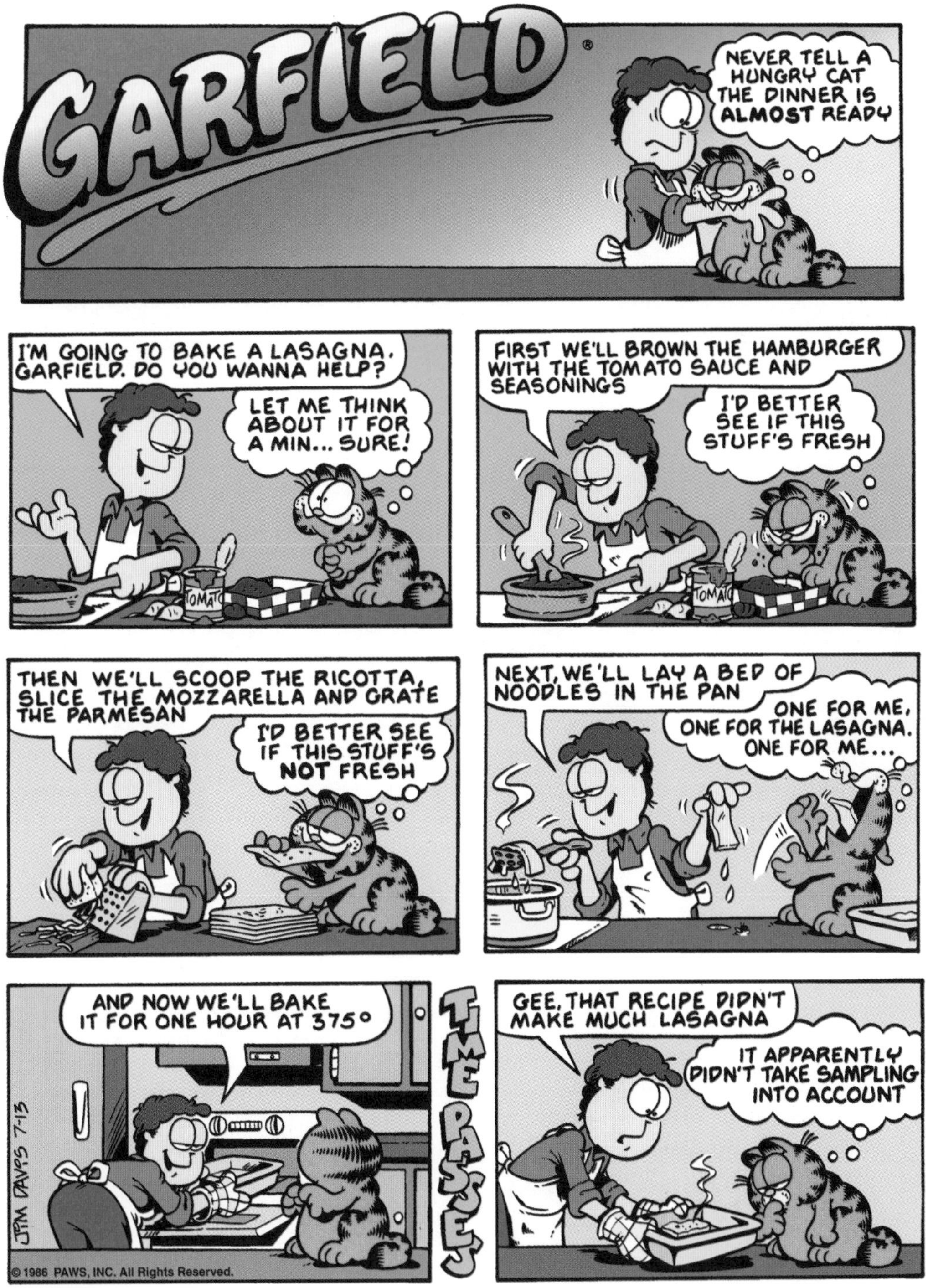
GARFIELD®
NEVER TELL A HUNGRY CAT THE DINNER IS **ALMOST** READY
I'M GOING TO BAKE A LASAGNA, GARFIELD. DO YOU WANNA HELP?
LET ME THINK ABOUT IT FOR A MIN... SURE!
FIRST WE'LL BROWN THE HAMBURGER WITH THE TOMATO SAUCE AND SEASONINGS
I'D BETTER SEE IF THIS STUFF'S FRESH
THEN WE'LL SCOOP THE RICOTTA, SLICE THE MOZZARELLA AND GRATE THE PARMESAN
I'D BETTER SEE IF THIS STUFF'S **NOT** FRESH
NEXT, WE'LL LAY A BED OF NOODLES IN THE PAN
ONE FOR ME, ONE FOR THE LASAGNA. ONE FOR ME...
AND NOW WE'LL BAKE IT FOR ONE HOUR AT 375°
JIM DAVIS 7-13
© 1986 PAWS, INC. All Rights Reserved.
TIME PASSES
GEE, THAT RECIPE DIDN'T MAKE MUCH LASAGNA
IT APPARENTLY DIDN'T TAKE SAMPLING INTO ACCOUNT

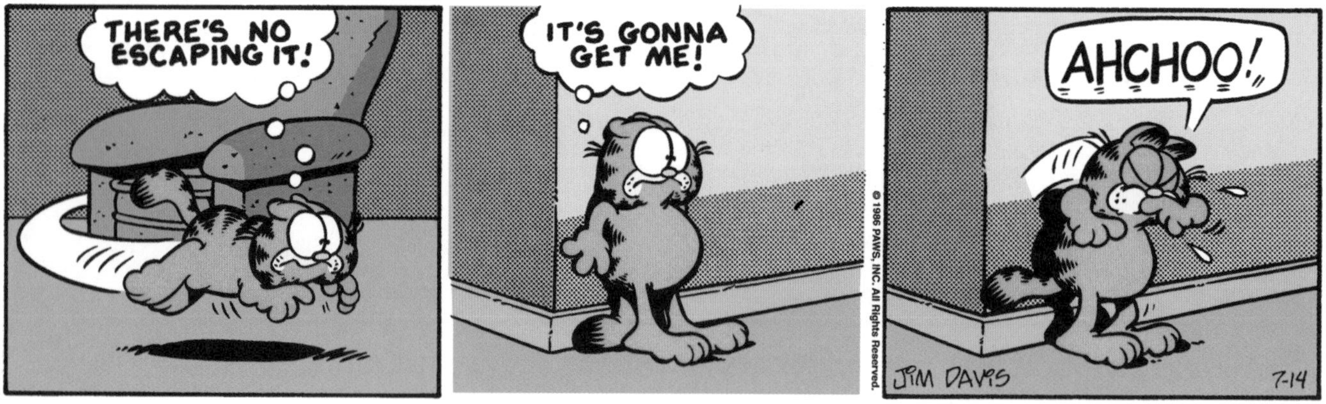
THERE'S NO ESCAPING IT!
IT'S GONNA GET ME!
© 1986 PAWS, INC. All Rights Reserved.
AHCHOO!
JIM DAVIS
7-14

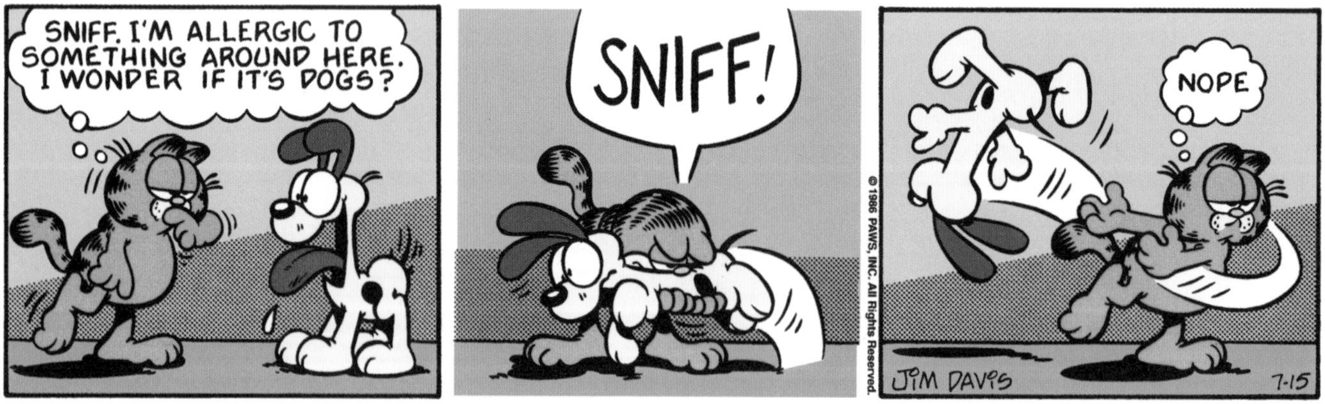
SNIFF. I'M ALLERGIC TO SOMETHING AROUND HERE. I WONDER IF IT'S DOGS?
SNIFF!
© 1986 PAWS, INC. All Rights Reserved.
NOPE
JIM DAVIS
7-15

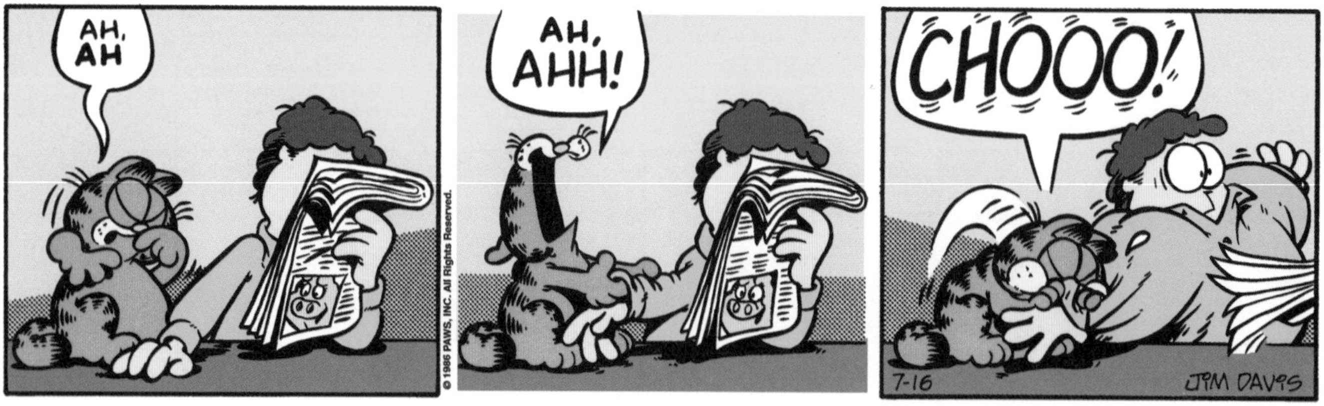
AH, AH
© 1986 PAWS, INC. All Rights Reserved.
AH, AHH!
CHOOO!
7-16
JIM DAVIS

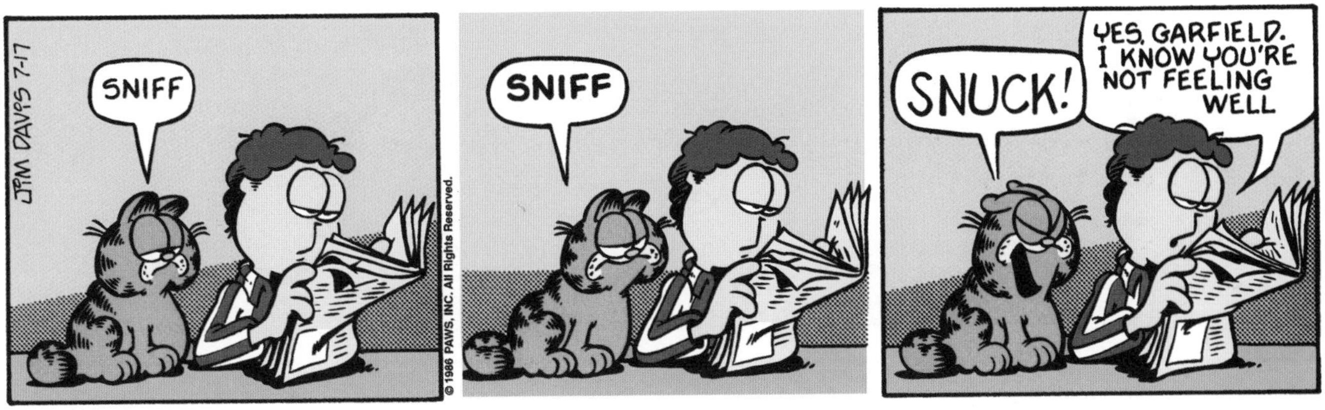
JIM DAVIS 7-17
SNIFF
© 1986 PAWS, INC. All Rights Reserved.
SNIFF
SNUCK!
YES, GARFIELD. I KNOW YOU'RE NOT FEELING WELL

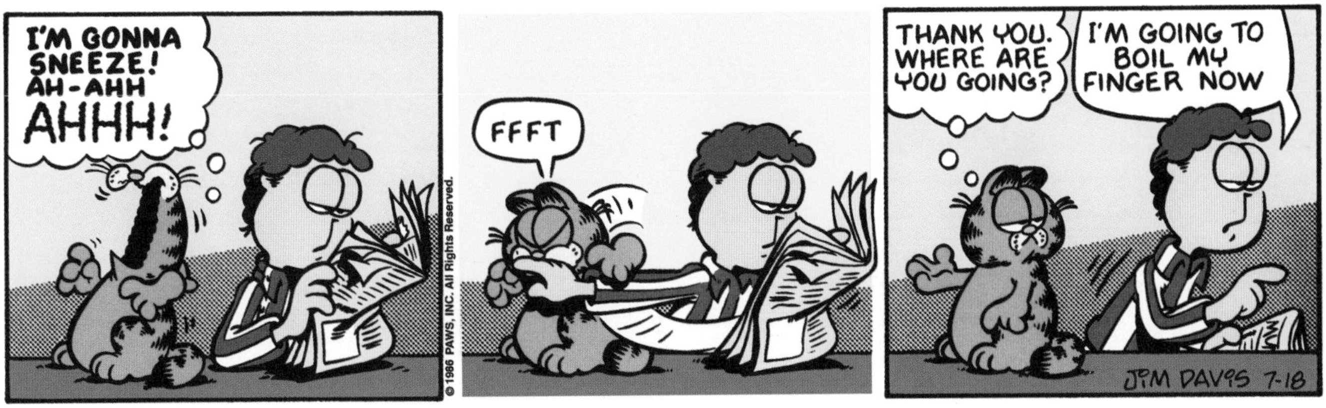
I'M GONNA SNEEZE! AH-AHH AHHH!
© 1986 PAWS, INC. All Rights Reserved.
FFFT
THANK YOU. WHERE ARE YOU GOING?
I'M GOING TO BOIL MY FINGER NOW
JIM DAVIS 7-18

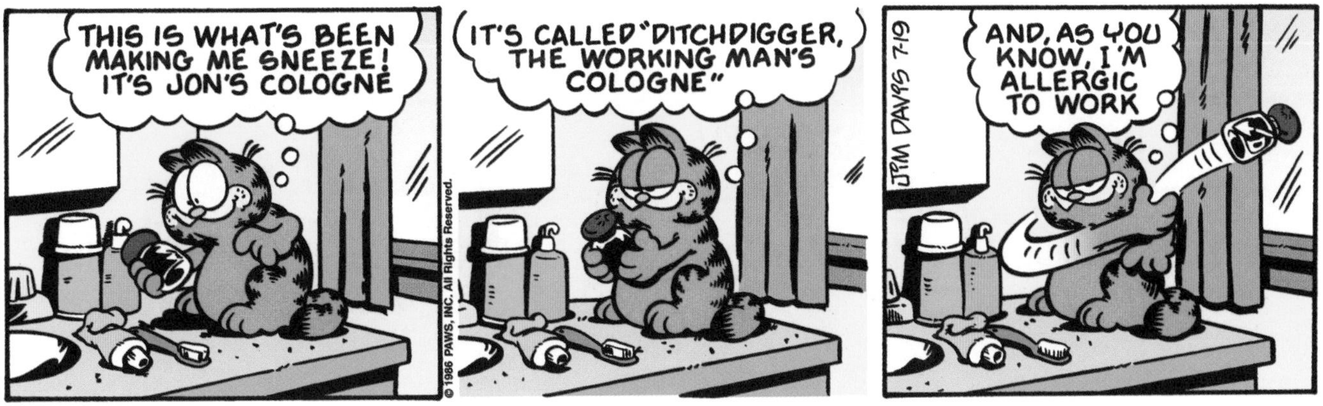
THIS IS WHAT'S BEEN MAKING ME SNEEZE! IT'S JON'S COLOGNE
© 1986 PAWS, INC. All Rights Reserved.
IT'S CALLED "DITCHDIGGER, THE WORKING MAN'S COLOGNE"
JIM DAVIS 7-19
AND, AS YOU KNOW, I'M ALLERGIC TO WORK

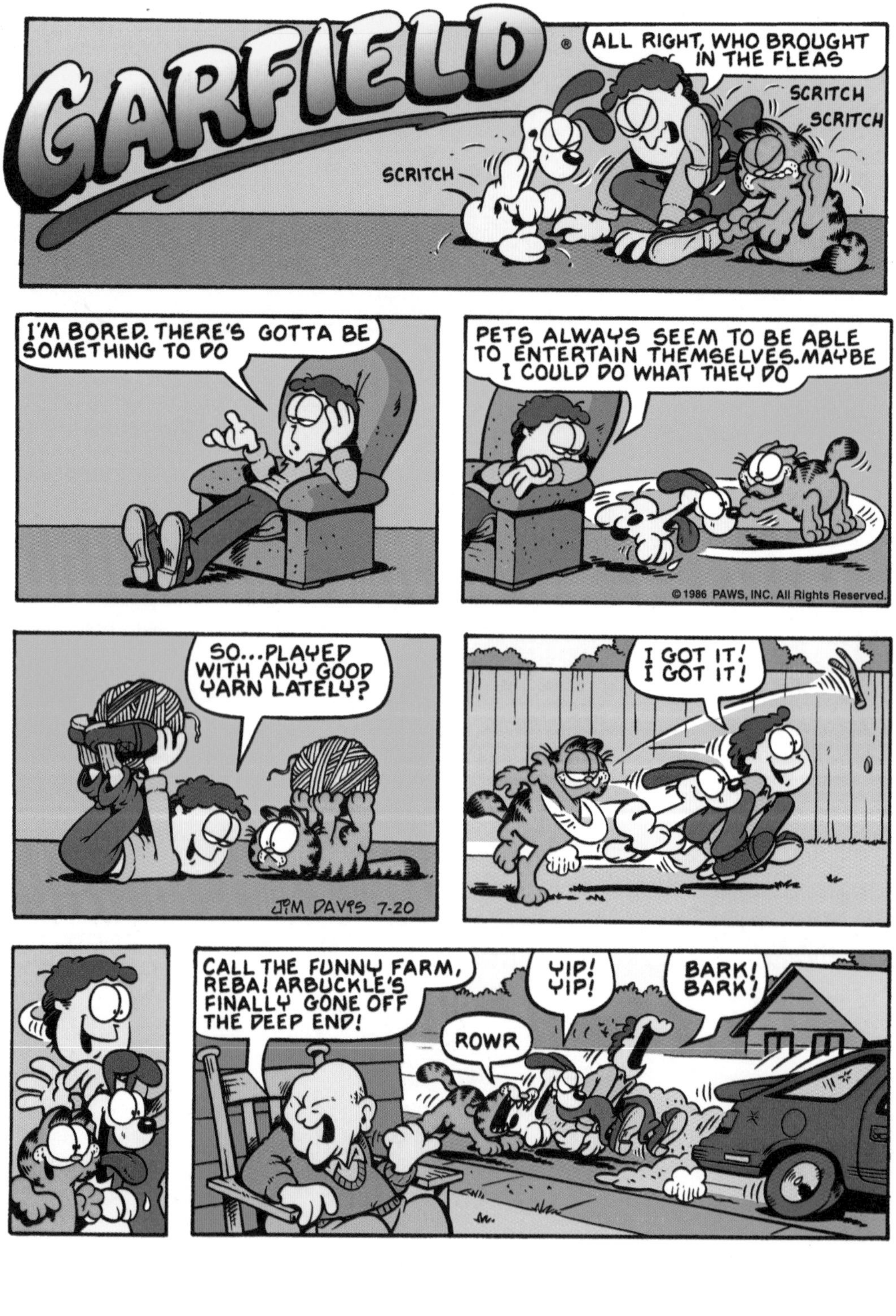
GARFIELD
ALL RIGHT, WHO BROUGHT IN THE FLEAS
SCRITCH
SCRITCH
SCRITCH
I'M BORED. THERE'S GOTTA BE SOMETHING TO DO
PETS ALWAYS SEEM TO BE ABLE TO ENTERTAIN THEMSELVES. MAYBE I COULD DO WHAT THEY DO
© 1986 PAWS, INC. All Rights Reserved.
SO...PLAYED WITH ANY GOOD YARN LATELY?
JIM DAVIS 7-20
I GOT IT! I GOT IT!
CALL THE FUNNY FARM, REBA! ARBUCKLE'S FINALLY GONE OFF THE DEEP END!
ROWR
YIP! YIP!
BARK! BARK!

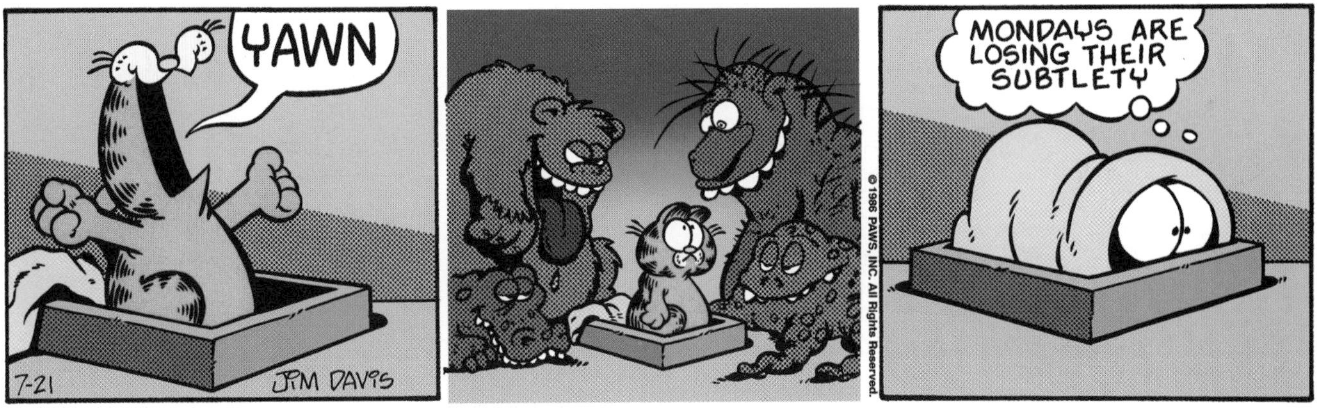
YAWN
7-21
JIM DAVIS
© 1986 PAWS, INC. All Rights Reserved.
MONDAYS ARE LOSING THEIR SUBTLETY

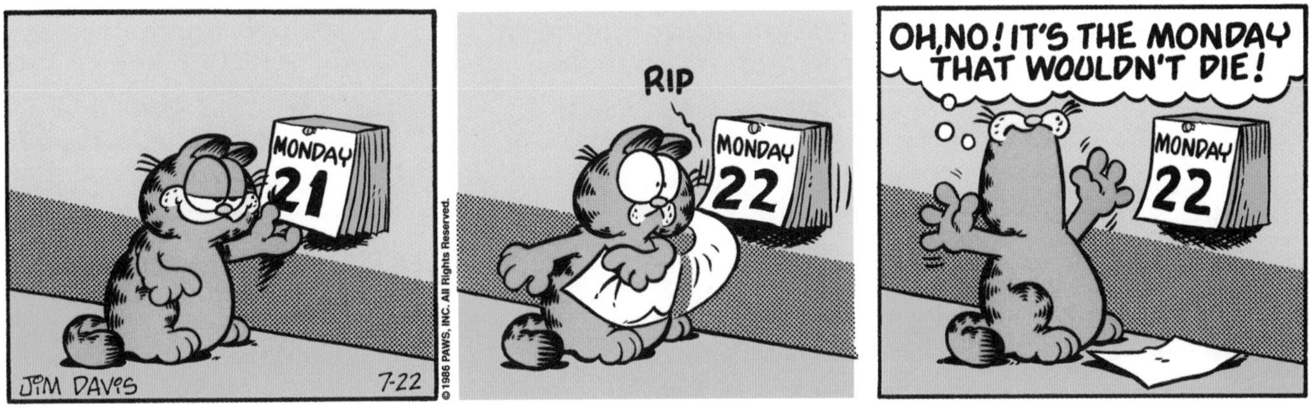
MONDAY
21
JIM DAVIS
7-22
© 1986 PAWS, INC. All Rights Reserved.
RIP
MONDAY
22
OH, NO! IT'S THE MONDAY THAT WOULDN'T DIE!
MONDAY
22

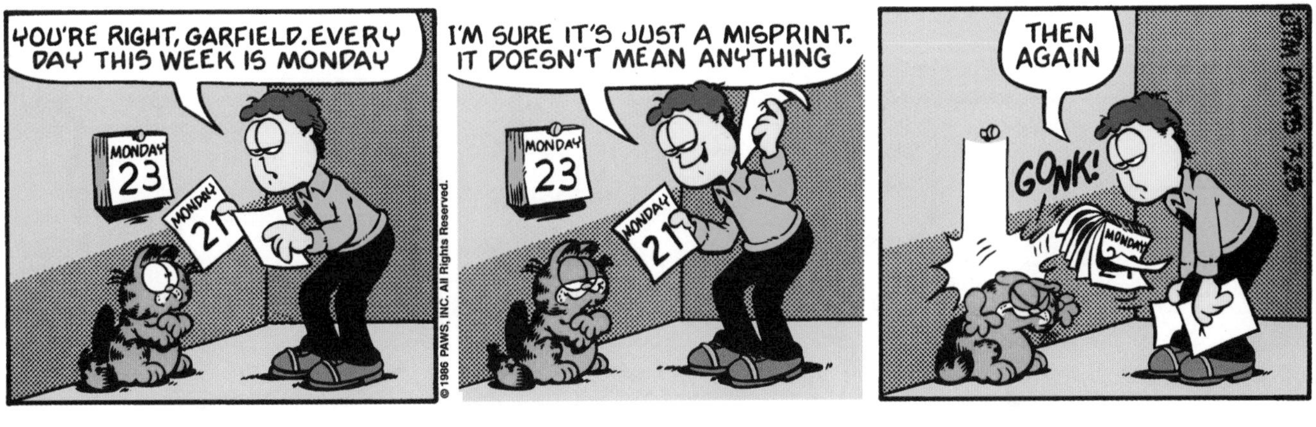
YOU'RE RIGHT, GARFIELD. EVERY DAY THIS WEEK IS MONDAY
MONDAY
23
MONDAY
21
© 1986 PAWS, INC. All Rights Reserved.
I'M SURE IT'S JUST A MISPRINT. IT DOESN'T MEAN ANYTHING
MONDAY
23
MONDAY
21
THEN AGAIN
GONK!
MONDAY
JIM DAVIS 7-23

I'D BETTER CHECK TO SEE IF IT'S STILL MONDAY OUT THERE
JIM DAVIS 7-24
© 1986 PAWS, INC. All Rights Reserved.
SPLUT!
YUP

IMAGINE HAVING TO SUFFER AN ENTIRE WEEK OF MONDAYS. WELL, THEY'RE NOT GETTING ME!
© 1986 PAWS, INC. All Rights Reserved.
I'M SPENDING THE REST OF THE WEEK IN BED
YOU GOTTA GET UP PRETTY EARLY TO PUT ONE OVER ON OLD GARFIELD
JIM DAVIS 7-25

JIM DAVIS 7-26
© 1986 PAWS, INC. All Rights Reserved.
IT MUST BE WONDERFUL TO BE THAT STUPID
FOR ODIE, EVERY DAY IS SATURDAY

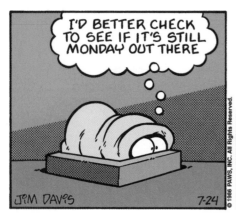

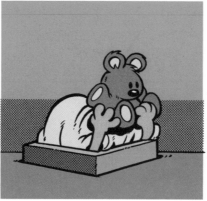

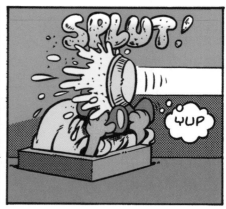

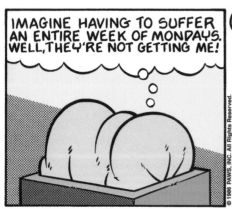

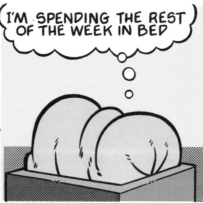

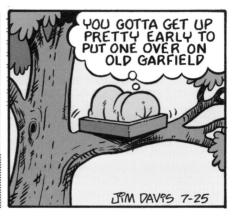

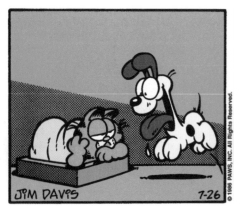

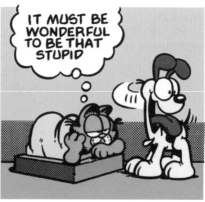

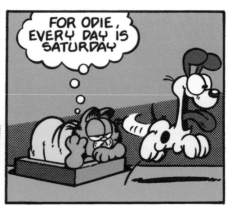

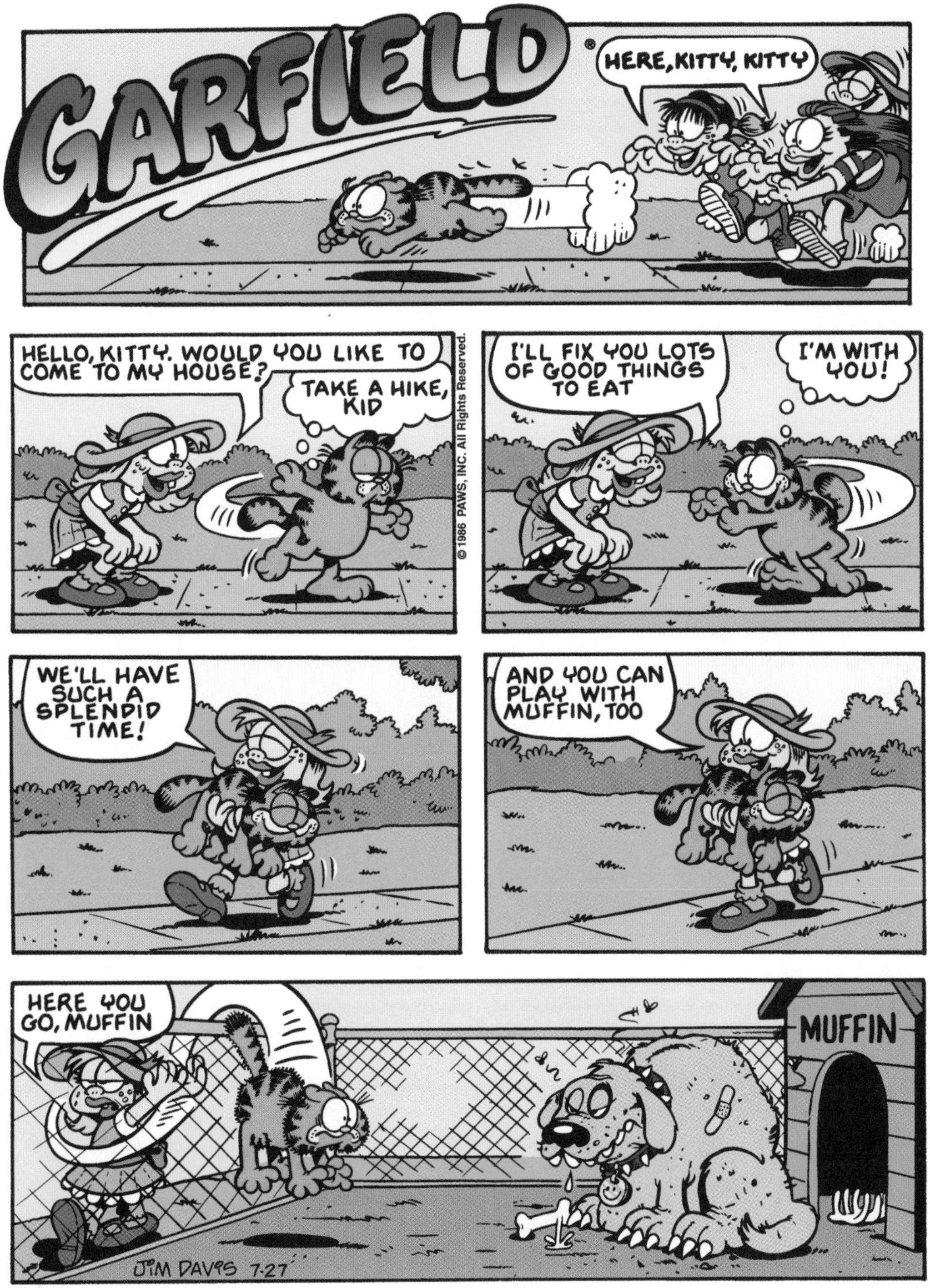
GARFIELD®
HERE, KITTY, KITTY
HELLO, KITTY. WOULD YOU LIKE TO COME TO MY HOUSE?
TAKE A HIKE, KID
© 1986 PAWS, INC. All Rights Reserved.
I'LL FIX YOU LOTS OF GOOD THINGS TO EAT
I'M WITH YOU!
WE'LL HAVE SUCH A SPLENDID TIME!
AND YOU CAN PLAY WITH MUFFIN, TOO
HERE YOU GO, MUFFIN
MUFFIN
JIM DAVIS 7-27

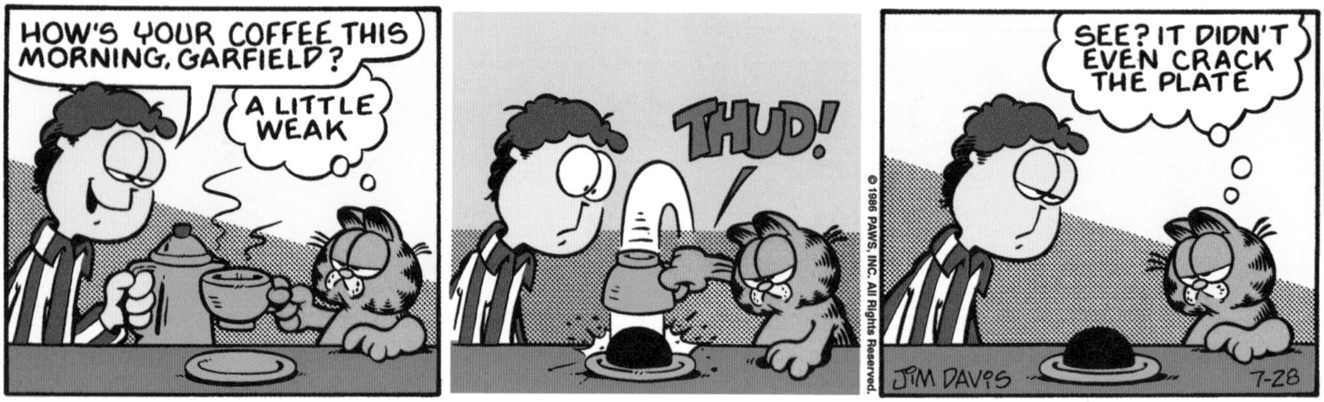
HOW'S YOUR COFFEE THIS MORNING, GARFIELD?
A LITTLE WEAK
THUD!
SEE? IT DIDN'T EVEN CRACK THE PLATE
© 1986 PAWS, INC. All Rights Reserved.
JIM DAVIS 7-28

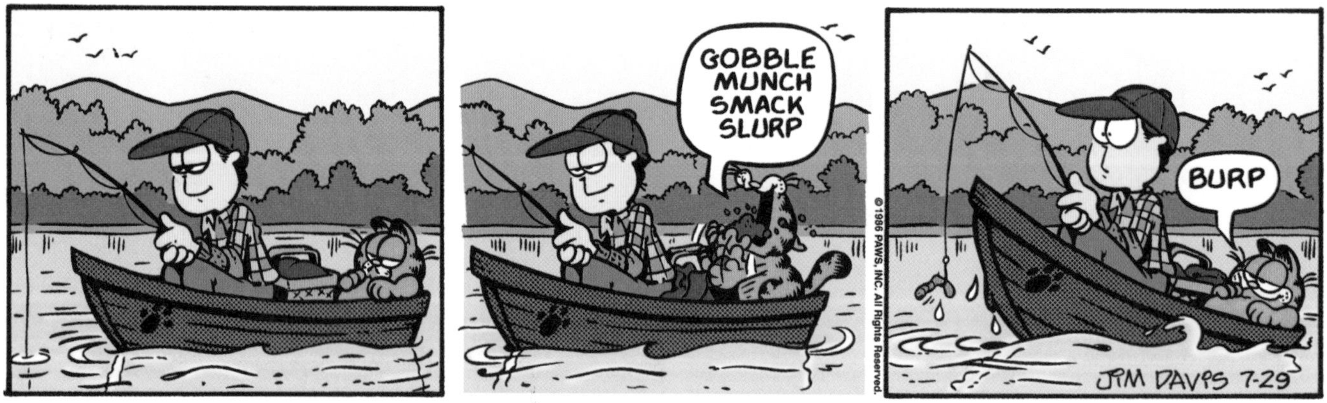
GOBBLE MUNCH SMACK SLURP
BURP
© 1986 PAWS, INC. All Rights Reserved.
JIM DAVIS 7-29

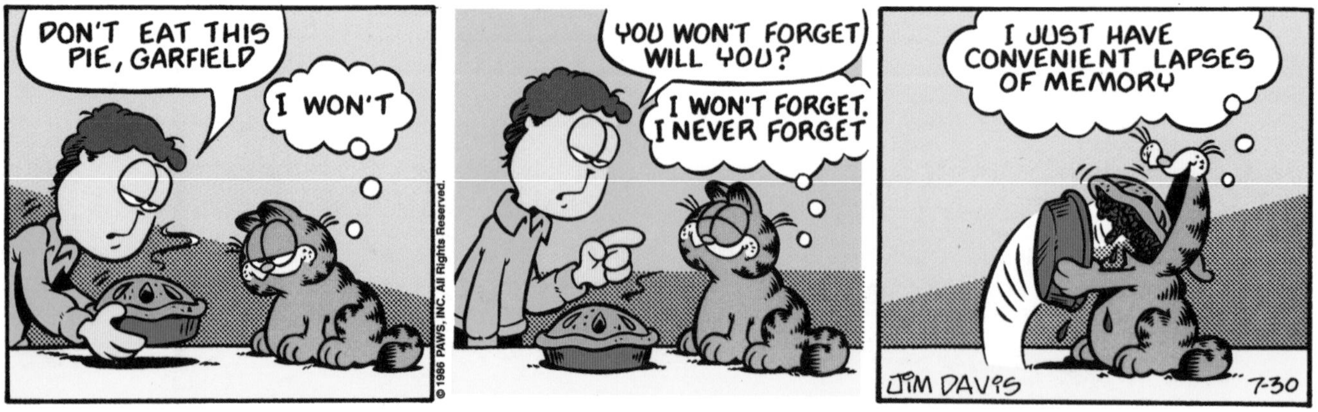
DON'T EAT THIS PIE, GARFIELD
I WON'T
© 1986 PAWS, INC. All Rights Reserved.
YOU WON'T FORGET WILL YOU?
I WON'T FORGET. I NEVER FORGET
I JUST HAVE CONVENIENT LAPSES OF MEMORY
JIM DAVIS 7-30

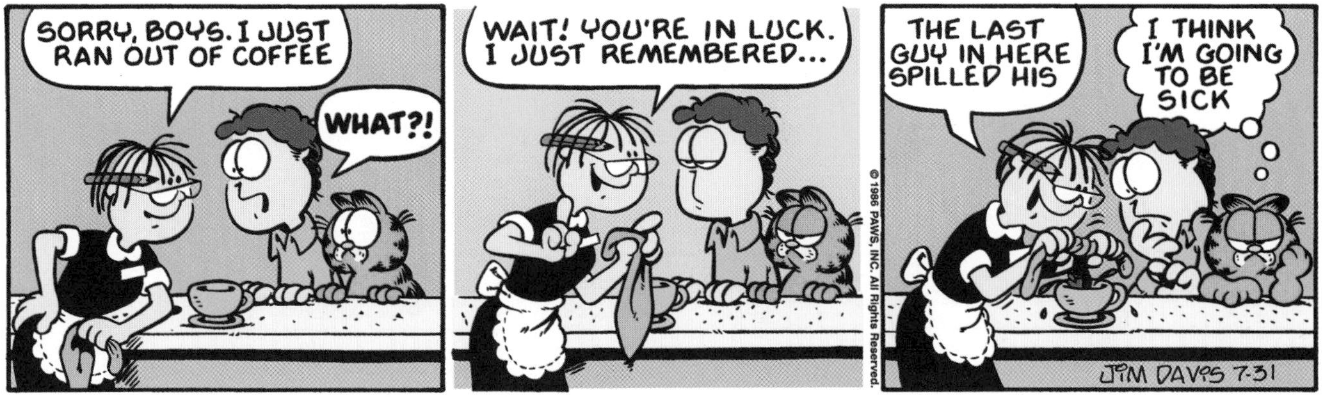
SORRY, BOYS. I JUST RAN OUT OF COFFEE
WHAT?!
WAIT! YOU'RE IN LUCK. I JUST REMEMBERED...
THE LAST GUY IN HERE SPILLED HIS
I THINK I'M GOING TO BE SICK
© 1986 PAWS, INC. All Rights Reserved.
JIM DAVIS 7-31

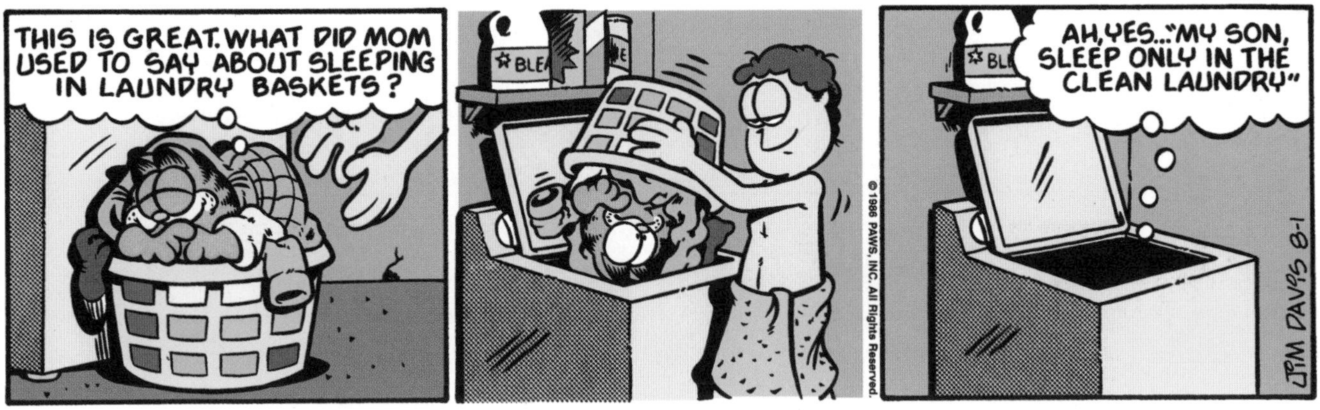
THIS IS GREAT. WHAT DID MOM USED TO SAY ABOUT SLEEPING IN LAUNDRY BASKETS?
© 1986 PAWS, INC. All Rights Reserved.
AH, YES..."MY SON, SLEEP ONLY IN THE CLEAN LAUNDRY"
JIM DAVIS 8-1

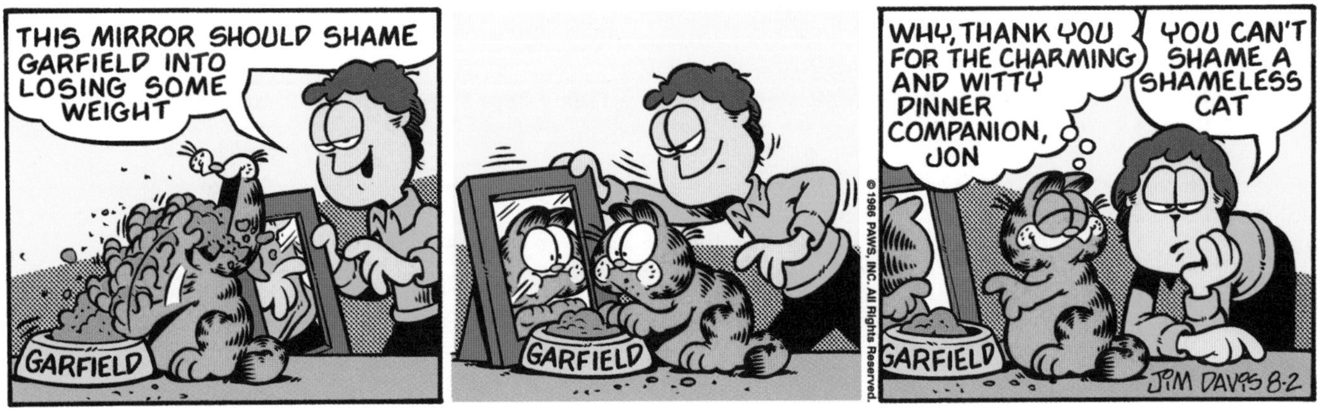
THIS MIRROR SHOULD SHAME GARFIELD INTO LOSING SOME WEIGHT
GARFIELD
GARFIELD
© 1986 PAWS, INC. All Rights Reserved.
WHY, THANK YOU FOR THE CHARMING AND WITTY DINNER COMPANION, JON
YOU CAN'T SHAME A SHAMELESS CAT
GARFIELD
JIM DAVIS 8-2

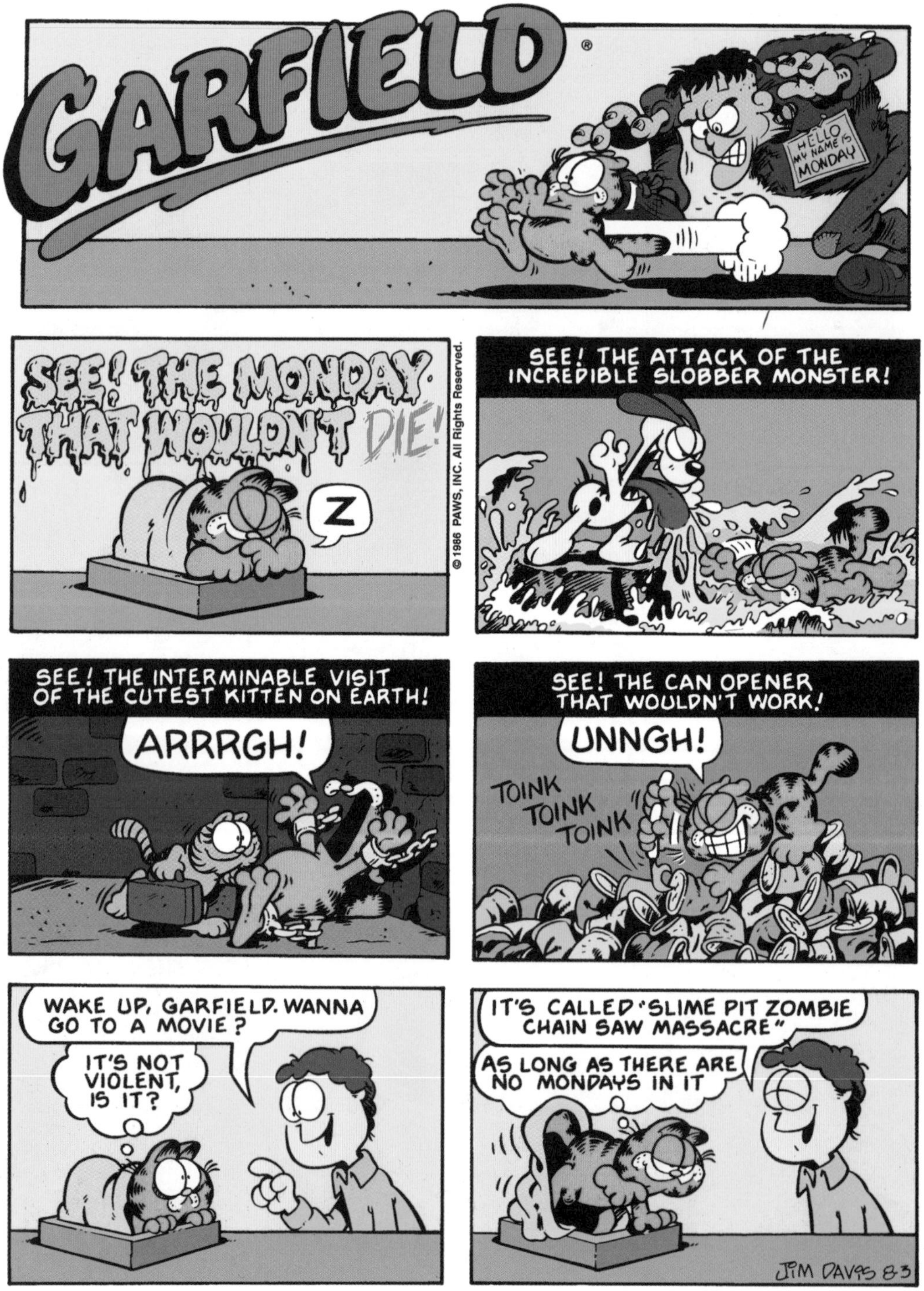
GARFIELD
HELLO MY NAME IS MONDAY
SEE! THE MONDAY THAT WOULDN'T DIE!
Z
© 1986 PAWS, INC. All Rights Reserved.
SEE! THE ATTACK OF THE INCREDIBLE SLOBBER MONSTER!
SEE! THE INTERMINABLE VISIT OF THE CUTEST KITTEN ON EARTH!
ARRRGH!
SEE! THE CAN OPENER THAT WOULDN'T WORK!
UNNGH!
TOINK TOINK TOINK
WAKE UP, GARFIELD. WANNA GO TO A MOVIE?
IT'S NOT VIOLENT, IS IT?
IT'S CALLED "SLIME PIT ZOMBIE CHAIN SAW MASSACRE"
AS LONG AS THERE ARE NO MONDAYS IN IT
JIM DAVIS 8-3

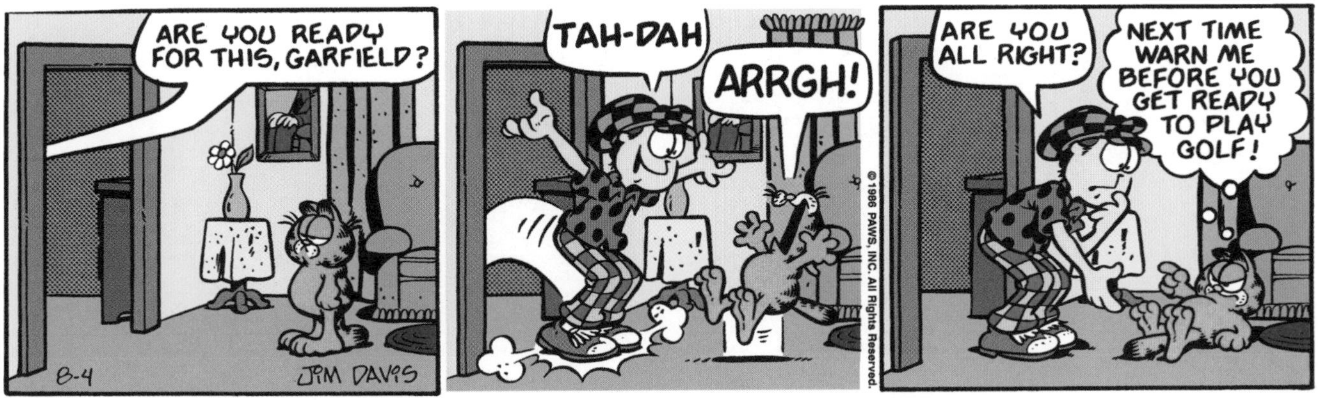
ARE YOU READY FOR THIS, GARFIELD?
8-4
JIM DAVIS
TAH-DAH
ARRGH!
© 1986 PAWS, INC. All Rights Reserved.
ARE YOU ALL RIGHT?
NEXT TIME WARN ME BEFORE YOU GET READY TO PLAY GOLF!

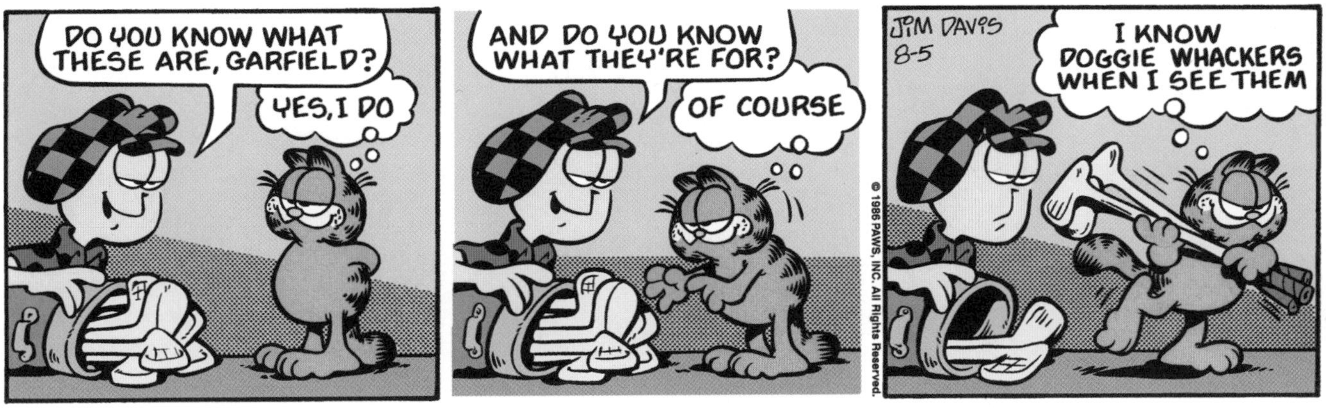
DO YOU KNOW WHAT THESE ARE, GARFIELD?
YES, I DO
AND DO YOU KNOW WHAT THEY'RE FOR?
OF COURSE
© 1986 PAWS, INC. All Rights Reserved.
JIM DAVIS
8-5
I KNOW DOGGIE WHACKERS WHEN I SEE THEM

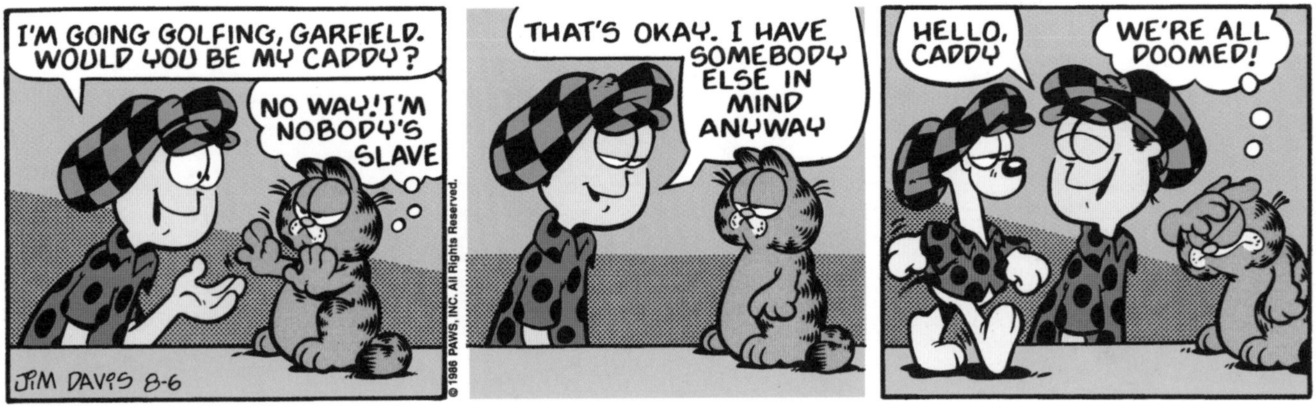
I'M GOING GOLFING, GARFIELD. WOULD YOU BE MY CADDY?
NO WAY! I'M NOBODY'S SLAVE
JIM DAVIS 8-6
© 1986 PAWS, INC. All Rights Reserved.
THAT'S OKAY. I HAVE SOMEBODY ELSE IN MIND ANYWAY
HELLO, CADDY
WE'RE ALL DOOMED!

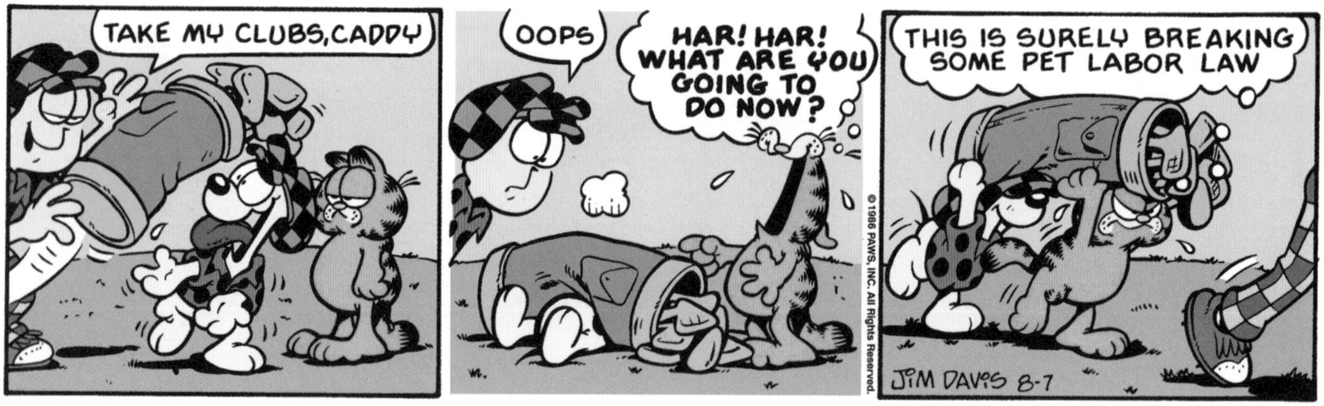
TAKE MY CLUBS, CADDY
OOPS
HAR! HAR! WHAT ARE YOU GOING TO DO NOW?
THIS IS SURELY BREAKING SOME PET LABOR LAW
JIM DAVIS 8-7
© 1986 PAWS, INC. All Rights Reserved.

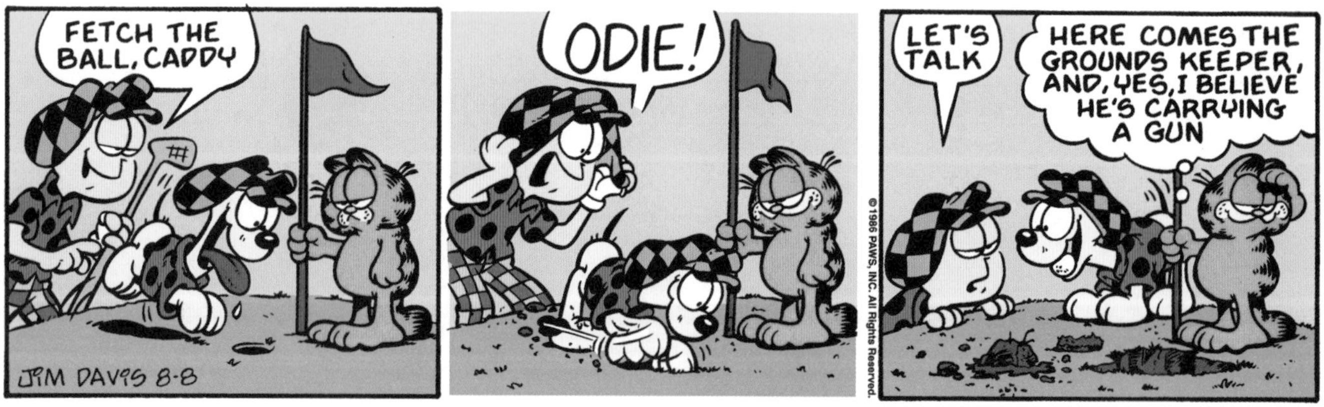
FETCH THE BALL, CADDY
JIM DAVIS 8-8
ODIE!
LET'S TALK
HERE COMES THE GROUNDS KEEPER, AND, YES, I BELIEVE HE'S CARRYING A GUN
© 1986 PAWS, INC. All Rights Reserved.

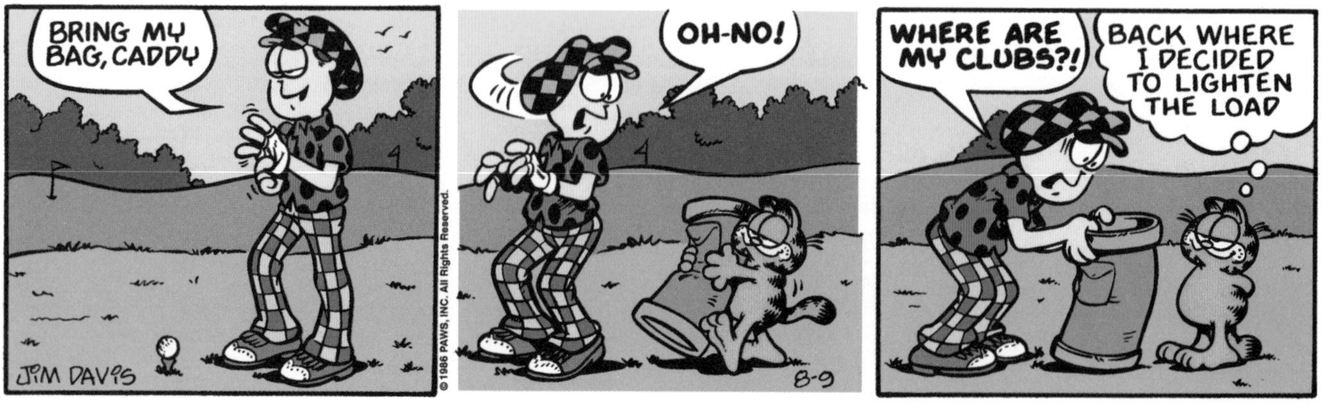
BRING MY BAG, CADDY
JIM DAVIS
OH-NO!
8-9
WHERE ARE MY CLUBS?!
BACK WHERE I DECIDED TO LIGHTEN THE LOAD
© 1986 PAWS, INC. All Rights Reserved.

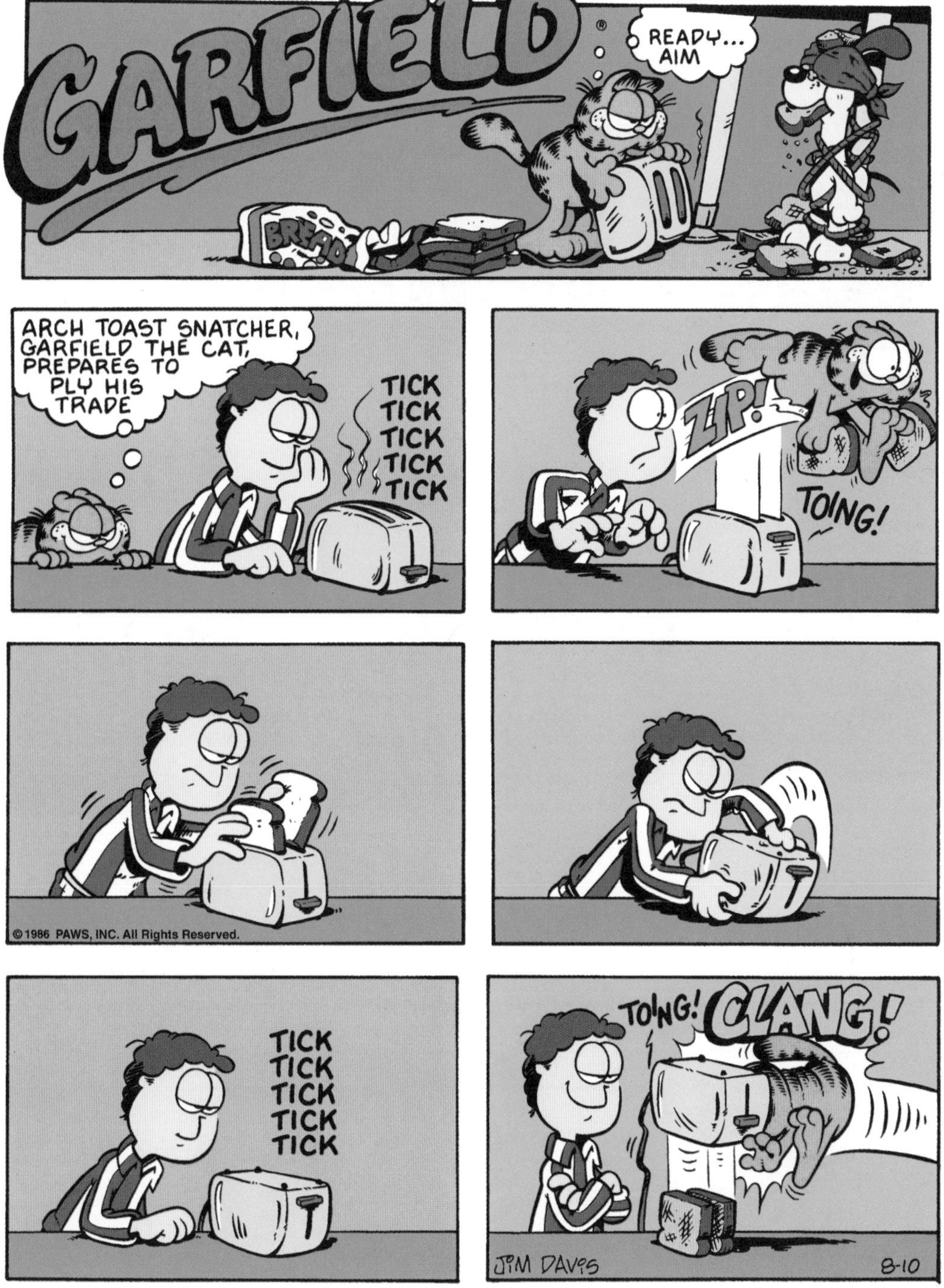
GARFIELD
READY... AIM
BREAD
ARCH TOAST SNATCHER, GARFIELD THE CAT, PREPARES TO PLY HIS TRADE
TICK TICK TICK TICK TICK
ZIP!
TOING!
TICK TICK TICK TICK TICK
TOING!
CLANG!
JIM DAVIS
8-10

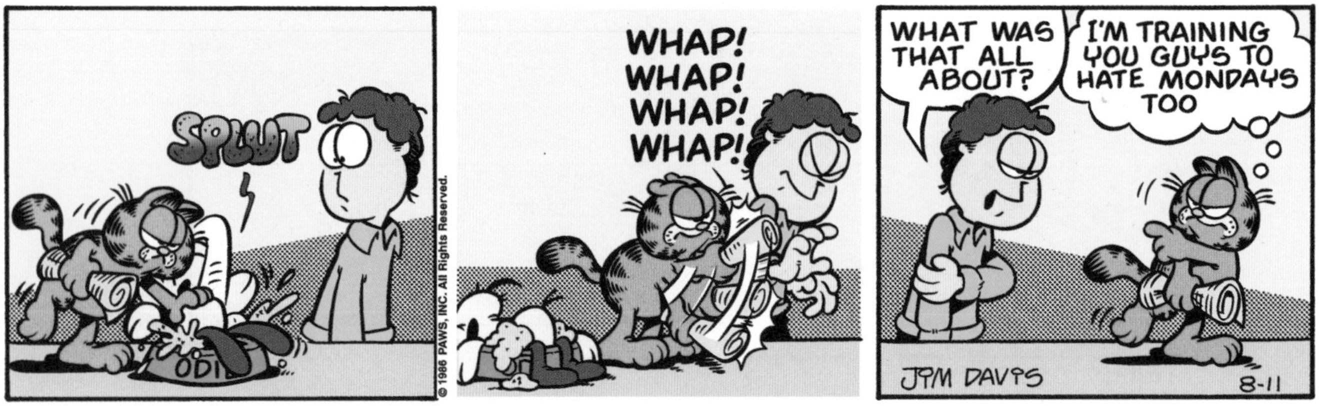
SPLUT
ODI
© 1986 PAWS, INC. All Rights Reserved.
WHAP! WHAP! WHAP! WHAP!
WHAT WAS THAT ALL ABOUT?
I'M TRAINING YOU GUYS TO HATE MONDAYS TOO
JIM DAVIS
8-11

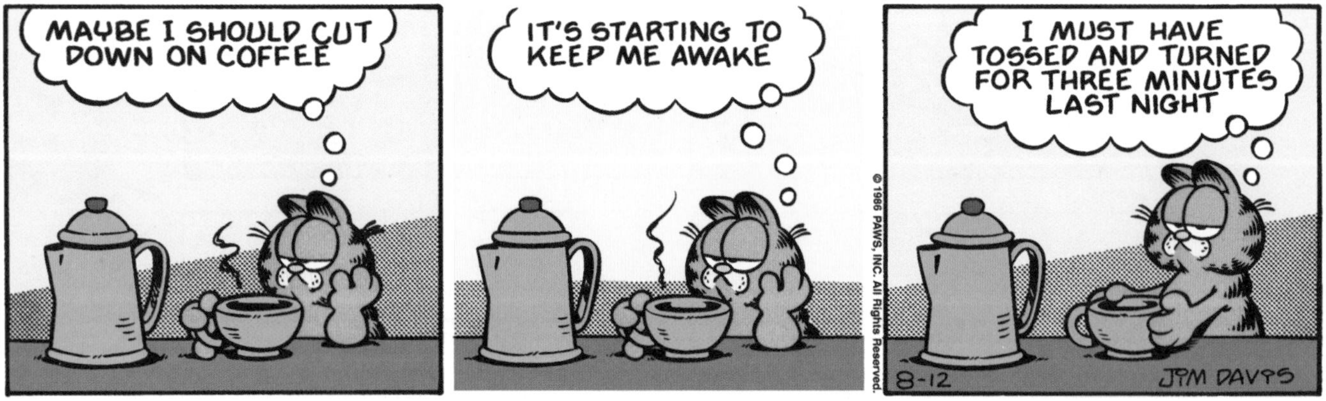
MAYBE I SHOULD CUT DOWN ON COFFEE
IT'S STARTING TO KEEP ME AWAKE
© 1986 PAWS, INC. All Rights Reserved.
I MUST HAVE TOSSED AND TURNED FOR THREE MINUTES LAST NIGHT
8-12
JIM DAVIS

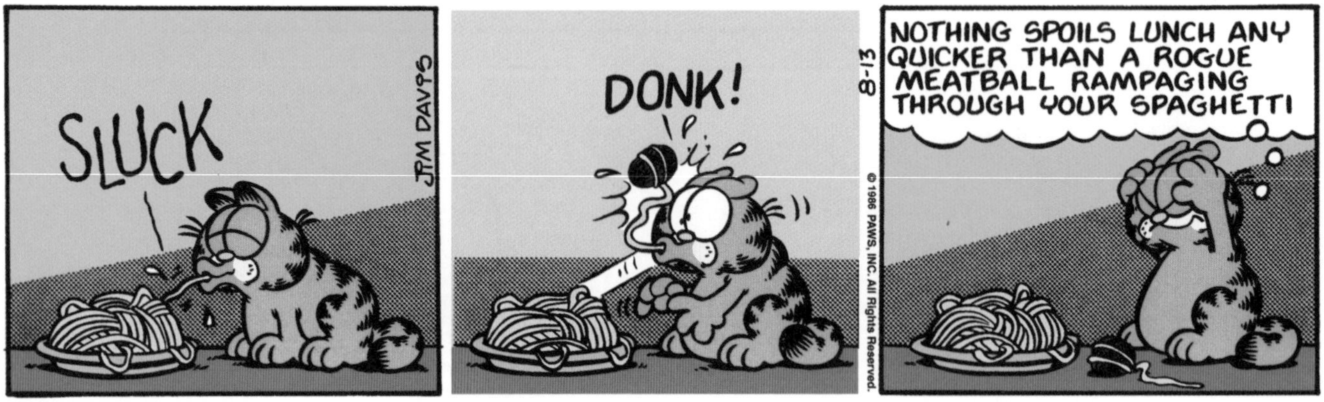
SLUCK
JIM DAVIS
DONK!
8-13
© 1986 PAWS, INC. All Rights Reserved.
NOTHING SPOILS LUNCH ANY QUICKER THAN A ROGUE MEATBALL RAMPAGING THROUGH YOUR SPAGHETTI

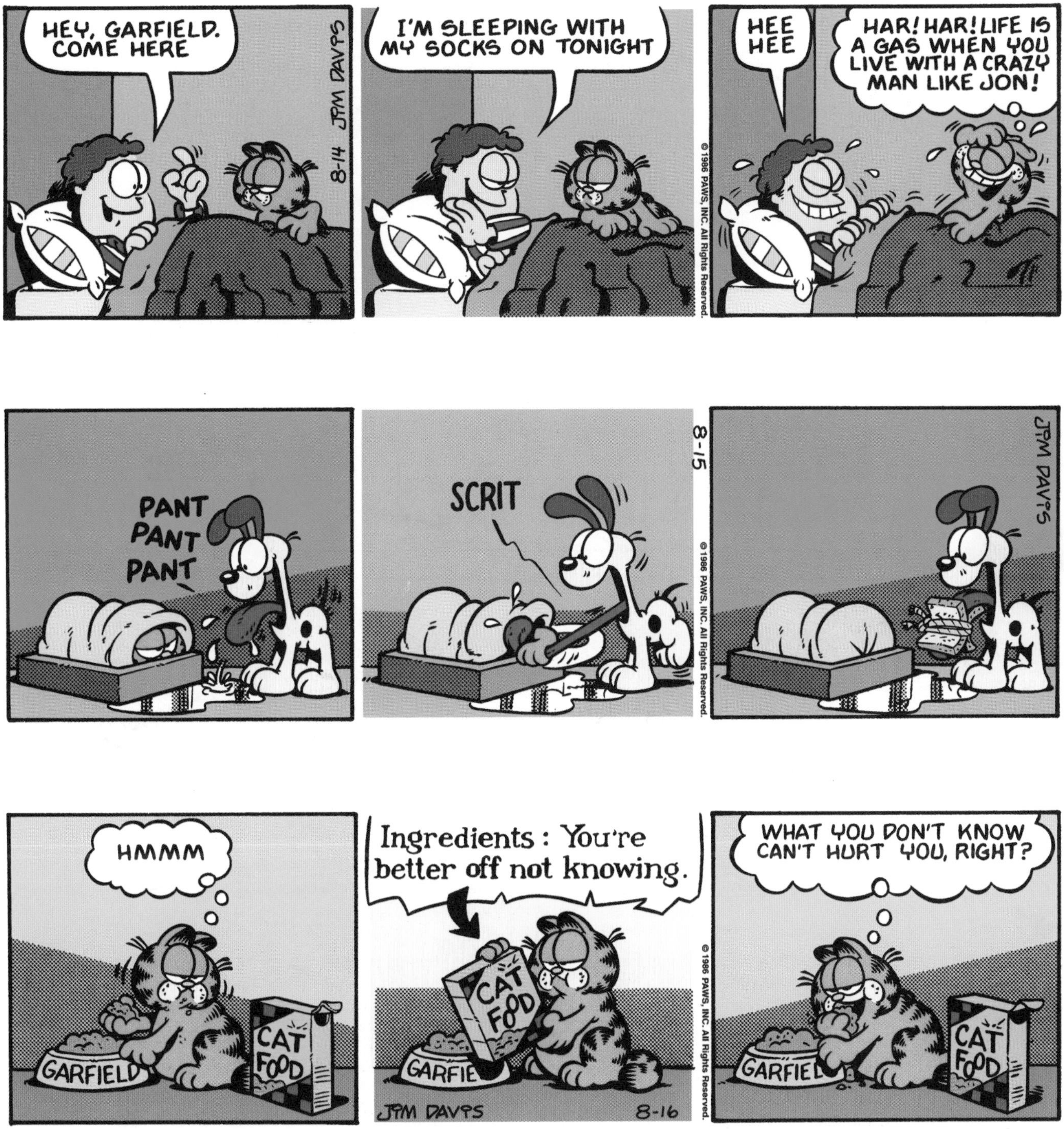
HEY, GARFIELD. COME HERE
JPM DAVPS 8-14
I'M SLEEPING WITH MY SOCKS ON TONIGHT
© 1986 PAWS, INC. All Rights Reserved.
HEE HEE
HAR! HAR! LIFE IS A GAS WHEN YOU LIVE WITH A CRAZY MAN LIKE JON!
PANT PANT PANT
SCRIT
8-15
© 1986 PAWS, INC. All Rights Reserved.
JPM DAVPS
HMMM
GARFIELD
CAT FOOD
Ingredients : You're better off not knowing.
CAT FOOD
GARFIE
JPM DAVPS 8-16
© 1986 PAWS, INC. All Rights Reserved.
WHAT YOU DON'T KNOW CAN'T HURT YOU, RIGHT?
GARFIEL
CAT FOOD

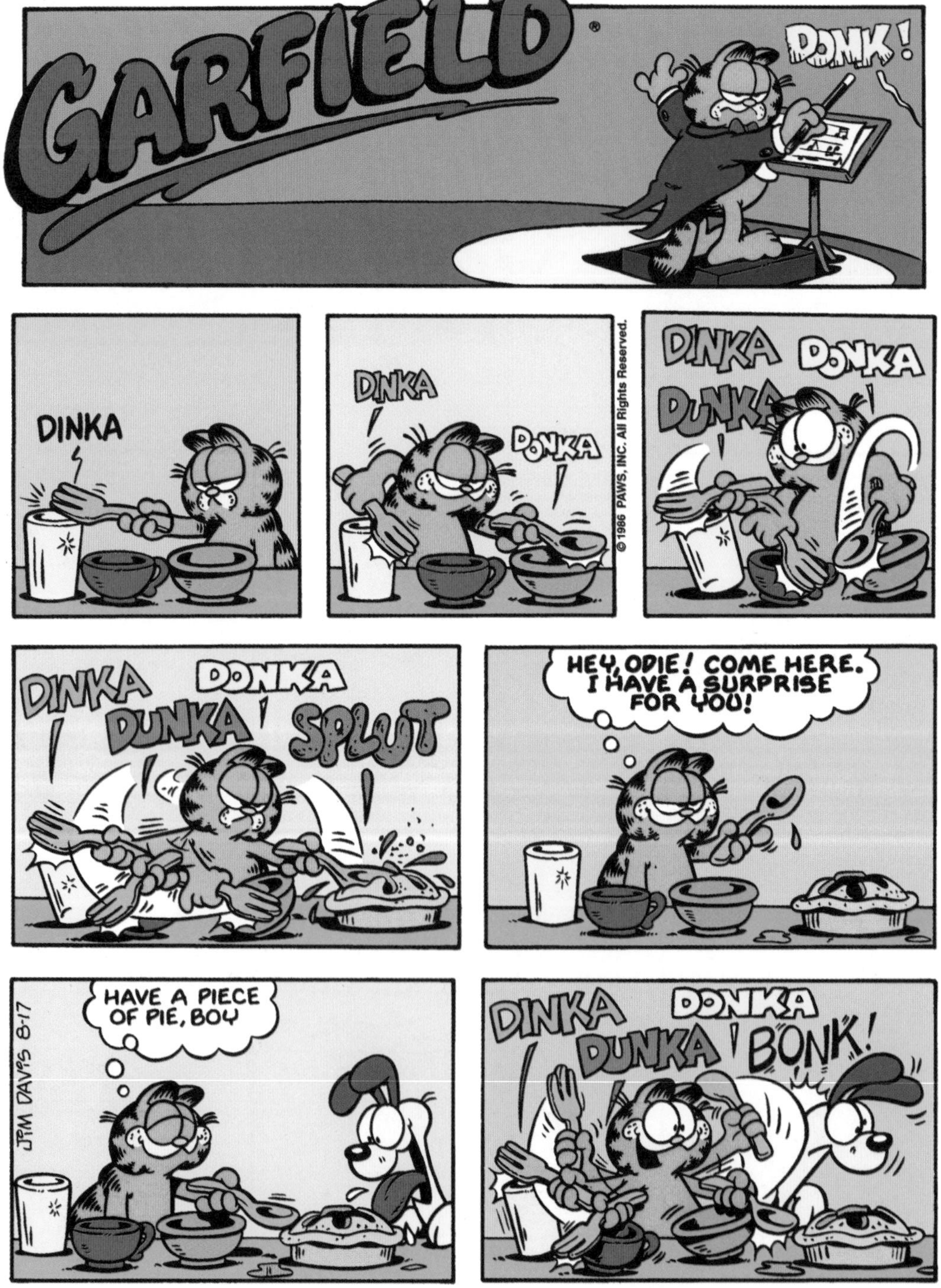
GARFIELD®
DONK!
DINKA
DINKA
DONKA
© 1986 PAWS, INC. All Rights Reserved.
DINKA DONKA
DUNKA
DINKA DONKA
DUNKA
SPLUT
HEY, ODIE! COME HERE. I HAVE A SURPRISE FOR YOU!
JIM DAVIS 8-17
HAVE A PIECE OF PIE, BOY
DINKA DONKA
DUNKA
BONK!

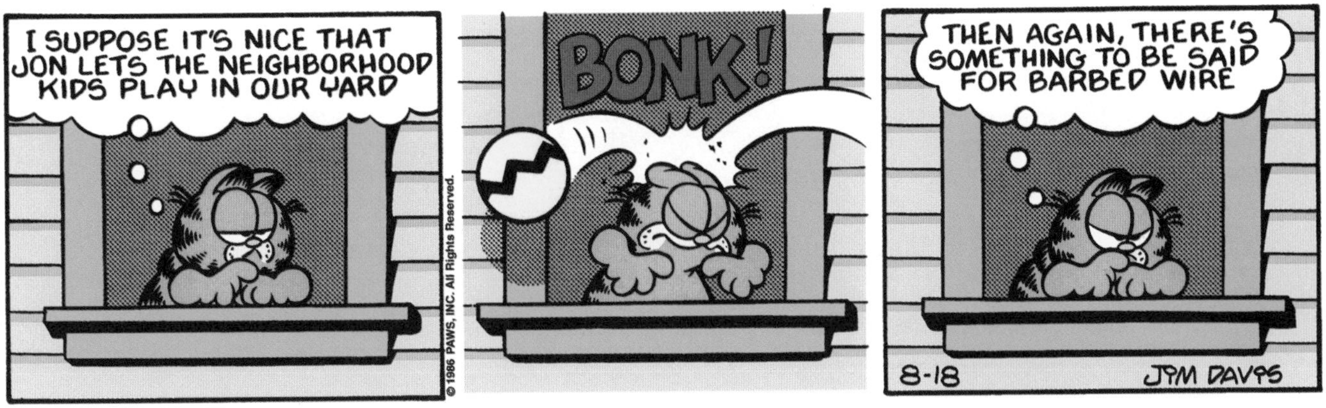
I SUPPOSE IT'S NICE THAT JON LETS THE NEIGHBORHOOD KIDS PLAY IN OUR YARD
BONK!
THEN AGAIN, THERE'S SOMETHING TO BE SAID FOR BARBED WIRE
8-18
JIM DAVIS

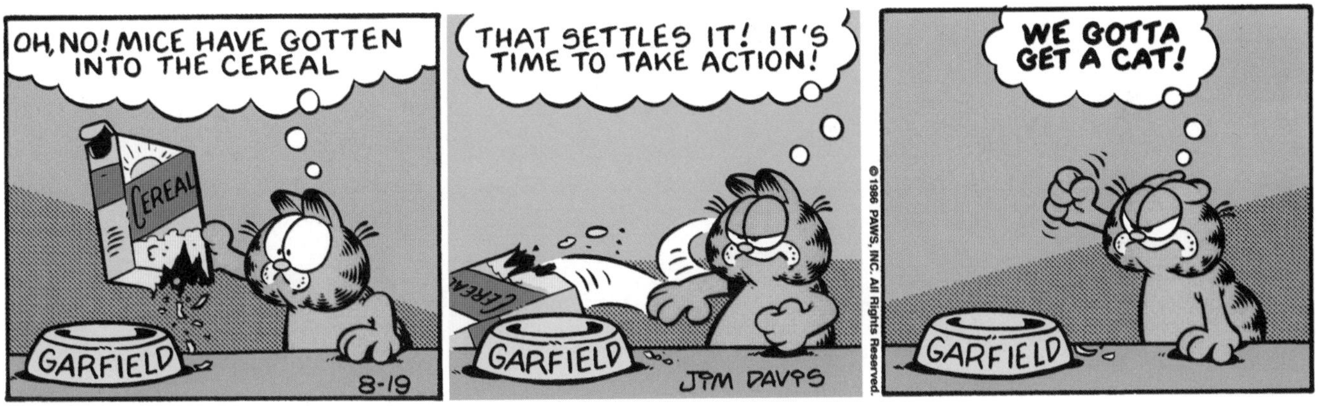
OH, NO! MICE HAVE GOTTEN INTO THE CEREAL
CEREAL
GARFIELD
8-19
THAT SETTLES IT! IT'S TIME TO TAKE ACTION!
GARFIELD
JIM DAVIS
WE GOTTA GET A CAT!
GARFIELD

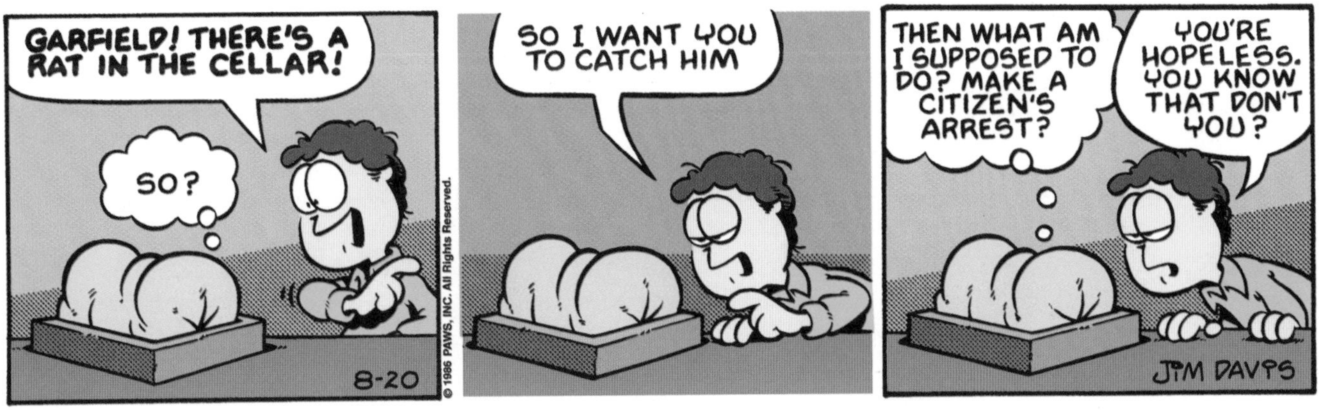
GARFIELD! THERE'S A RAT IN THE CELLAR!
SO?
8-20
SO I WANT YOU TO CATCH HIM
THEN WHAT AM I SUPPOSED TO DO? MAKE A CITIZEN'S ARREST?
YOU'RE HOPELESS. YOU KNOW THAT DON'T YOU?
JIM DAVIS

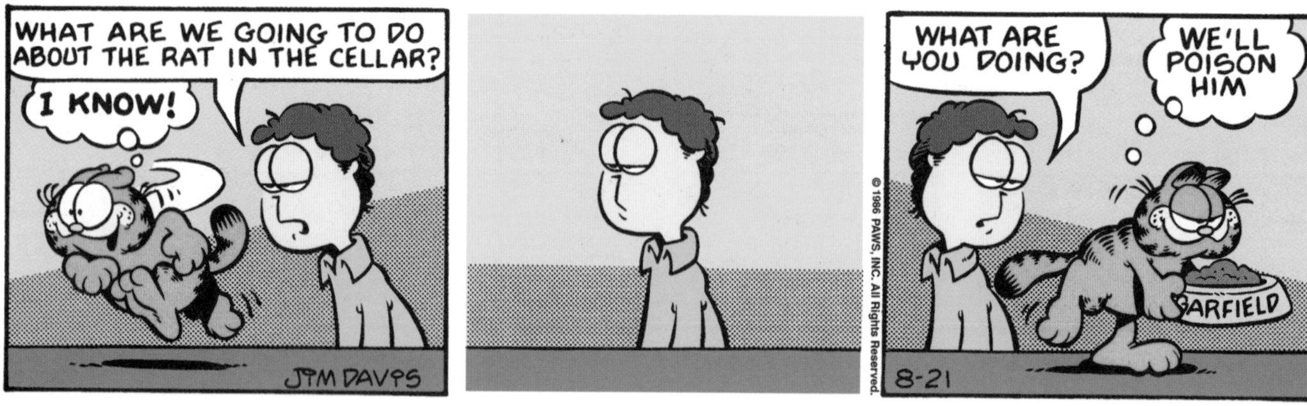
WHAT ARE WE GOING TO DO ABOUT THE RAT IN THE CELLAR?
I KNOW!
JIM DAVIS
© 1986 PAWS, INC. All Rights Reserved.
WHAT ARE YOU DOING?
WE'LL POISON HIM
GARFIELD
8-21

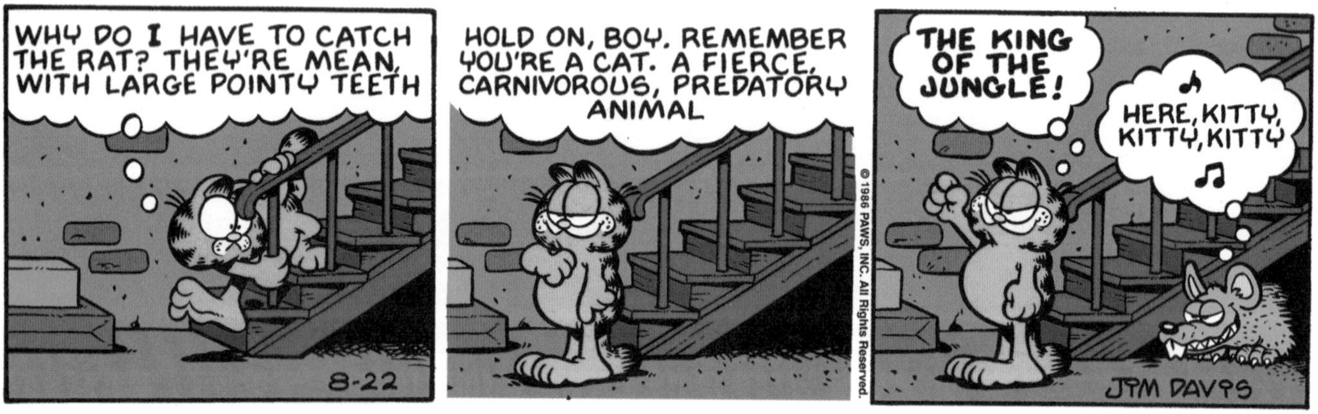
WHY DO I HAVE TO CATCH THE RAT? THEY'RE MEAN, WITH LARGE POINTY TEETH
8-22
HOLD ON, BOY. REMEMBER YOU'RE A CAT. A FIERCE, CARNIVOROUS, PREDATORY ANIMAL
© 1986 PAWS, INC. All Rights Reserved.
THE KING OF THE JUNGLE!
HERE, KITTY, KITTY, KITTY
JIM DAVIS

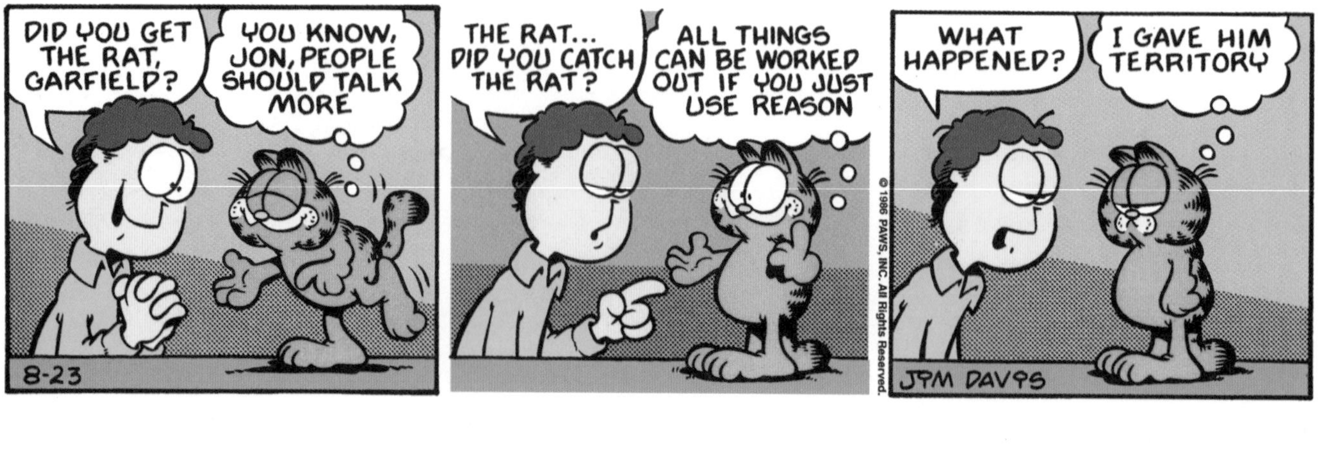
DID YOU GET THE RAT, GARFIELD?
YOU KNOW, JON, PEOPLE SHOULD TALK MORE
8-23
THE RAT... DID YOU CATCH THE RAT?
ALL THINGS CAN BE WORKED OUT IF YOU JUST USE REASON
© 1986 PAWS, INC. All Rights Reserved.
WHAT HAPPENED?
I GAVE HIM TERRITORY
JIM DAVIS

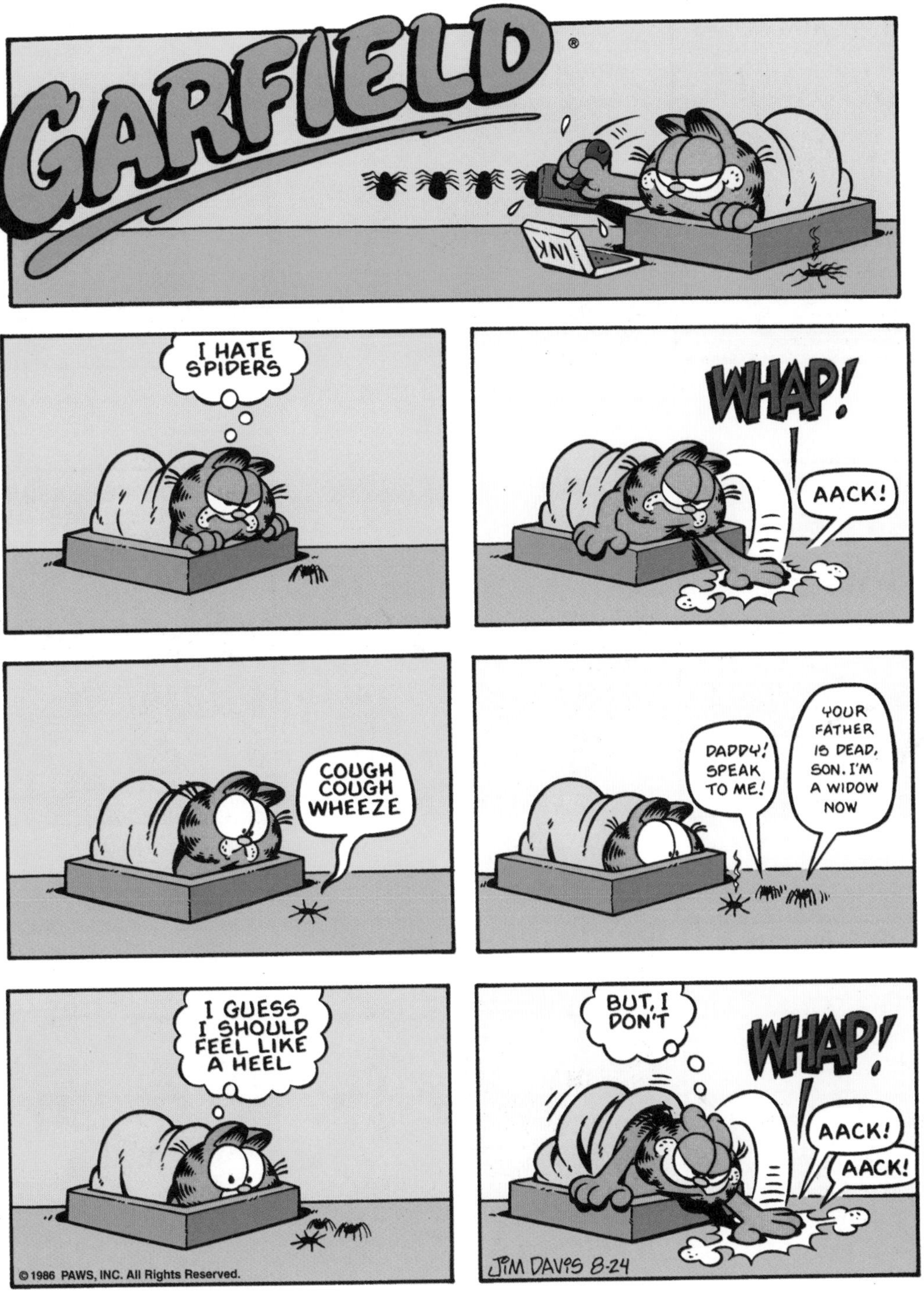
GARFIELD®
INK
I HATE SPIDERS
WHAP!
AACK!
COUGH COUGH WHEEZE
DADDY! SPEAK TO ME!
YOUR FATHER IS DEAD, SON. I'M A WIDOW NOW
I GUESS I SHOULD FEEL LIKE A HEEL
BUT, I DON'T
WHAP!
AACK!
AACK!
JIM DAVIS 8-24

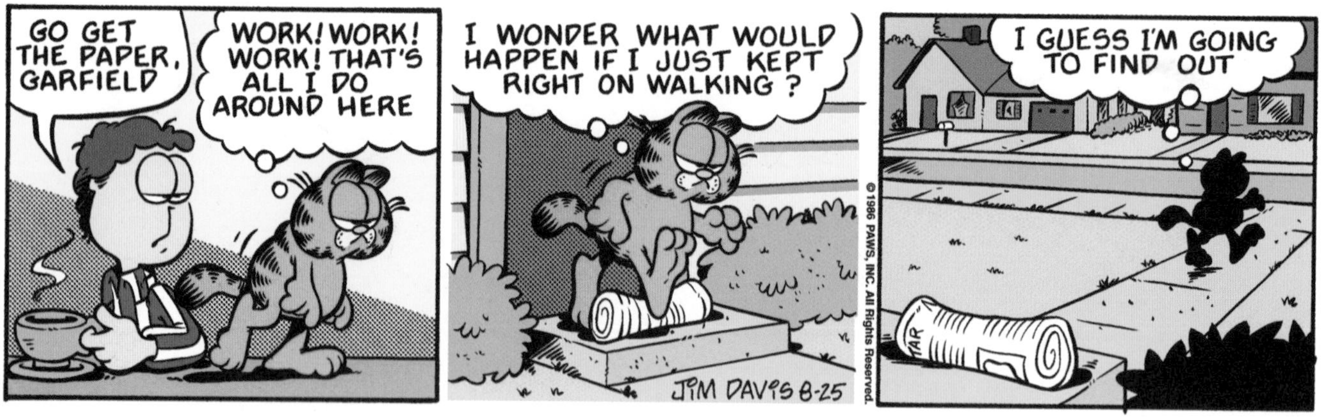
GO GET THE PAPER, GARFIELD
WORK! WORK! WORK! THAT'S ALL I DO AROUND HERE
I WONDER WHAT WOULD HAPPEN IF I JUST KEPT RIGHT ON WALKING ?
JIM DAVIS 8-25
© 1986 PAWS, INC. All Rights Reserved.
I GUESS I'M GOING TO FIND OUT

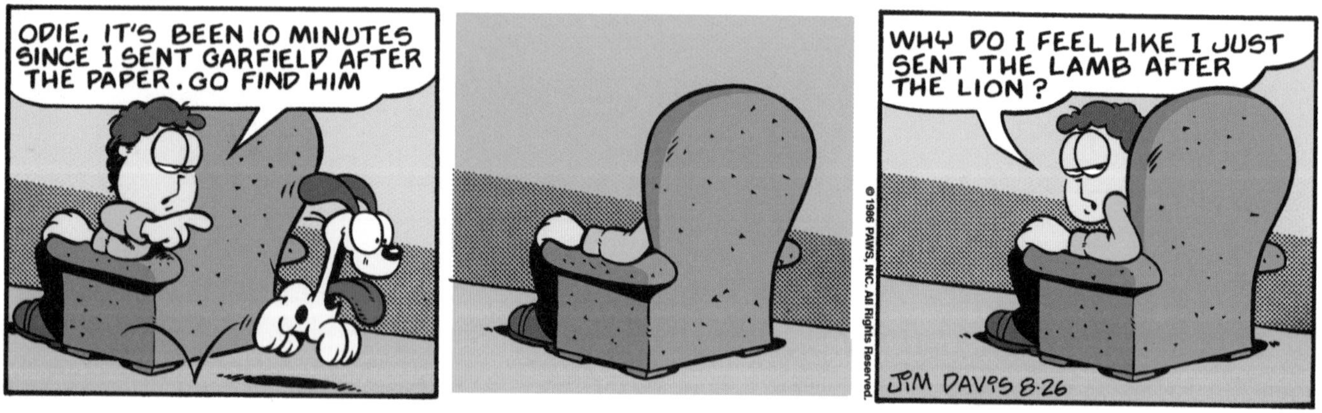
ODIE, IT'S BEEN 10 MINUTES SINCE I SENT GARFIELD AFTER THE PAPER. GO FIND HIM
© 1986 PAWS, INC. All Rights Reserved.
WHY DO I FEEL LIKE I JUST SENT THE LAMB AFTER THE LION ?
JIM DAVIS 8-26

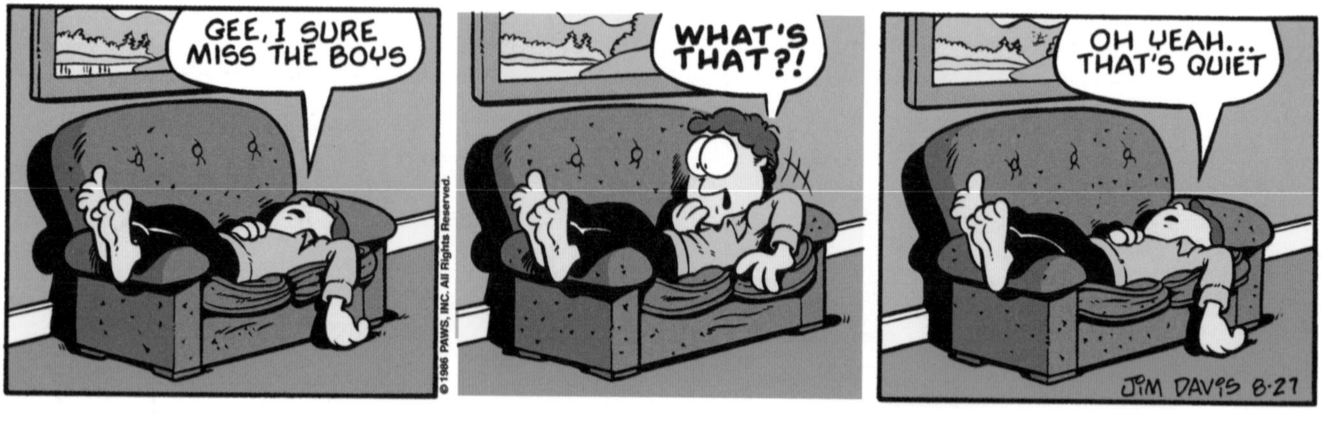
GEE, I SURE MISS THE BOYS
© 1986 PAWS, INC. All Rights Reserved.
WHAT'S THAT?!
OH YEAH... THAT'S QUIET
JIM DAVIS 8-27

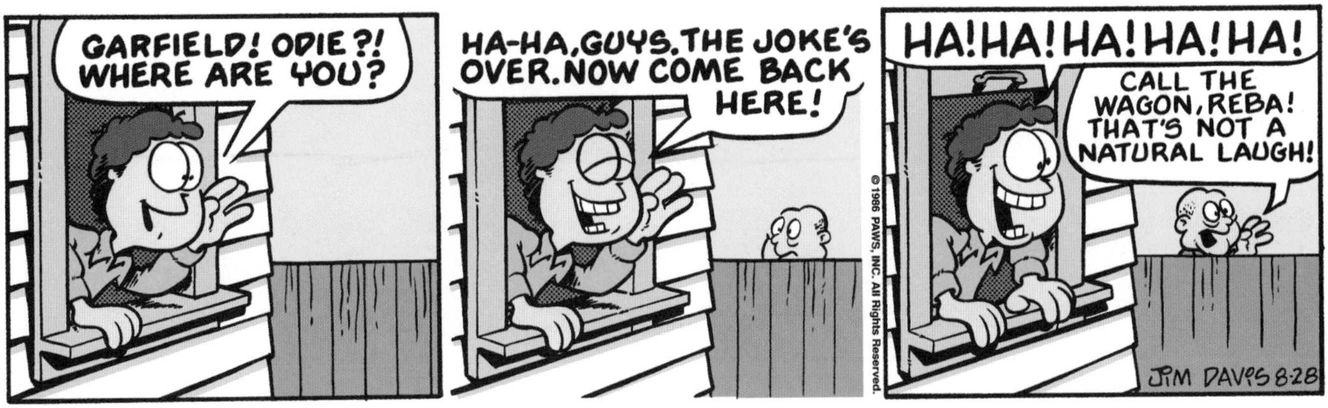
GARFIELD! ODIE?! WHERE ARE YOU?
HA-HA, GUYS. THE JOKE'S OVER. NOW COME BACK HERE!
HA! HA! HA! HA! HA!
CALL THE WAGON, REBA! THAT'S NOT A NATURAL LAUGH!
JIM DAVIS 8-28

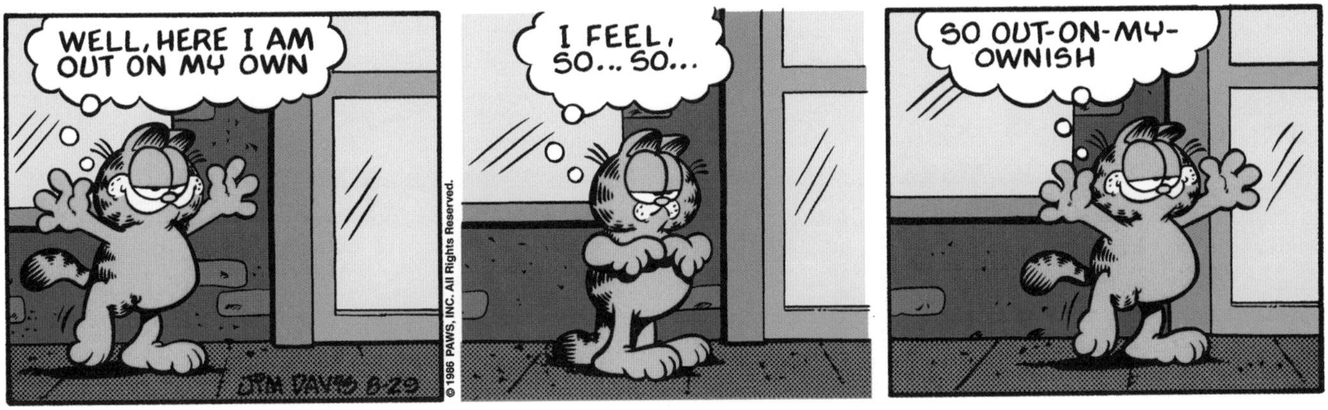
WELL, HERE I AM OUT ON MY OWN
JIM DAVIS 8-29
I FEEL, SO... SO...
SO OUT-ON-MY-OWNISH

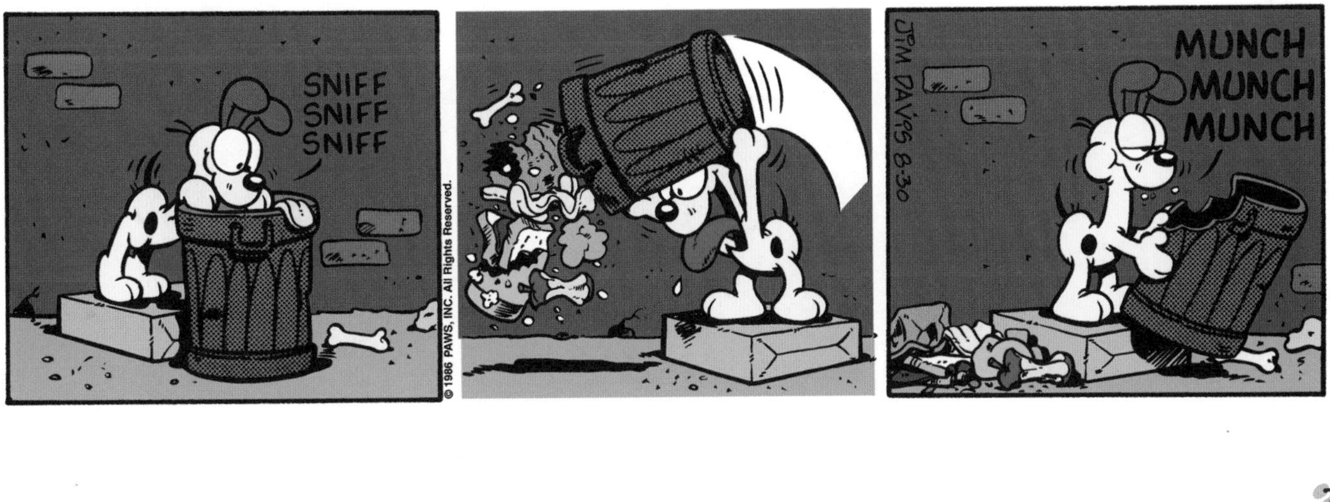
SNIFF
SNIFF
SNIFF
JIM DAVIS 8-30
MUNCH
MUNCH
MUNCH

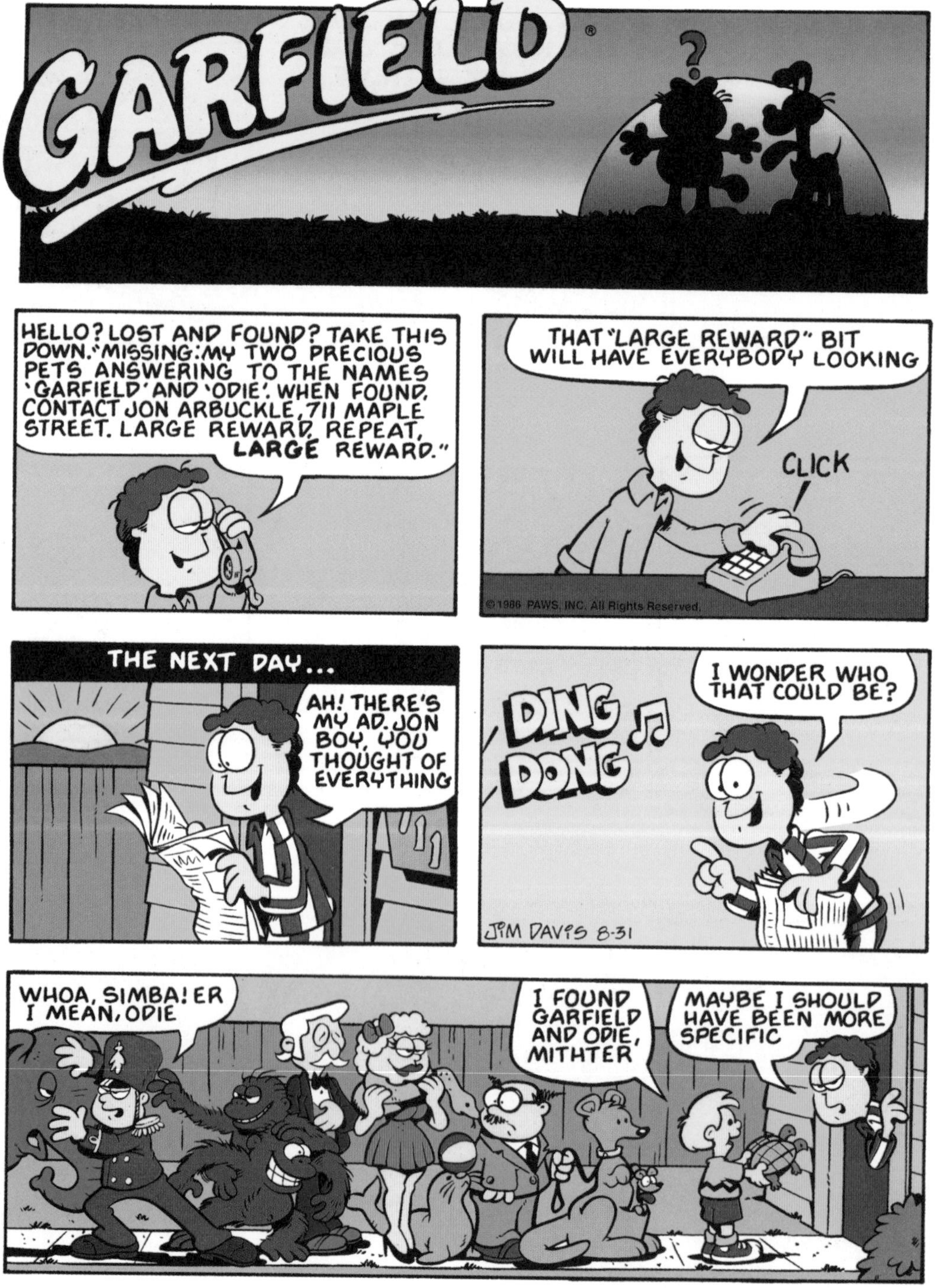
GARFIELD
?
HELLO? LOST AND FOUND? TAKE THIS DOWN. "MISSING: MY TWO PRECIOUS PETS ANSWERING TO THE NAMES 'GARFIELD' AND 'ODIE'. WHEN FOUND, CONTACT JON ARBUCKLE, 711 MAPLE STREET. LARGE REWARD. REPEAT, LARGE REWARD."
THAT "LARGE REWARD" BIT WILL HAVE EVERYBODY LOOKING
CLICK
© 1986 PAWS, INC. All Rights Reserved.
THE NEXT DAY...
AH! THERE'S MY AD. JON BOY, YOU THOUGHT OF EVERYTHING
DING DONG
I WONDER WHO THAT COULD BE?
JIM DAVIS 8-31
WHOA, SIMBA! ER I MEAN, ODIE
I FOUND GARFIELD AND ODIE, MITHTER
MAYBE I SHOULD HAVE BEEN MORE SPECIFIC

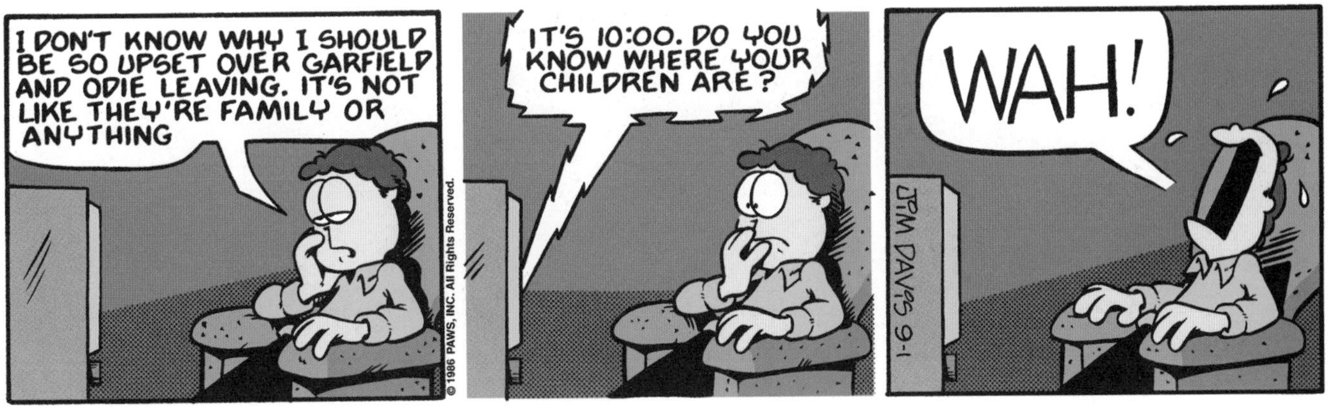
I DON'T KNOW WHY I SHOULD BE SO UPSET OVER GARFIELD AND ODIE LEAVING. IT'S NOT LIKE THEY'RE FAMILY OR ANYTHING
© 1986 PAWS, INC. All Rights Reserved.
IT'S 10:00. DO YOU KNOW WHERE YOUR CHILDREN ARE?
WAH!
JIM DAVIS 9-1

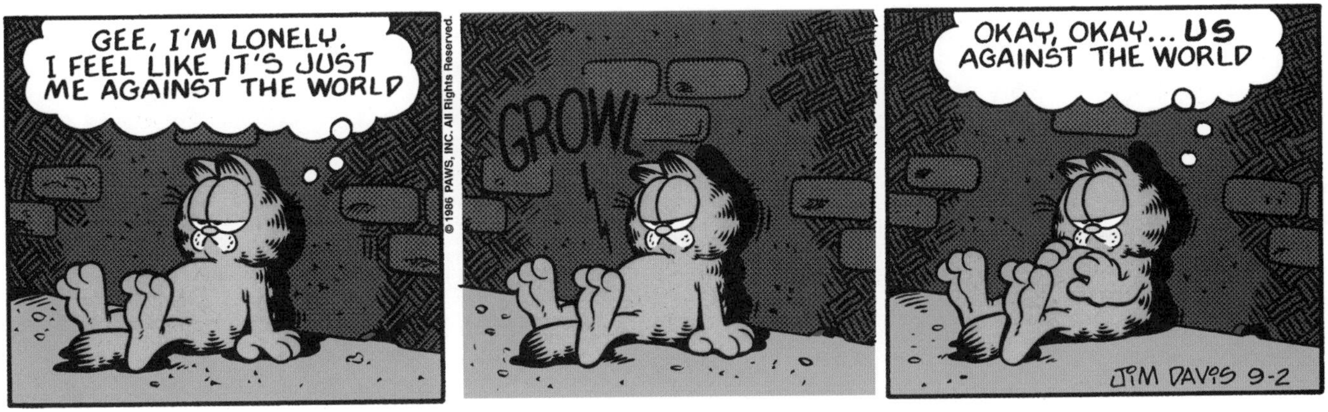
GEE, I'M LONELY. I FEEL LIKE IT'S JUST ME AGAINST THE WORLD
© 1986 PAWS, INC. All Rights Reserved.
GROWL
OKAY, OKAY... **US** AGAINST THE WORLD
JIM DAVIS 9-2

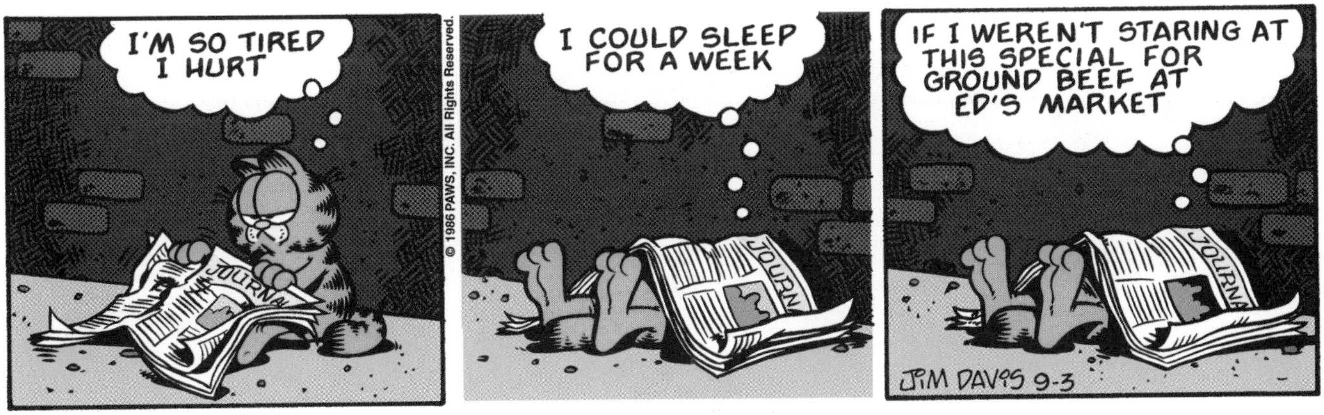
I'M SO TIRED I HURT
© 1986 PAWS, INC. All Rights Reserved.
I COULD SLEEP FOR A WEEK
IF I WEREN'T STARING AT THIS SPECIAL FOR GROUND BEEF AT ED'S MARKET
JIM DAVIS 9-3

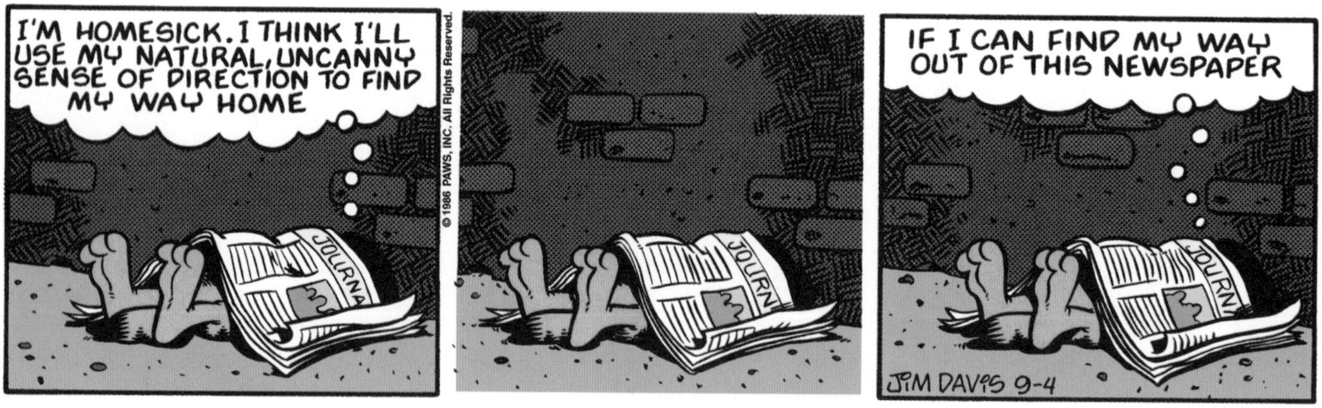
I'M HOMESICK. I THINK I'LL USE MY NATURAL, UNCANNY SENSE OF DIRECTION TO FIND MY WAY HOME
© 1986 PAWS, INC. All Rights Reserved.
IF I CAN FIND MY WAY OUT OF THIS NEWSPAPER
JIM DAVIS 9-4

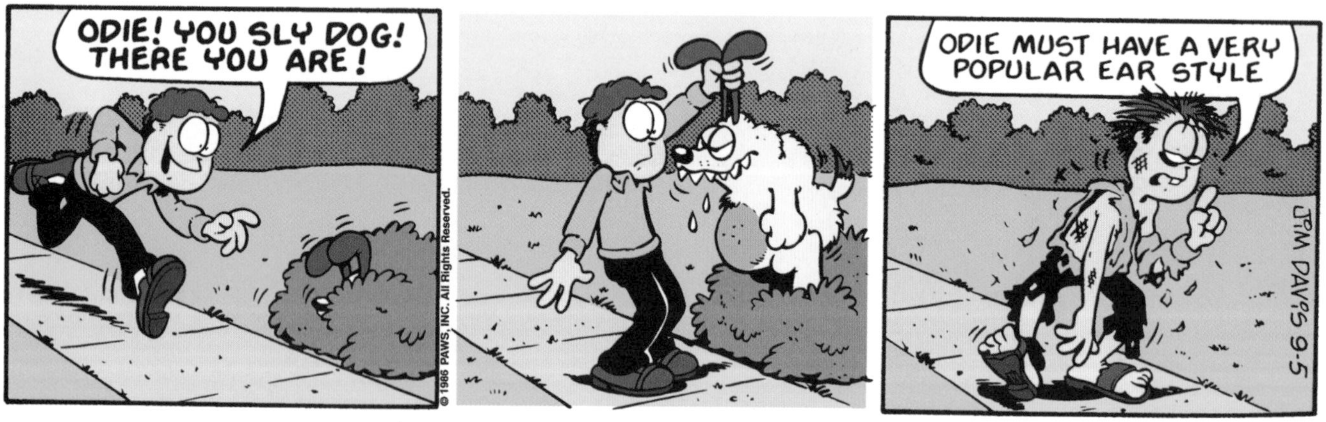
ODIE! YOU SLY DOG! THERE YOU ARE!
© 1986 PAWS, INC. All Rights Reserved.
ODIE MUST HAVE A VERY POPULAR EAR STYLE
JIM DAVIS 9-5

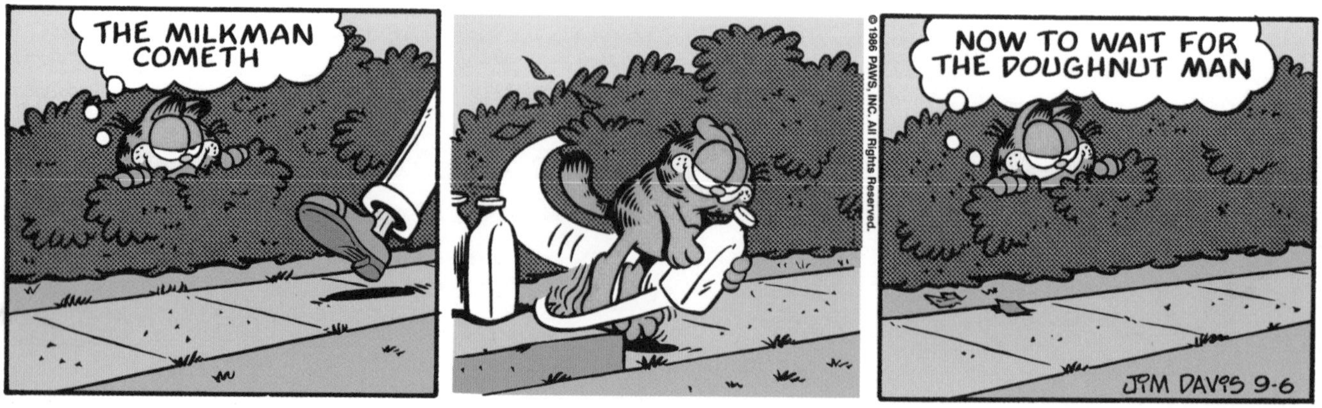
THE MILKMAN COMETH
© 1986 PAWS, INC. All Rights Reserved.
NOW TO WAIT FOR THE DOUGHNUT MAN
JIM DAVIS 9-6

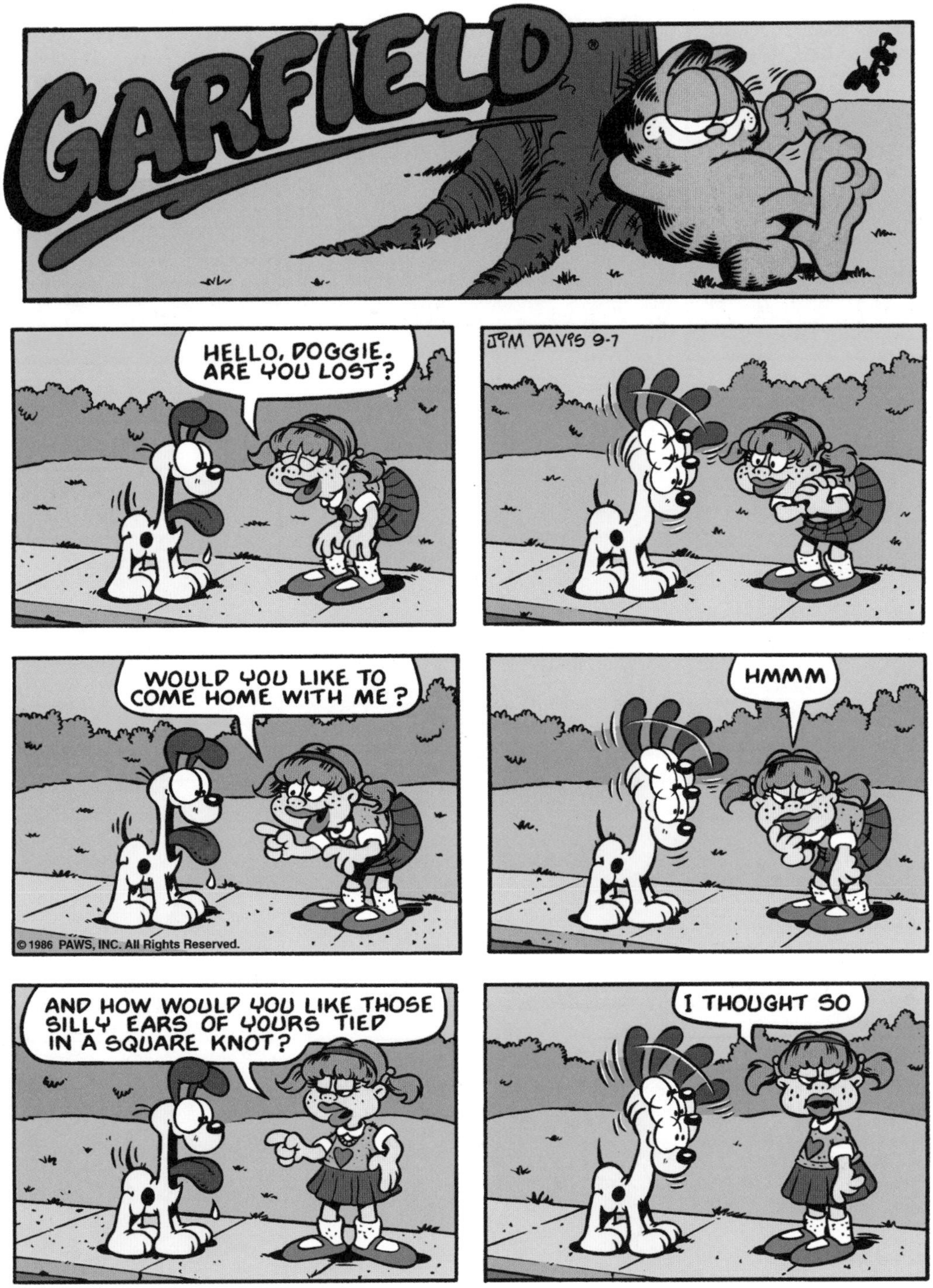
GARFIELD
HELLO, DOGGIE. ARE YOU LOST?
JIM DAVIS 9-7
WOULD YOU LIKE TO COME HOME WITH ME?
HMMM
© 1986 PAWS, INC. All Rights Reserved.
AND HOW WOULD YOU LIKE THOSE SILLY EARS OF YOURS TIED IN A SQUARE KNOT?
I THOUGHT SO

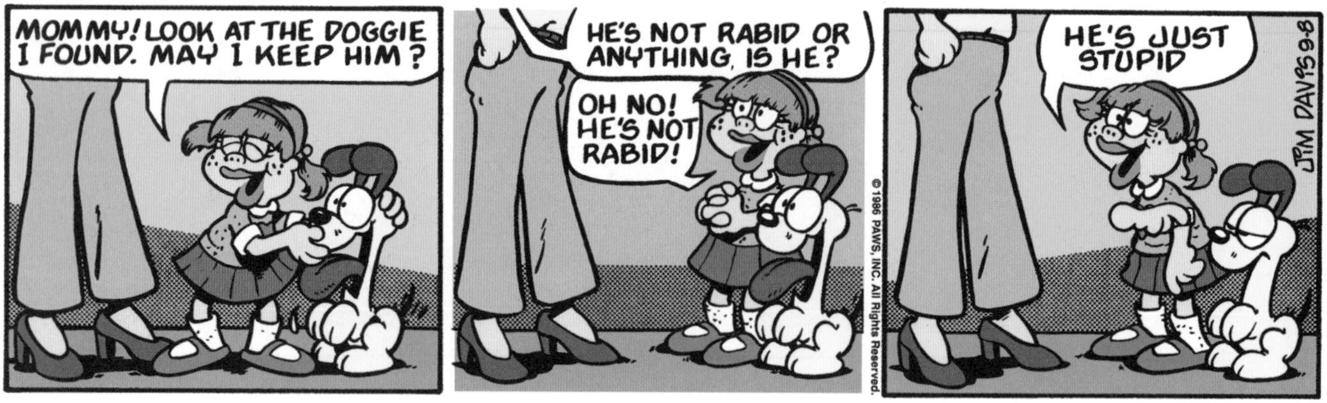
MOMMY! LOOK AT THE DOGGIE I FOUND. MAY I KEEP HIM?
HE'S NOT RABID OR ANYTHING, IS HE?
OH NO! HE'S NOT RABID!
© 1986 PAWS, INC. All Rights Reserved.
HE'S JUST STUPID
JIM DAVIS 9-8

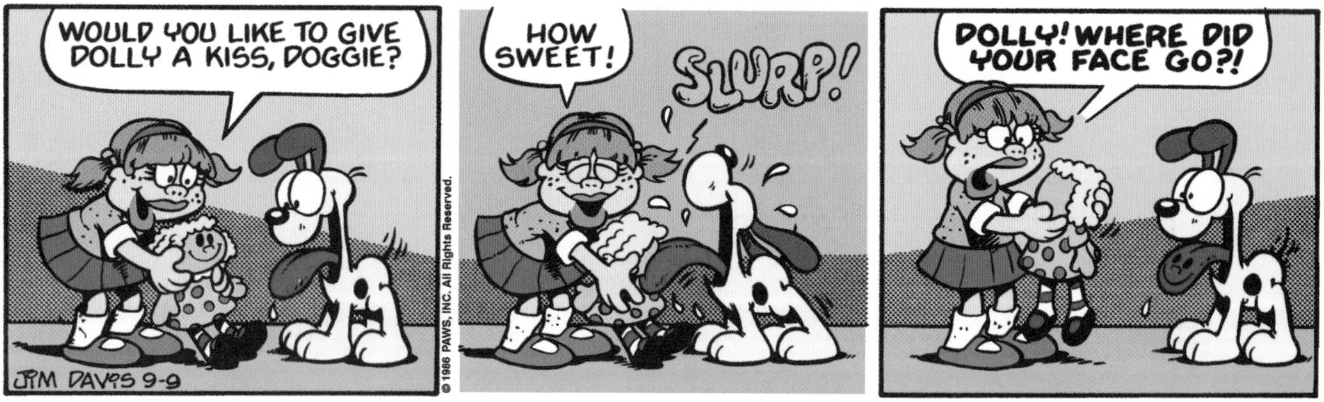
WOULD YOU LIKE TO GIVE DOLLY A KISS, DOGGIE?
JIM DAVIS 9-9
© 1986 PAWS, INC. All Rights Reserved.
HOW SWEET!
SLURP!
DOLLY! WHERE DID YOUR FACE GO?!

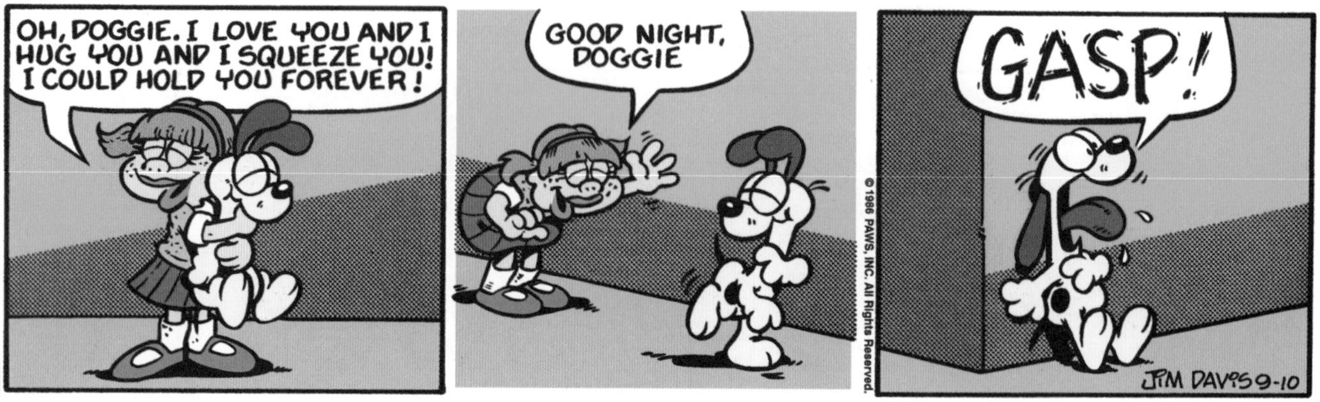
OH, DOGGIE. I LOVE YOU AND I HUG YOU AND I SQUEEZE YOU! I COULD HOLD YOU FOREVER!
GOOD NIGHT, DOGGIE
© 1986 PAWS, INC. All Rights Reserved.
GASP!
JIM DAVIS 9-10

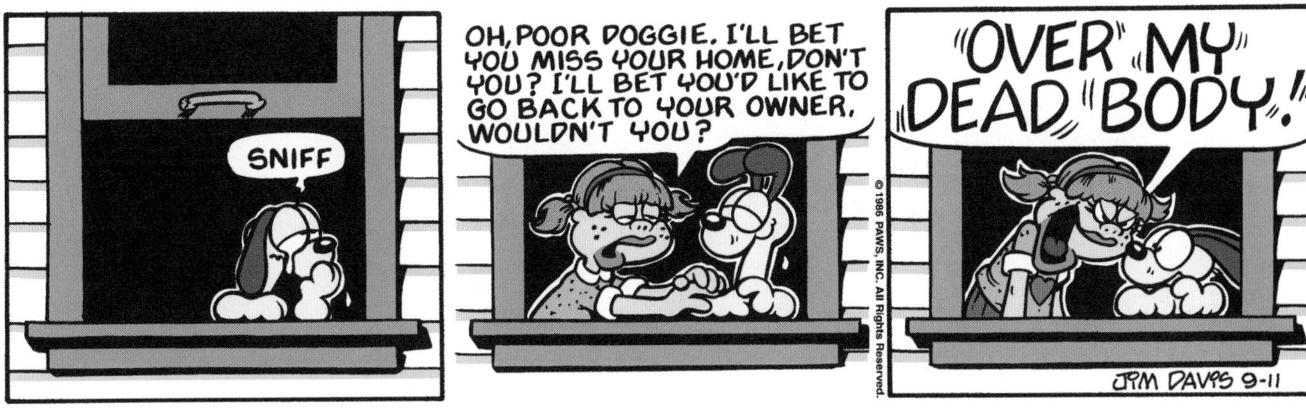
SNIFF
OH, POOR DOGGIE. I'LL BET YOU MISS YOUR HOME, DON'T YOU? I'LL BET YOU'D LIKE TO GO BACK TO YOUR OWNER, WOULDN'T YOU?
"OVER" MY "DEAD" BODY!"
© 1986 PAWS, INC. All Rights Reserved.
JIM DAVIS 9-11

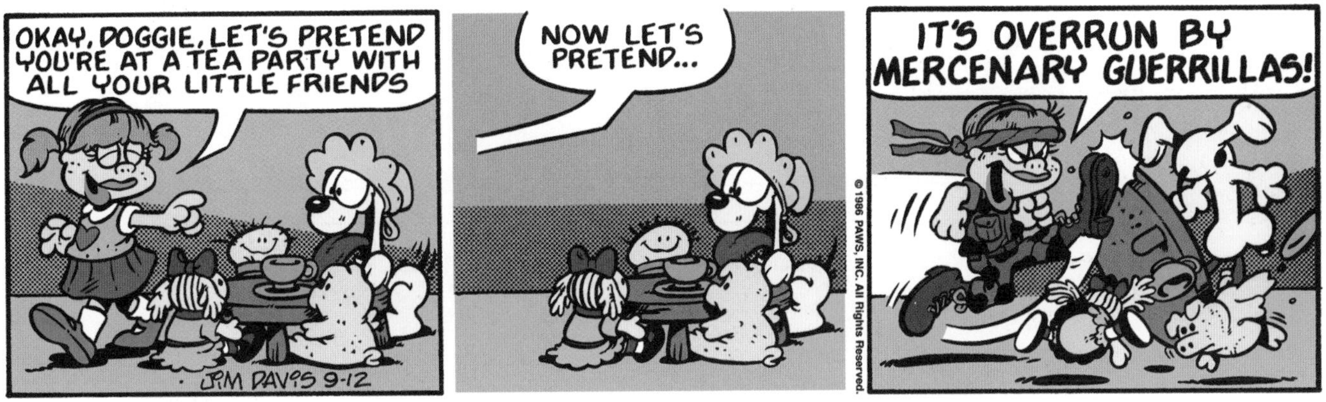
OKAY, DOGGIE, LET'S PRETEND YOU'RE AT A TEA PARTY WITH ALL YOUR LITTLE FRIENDS
JIM DAVIS 9-12
NOW LET'S PRETEND...
© 1986 PAWS, INC. All Rights Reserved.
IT'S OVERRUN BY MERCENARY GUERRILLAS!

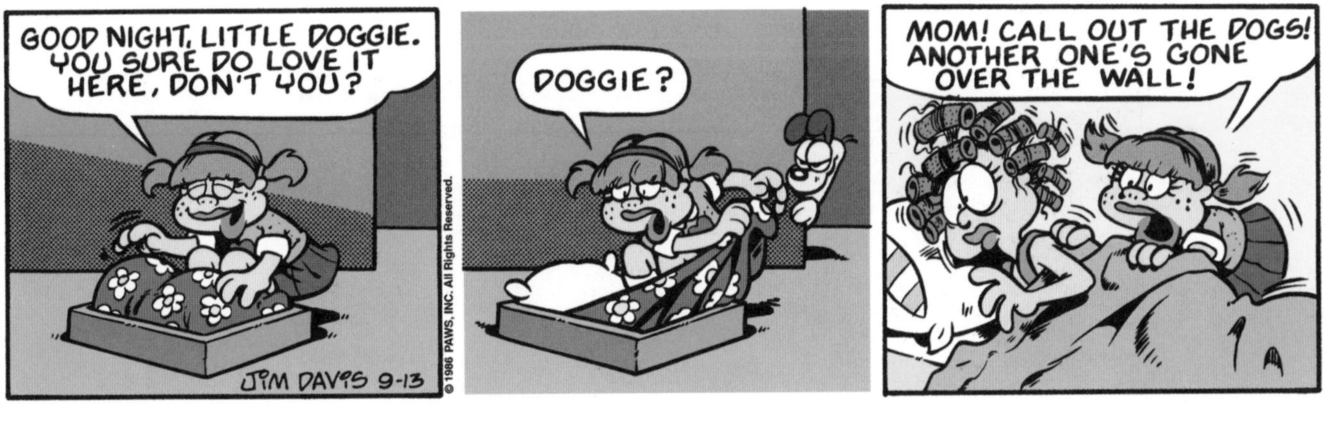
GOOD NIGHT, LITTLE DOGGIE. YOU SURE DO LOVE IT HERE, DON'T YOU?
JIM DAVIS 9-13
© 1986 PAWS, INC. All Rights Reserved.
DOGGIE?
MOM! CALL OUT THE DOGS! ANOTHER ONE'S GONE OVER THE WALL!

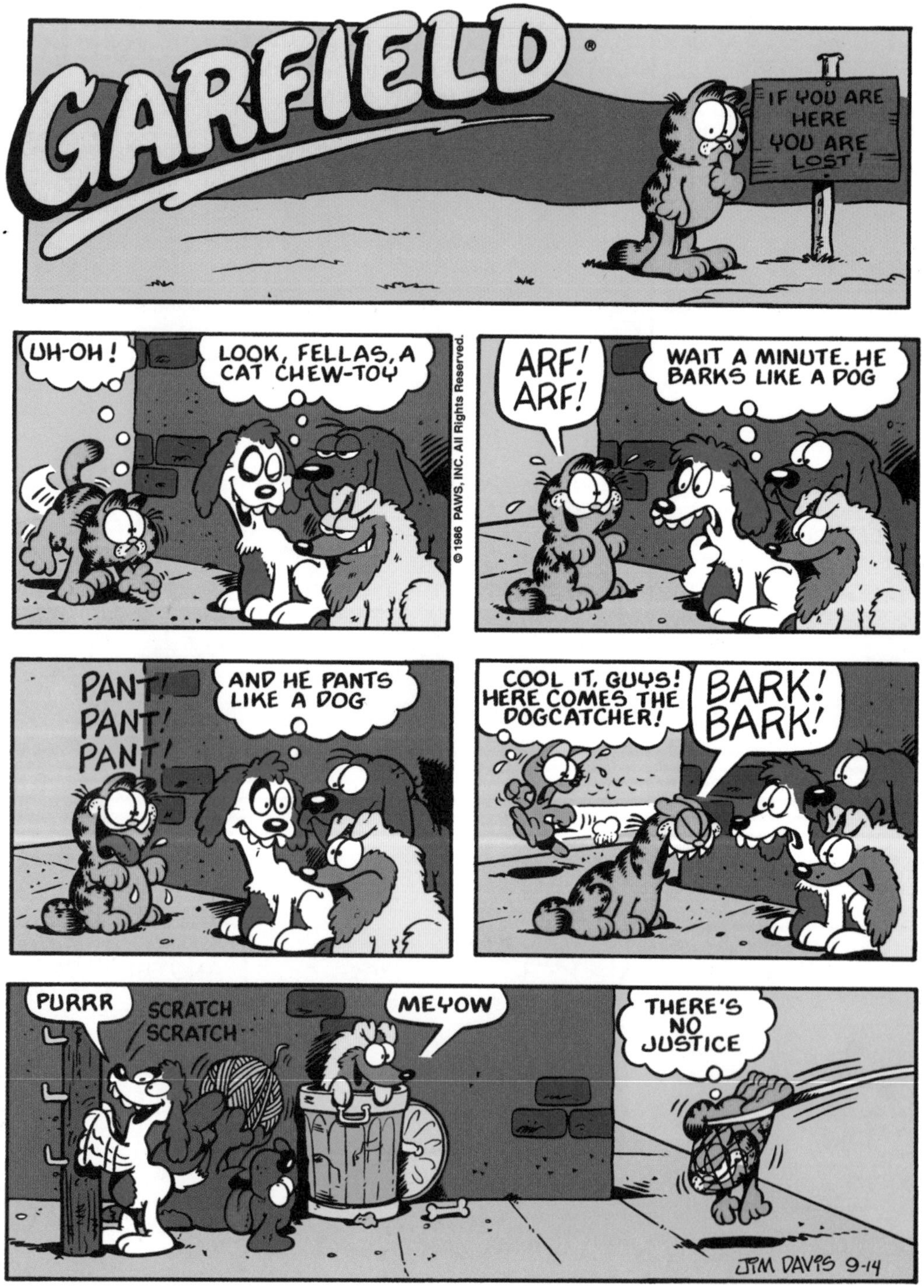
GARFIELD®
IF YOU ARE HERE YOU ARE LOST!
UH-OH!
LOOK, FELLAS, A CAT CHEW-TOY
© 1986 PAWS, INC. All Rights Reserved.
ARF! ARF!
WAIT A MINUTE. HE BARKS LIKE A DOG
PANT! PANT! PANT!
AND HE PANTS LIKE A DOG
COOL IT, GUYS! HERE COMES THE DOGCATCHER!
BARK! BARK!
PURRR
SCRATCH SCRATCH
MEYOW
THERE'S NO JUSTICE
JIM DAVIS 9-14

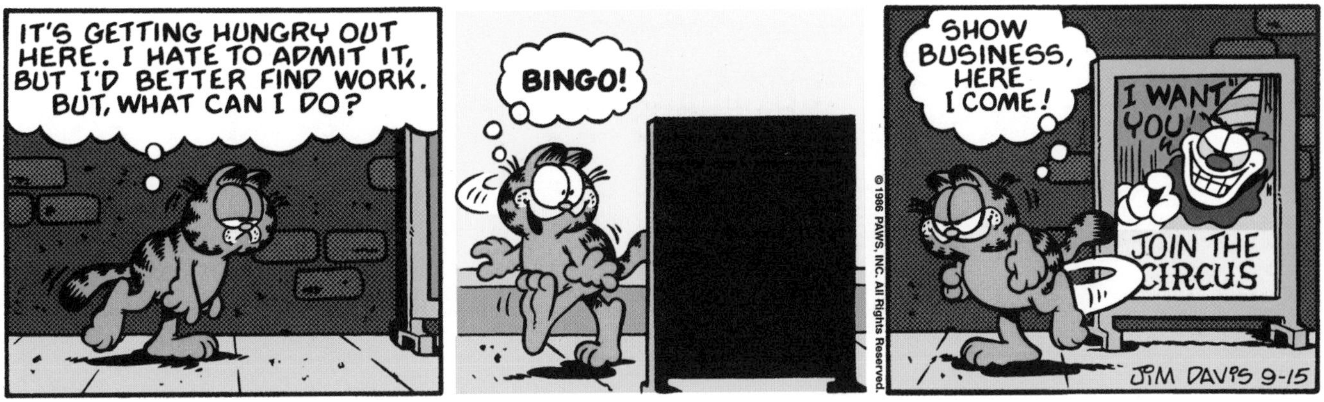
IT'S GETTING HUNGRY OUT HERE. I HATE TO ADMIT IT, BUT I'D BETTER FIND WORK. BUT, WHAT CAN I DO?
BINGO!
© 1986 PAWS, INC. All Rights Reserved.
SHOW BUSINESS, HERE I COME!
I WANT YOU!
JOIN THE CIRCUS
JIM DAVIS 9-15

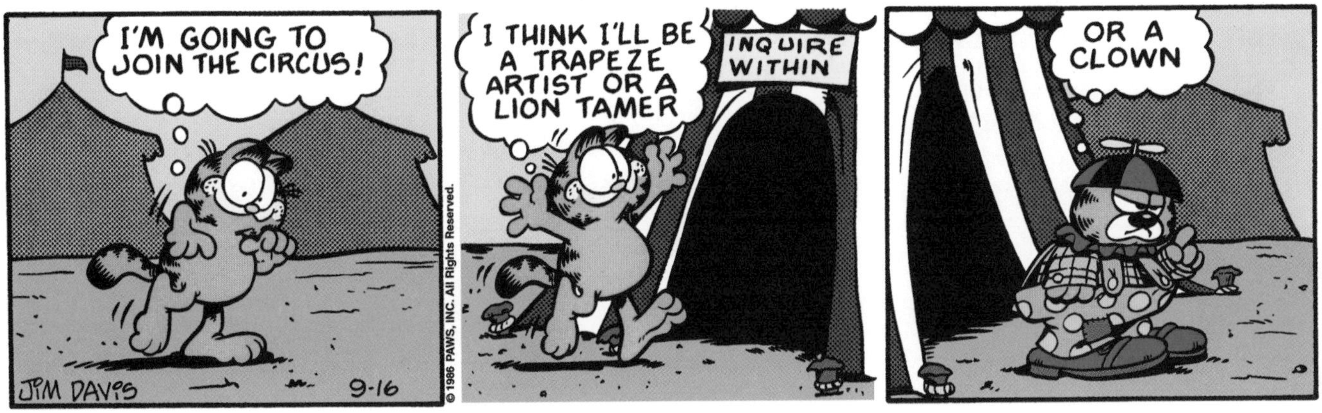
I'M GOING TO JOIN THE CIRCUS!
JIM DAVIS 9-16
© 1986 PAWS, INC. All Rights Reserved.
I THINK I'LL BE A TRAPEZE ARTIST OR A LION TAMER
INQUIRE WITHIN
OR A CLOWN

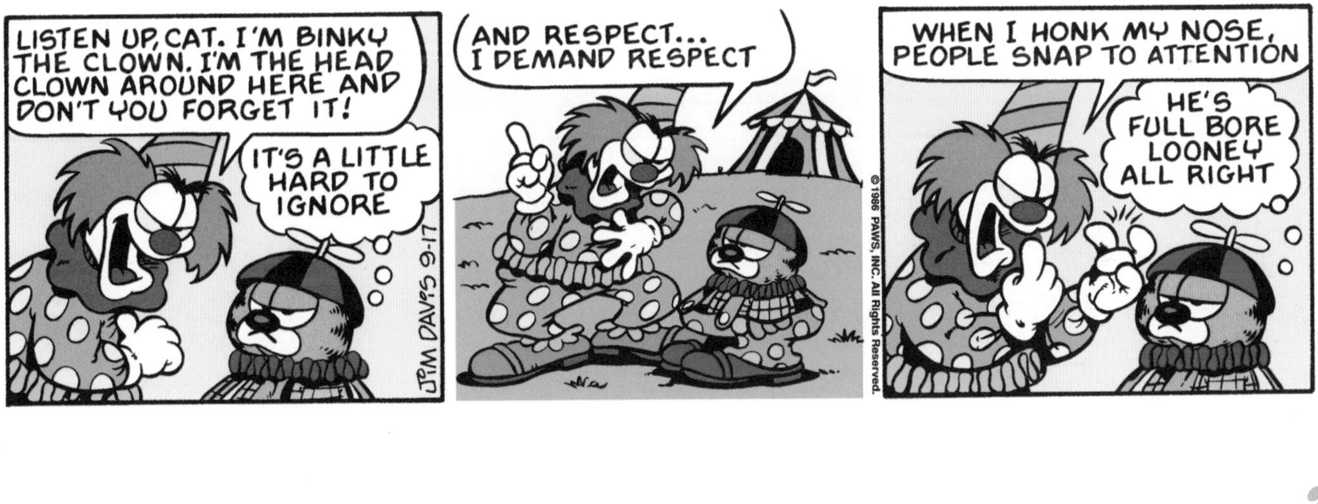
LISTEN UP, CAT. I'M BINKY THE CLOWN. I'M THE HEAD CLOWN AROUND HERE AND DON'T YOU FORGET IT!
IT'S A LITTLE HARD TO IGNORE
JIM DAVIS 9-17
AND RESPECT... I DEMAND RESPECT
© 1986 PAWS, INC. All Rights Reserved.
WHEN I HONK MY NOSE, PEOPLE SNAP TO ATTENTION
HE'S FULL BORE LOONEY ALL RIGHT

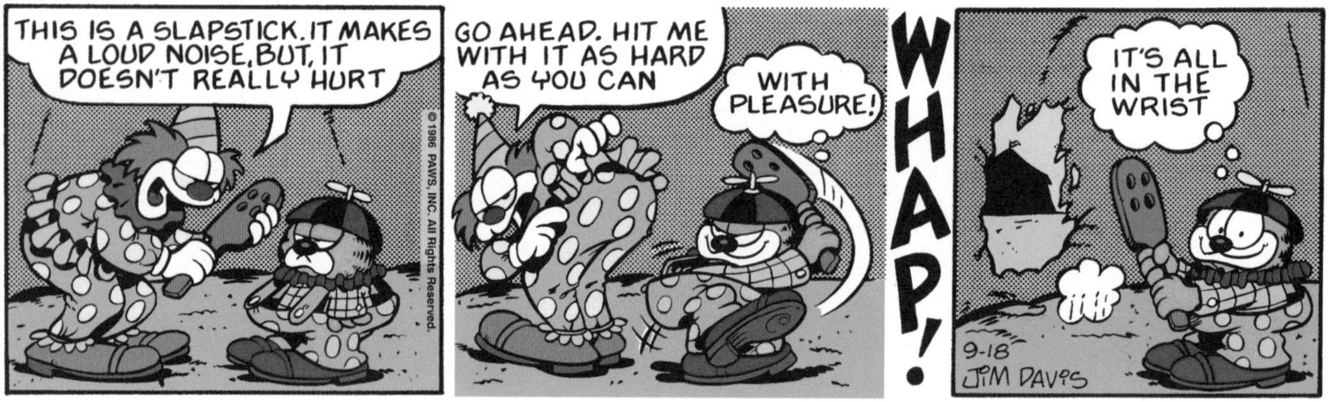
THIS IS A SLAPSTICK. IT MAKES A LOUD NOISE, BUT, IT DOESN'T REALLY HURT
© 1986 PAWS, INC. All Rights Reserved.
GO AHEAD. HIT ME WITH IT AS HARD AS YOU CAN
WITH PLEASURE!
WHAP!
IT'S ALL IN THE WRIST
9-18
JIM DAVIS

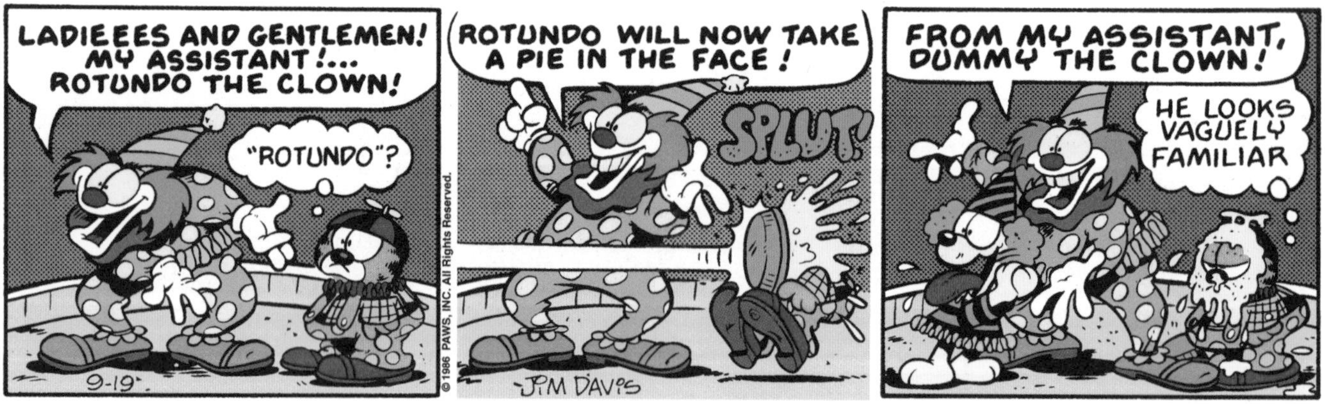
LADIEEES AND GENTLEMEN! MY ASSISTANT!... ROTUNDO THE CLOWN!
"ROTUNDO"?
9-19
© 1986 PAWS, INC. All Rights Reserved.
ROTUNDO WILL NOW TAKE A PIE IN THE FACE!
SPLUT!
JIM DAVIS
FROM MY ASSISTANT, DUMMY THE CLOWN!
HE LOOKS VAGUELY FAMILIAR

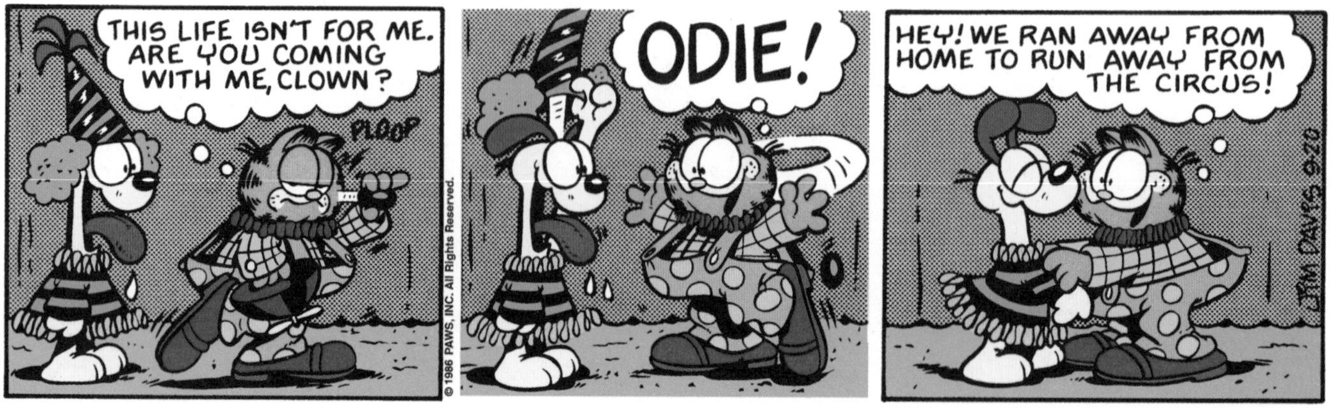
THIS LIFE ISN'T FOR ME. ARE YOU COMING WITH ME, CLOWN?
PLOOP
© 1986 PAWS, INC. All Rights Reserved.
ODIE!
HEY! WE RAN AWAY FROM HOME TO RUN AWAY FROM THE CIRCUS!
JIM DAVIS 9-20

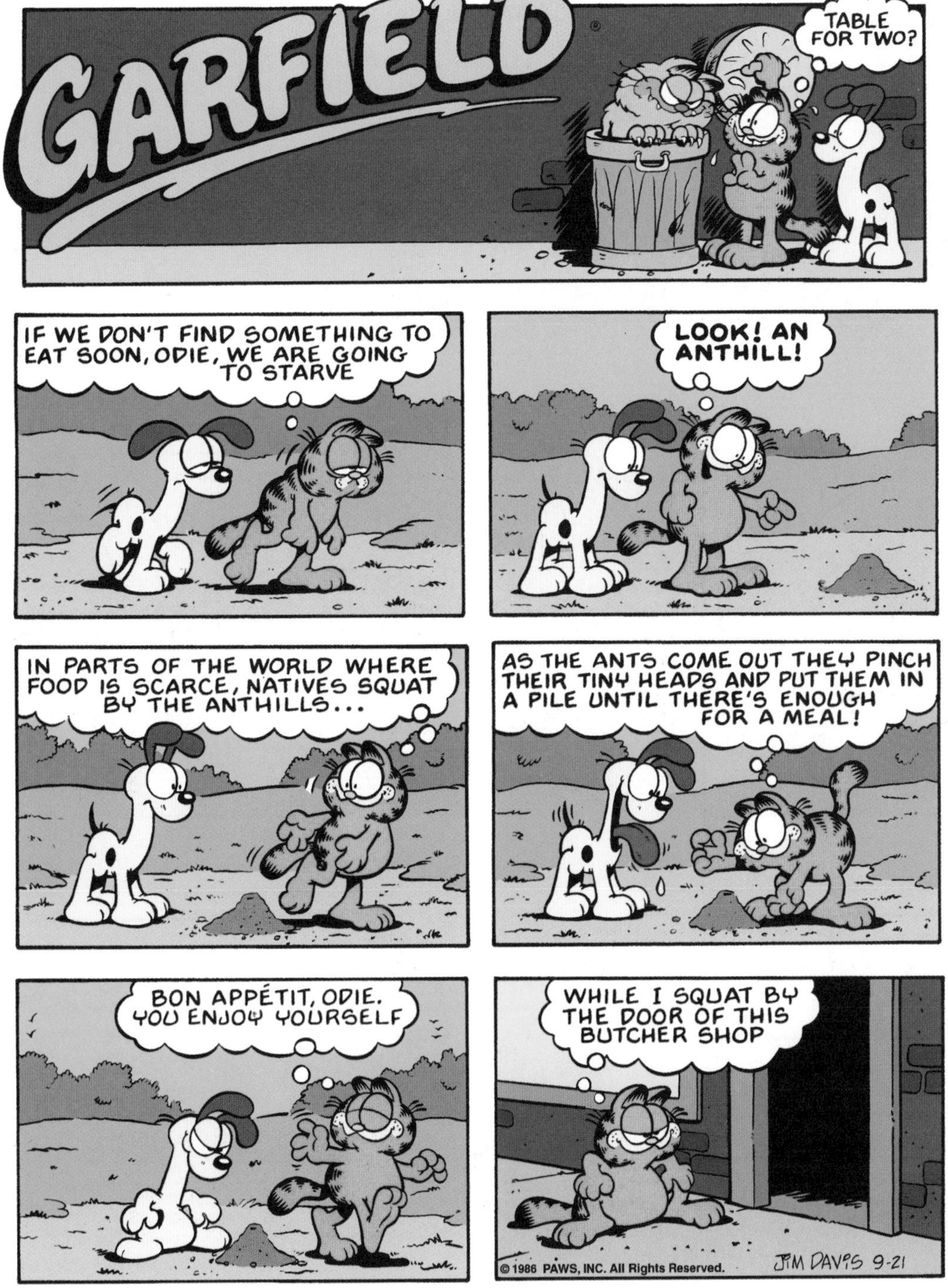
GARFIELD
TABLE FOR TWO?
IF WE DON'T FIND SOMETHING TO EAT SOON, ODIE, WE ARE GOING TO STARVE
LOOK! AN ANTHILL!
IN PARTS OF THE WORLD WHERE FOOD IS SCARCE, NATIVES SQUAT BY THE ANTHILLS...
AS THE ANTS COME OUT THEY PINCH THEIR TINY HEADS AND PUT THEM IN A PILE UNTIL THERE'S ENOUGH FOR A MEAL!
BON APPÉTIT, ODIE. YOU ENJOY YOURSELF
WHILE I SQUAT BY THE DOOR OF THIS BUTCHER SHOP
© 1986 PAWS, INC. All Rights Reserved.
JIM DAVIS 9-21

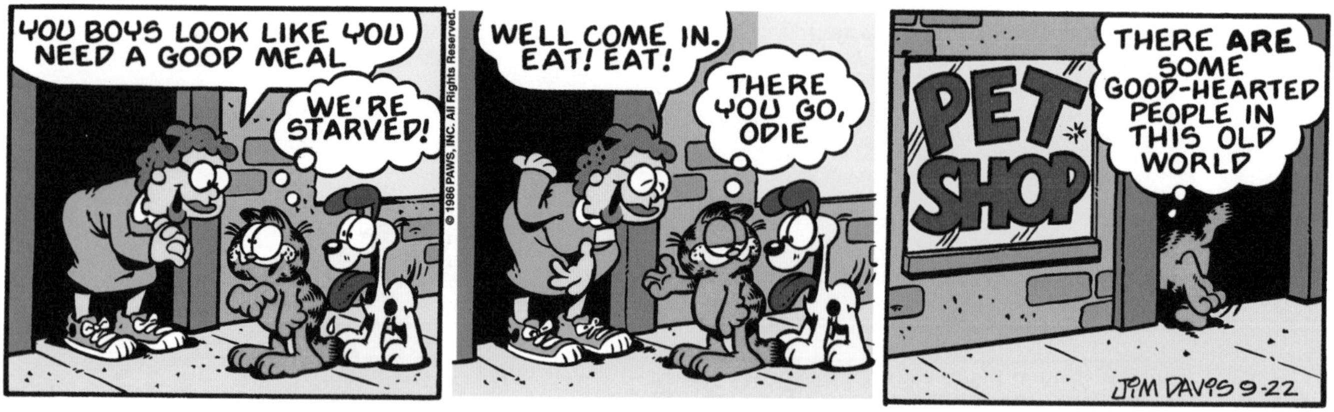
YOU BOYS LOOK LIKE YOU NEED A GOOD MEAL
WE'RE STARVED!
WELL COME IN. EAT! EAT!
THERE YOU GO, ODIE
PET SHOP
THERE ARE SOME GOOD-HEARTED PEOPLE IN THIS OLD WORLD
JIM DAVIS 9-22

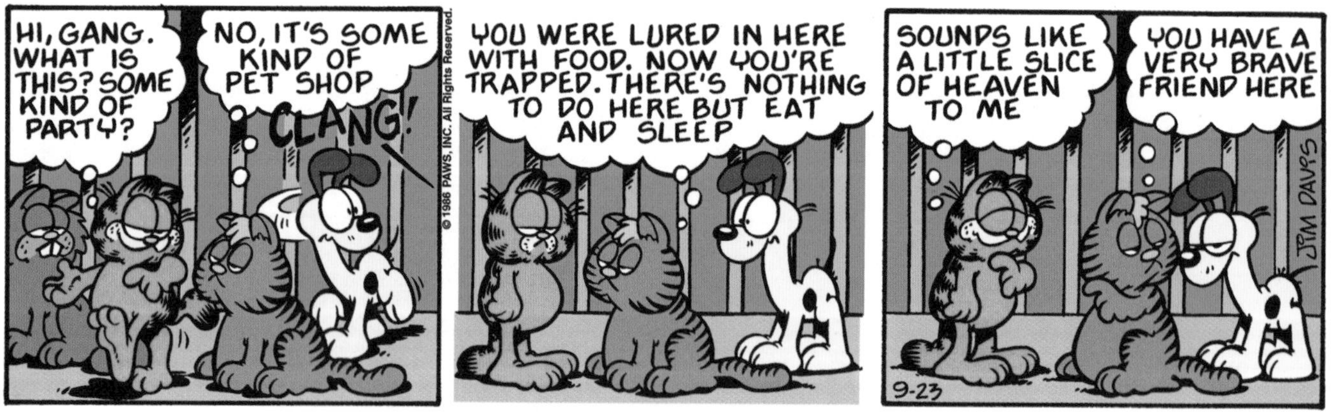
HI, GANG. WHAT IS THIS? SOME KIND OF PARTY?
NO, IT'S SOME KIND OF PET SHOP
CLANG!
YOU WERE LURED IN HERE WITH FOOD. NOW YOU'RE TRAPPED. THERE'S NOTHING TO DO HERE BUT EAT AND SLEEP
SOUNDS LIKE A LITTLE SLICE OF HEAVEN TO ME
YOU HAVE A VERY BRAVE FRIEND HERE
JIM DAVIS
9-23

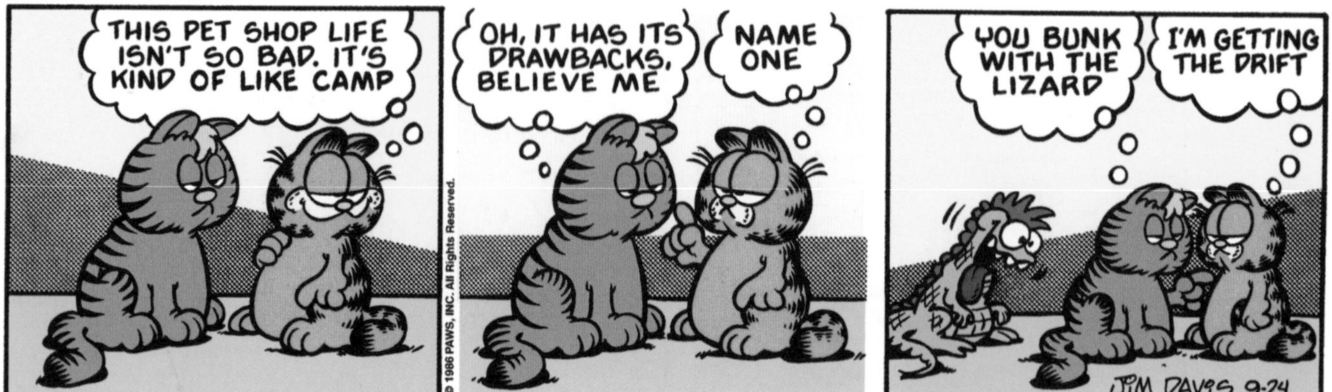
THIS PET SHOP LIFE ISN'T SO BAD. IT'S KIND OF LIKE CAMP
OH, IT HAS ITS DRAWBACKS, BELIEVE ME
NAME ONE
YOU BUNK WITH THE LIZARD
I'M GETTING THE DRIFT
JIM DAVIS 9-24

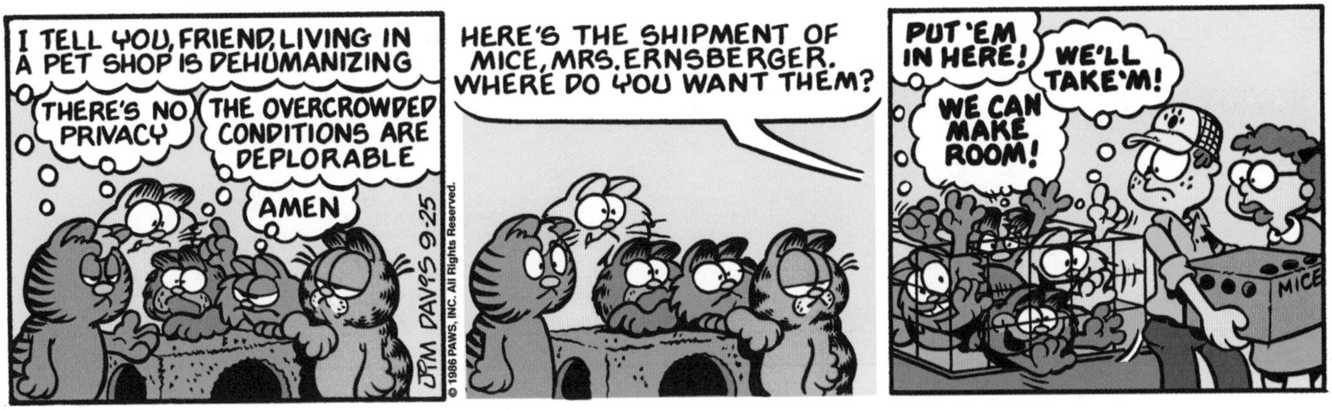
I TELL YOU, FRIEND, LIVING IN A PET SHOP IS DEHUMANIZING
THERE'S NO PRIVACY
THE OVERCROWDED CONDITIONS ARE DEPLORABLE
AMEN
JPM DAVPS 9-25
© 1986 PAWS, INC. All Rights Reserved.
HERE'S THE SHIPMENT OF MICE, MRS. ERNSBERGER. WHERE DO YOU WANT THEM?
PUT 'EM IN HERE!
WE'LL TAKE 'M!
WE CAN MAKE ROOM!
MICE

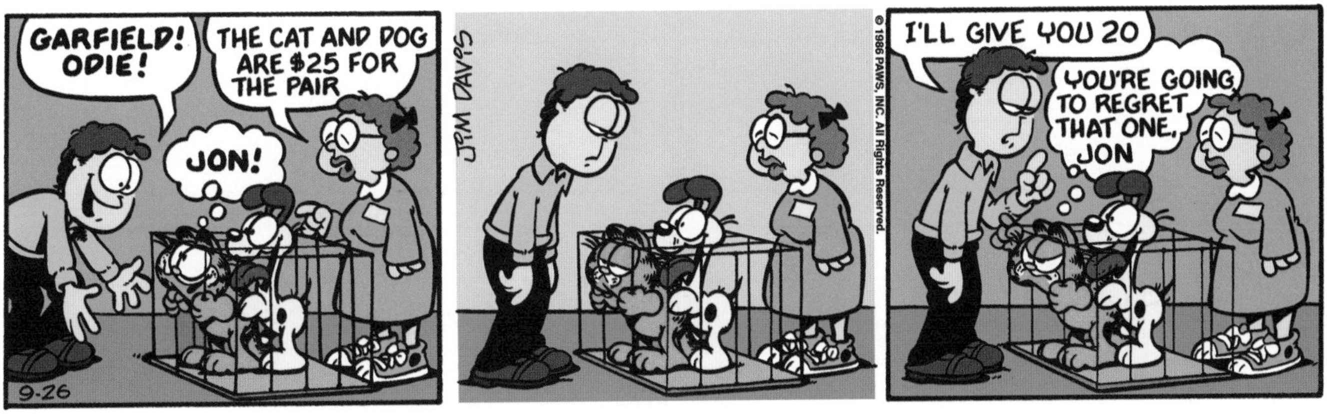
GARFIELD! ODIE!
THE CAT AND DOG ARE $25 FOR THE PAIR
JON!
9-26
JPM DAVPS
© 1986 PAWS, INC. All Rights Reserved.
I'LL GIVE YOU 20
YOU'RE GOING TO REGRET THAT ONE, JON

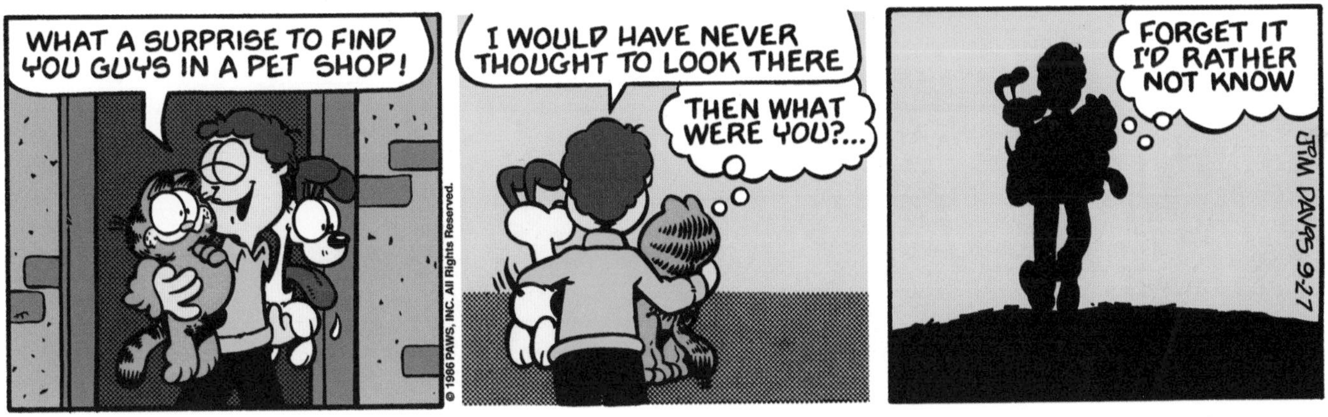
WHAT A SURPRISE TO FIND YOU GUYS IN A PET SHOP!
© 1986 PAWS, INC. All Rights Reserved.
I WOULD HAVE NEVER THOUGHT TO LOOK THERE
THEN WHAT WERE YOU?...
FORGET IT I'D RATHER NOT KNOW
JPM DAVPS 9-27

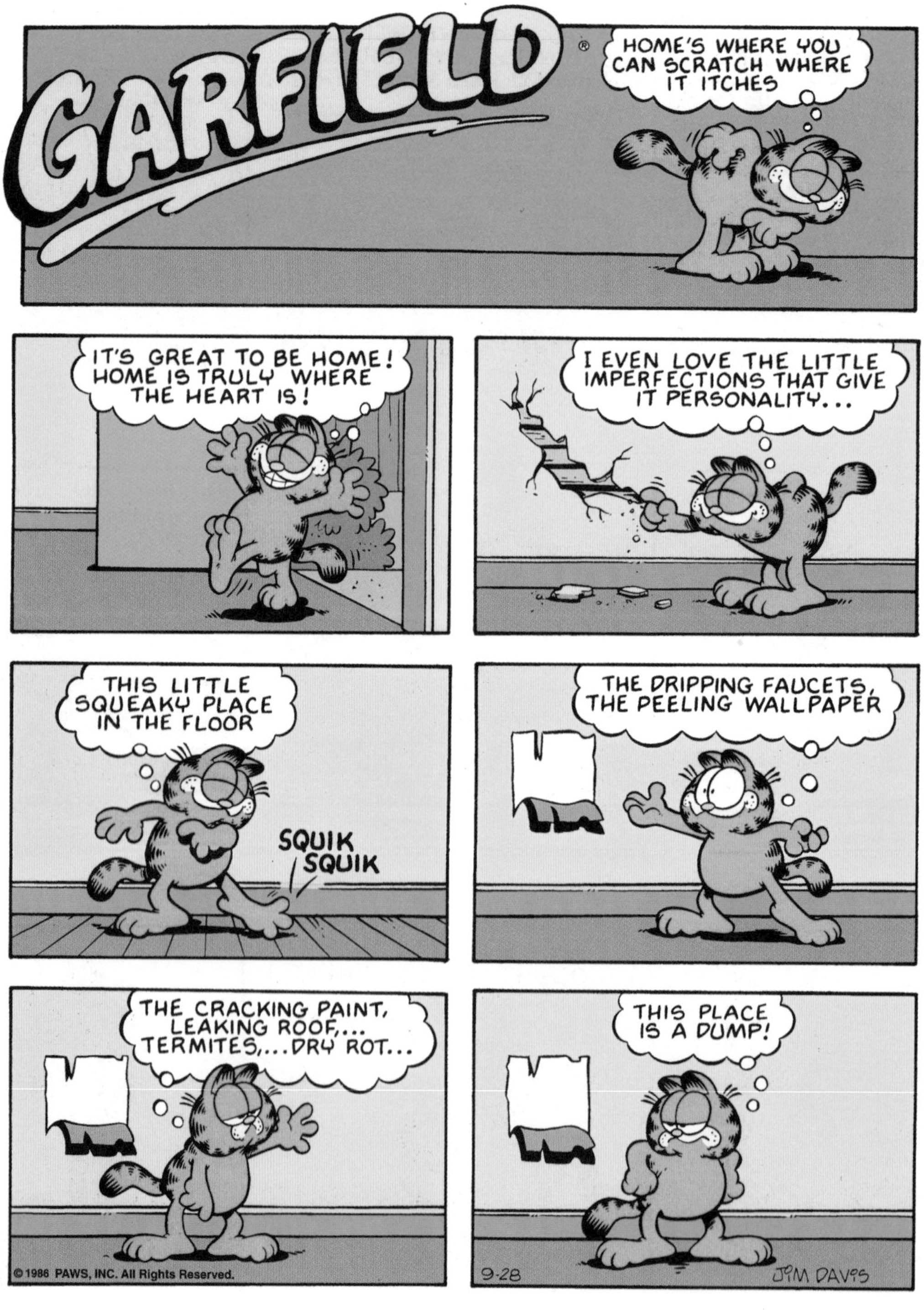
GARFIELD
HOME'S WHERE YOU CAN SCRATCH WHERE IT ITCHES
IT'S GREAT TO BE HOME! HOME IS TRULY WHERE THE HEART IS!
I EVEN LOVE THE LITTLE IMPERFECTIONS THAT GIVE IT PERSONALITY...
THIS LITTLE SQUEAKY PLACE IN THE FLOOR
SQUIK SQUIK
THE DRIPPING FAUCETS, THE PEELING WALLPAPER
THE CRACKING PAINT, LEAKING ROOF,... TERMITES,... DRY ROT...
THIS PLACE IS A DUMP!
9-28
JIM DAVIS

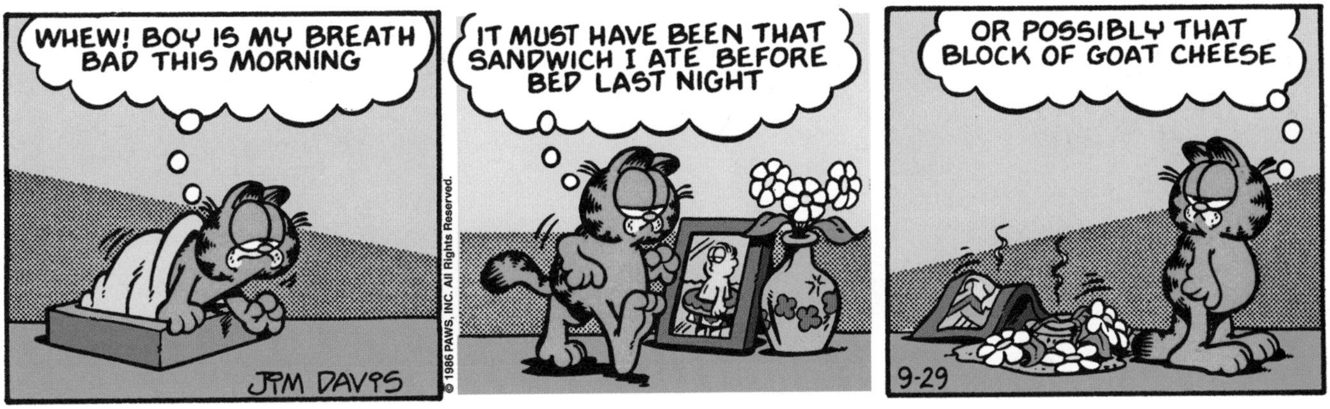
WHEW! BOY IS MY BREATH BAD THIS MORNING
IT MUST HAVE BEEN THAT SANDWICH I ATE BEFORE BED LAST NIGHT
OR POSSIBLY THAT BLOCK OF GOAT CHEESE
JIM DAVIS
© 1986 PAWS, INC. All Rights Reserved.
9-29

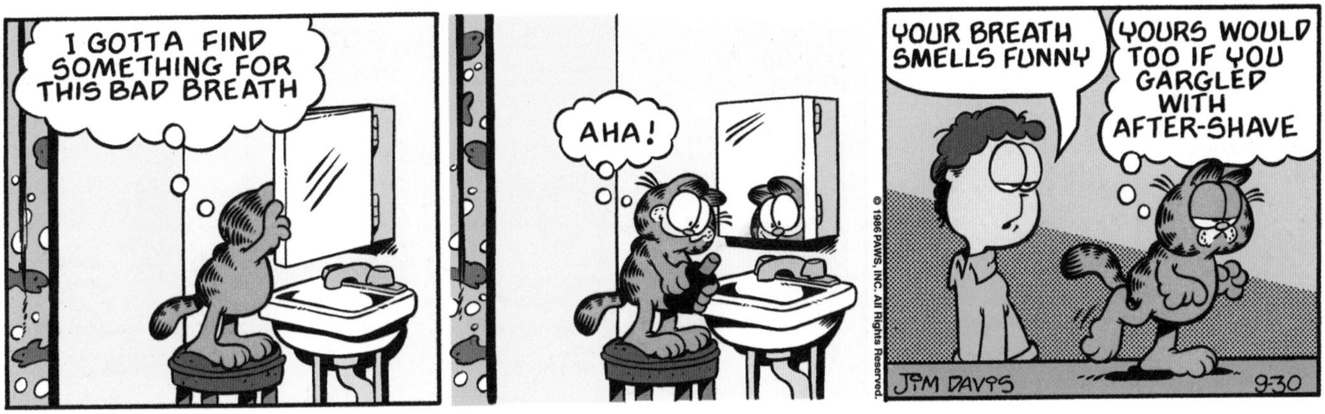
I GOTTA FIND SOMETHING FOR THIS BAD BREATH
AHA!
YOUR BREATH SMELLS FUNNY
YOURS WOULD TOO IF YOU GARGLED WITH AFTER-SHAVE
© 1986 PAWS, INC. All Rights Reserved.
JIM DAVIS
9-30

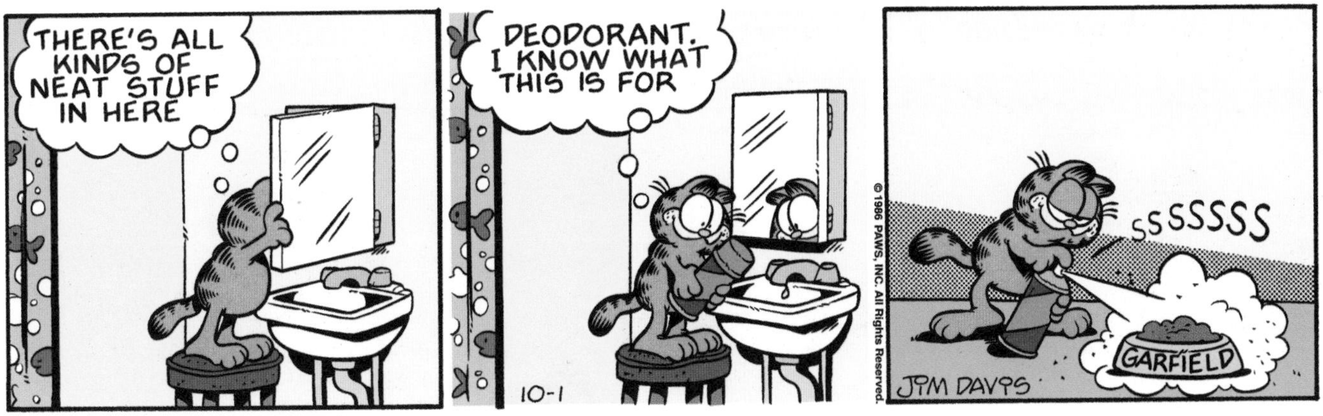
THERE'S ALL KINDS OF NEAT STUFF IN HERE
DEODORANT. I KNOW WHAT THIS IS FOR
10-1
© 1986 PAWS, INC. All Rights Reserved.
SSSSSSS
GARFIELD
JIM DAVIS

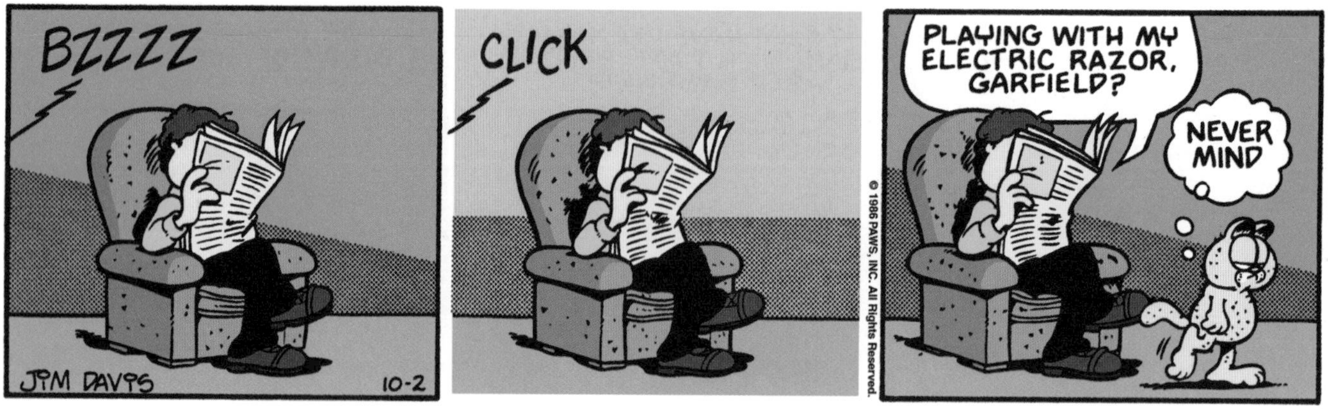
BZZZZ
JIM DAVIS
10-2
CLICK
PLAYING WITH MY ELECTRIC RAZOR, GARFIELD?
NEVER MIND
© 1986 PAWS, INC. All Rights Reserved.

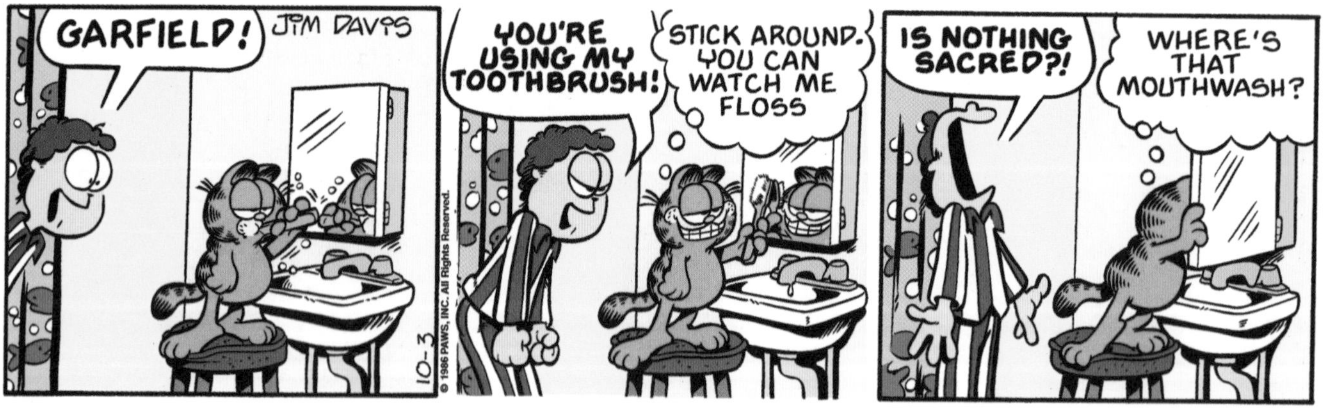
GARFIELD!
JIM DAVIS
10-3
© 1986 PAWS, INC. All Rights Reserved.
YOU'RE USING MY TOOTHBRUSH!
STICK AROUND. YOU CAN WATCH ME FLOSS
IS NOTHING SACRED?!
WHERE'S THAT MOUTHWASH?

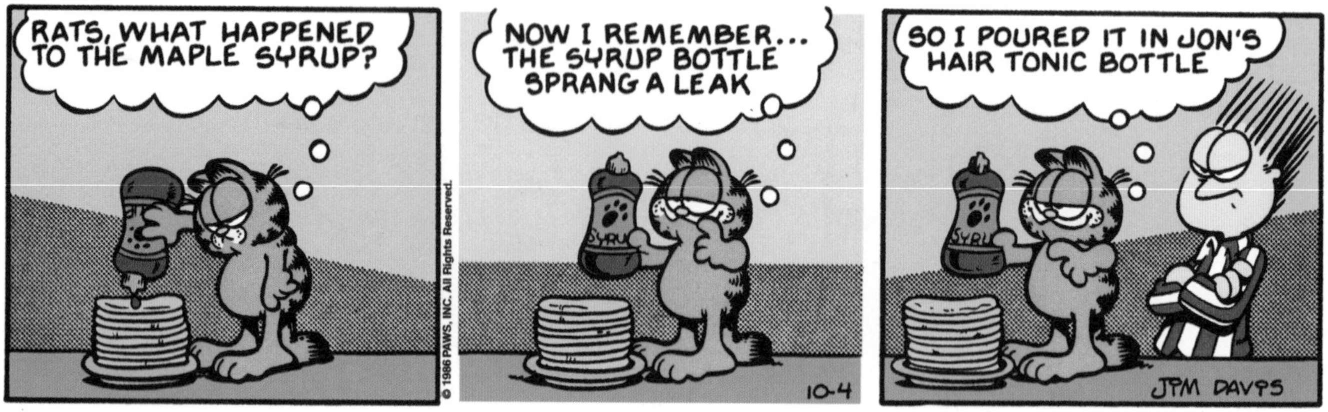
RATS, WHAT HAPPENED TO THE MAPLE SYRUP?
© 1986 PAWS, INC. All Rights Reserved.
NOW I REMEMBER... THE SYRUP BOTTLE SPRANG A LEAK
SYRUP
10-4
SO I POURED IT IN JON'S HAIR TONIC BOTTLE
JIM DAVIS

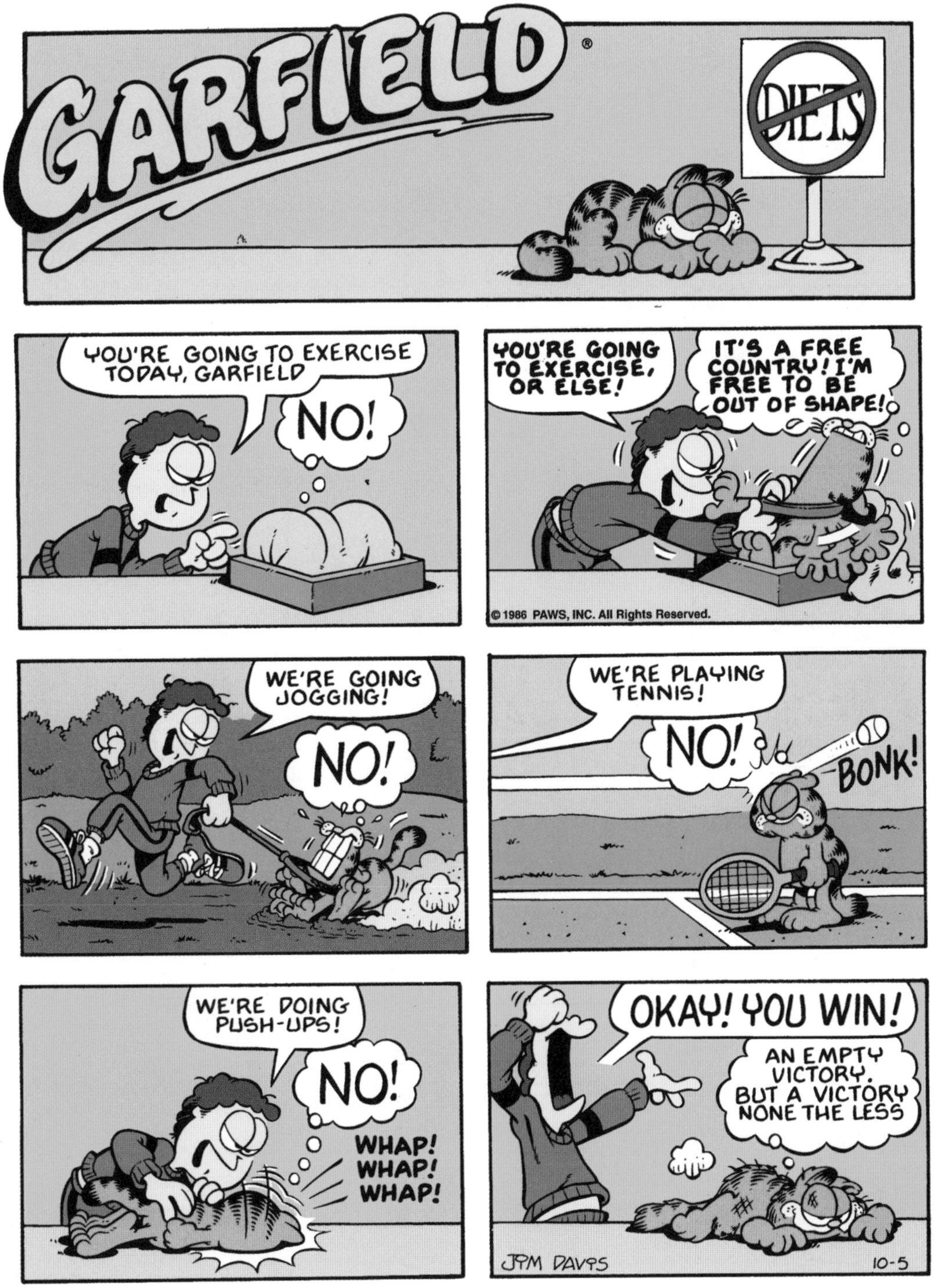
GARFIELD®
DIETS
YOU'RE GOING TO EXERCISE TODAY, GARFIELD
NO!
YOU'RE GOING TO EXERCISE, OR ELSE!
IT'S A FREE COUNTRY! I'M FREE TO BE OUT OF SHAPE!
© 1986 PAWS, INC. All Rights Reserved.
WE'RE GOING JOGGING!
NO!
WE'RE PLAYING TENNIS!
NO!
BONK!
WE'RE DOING PUSH-UPS!
NO!
WHAP! WHAP! WHAP!
OKAY! YOU WIN!
AN EMPTY VICTORY. BUT A VICTORY NONE THE LESS
JIM DAVIS
10-5

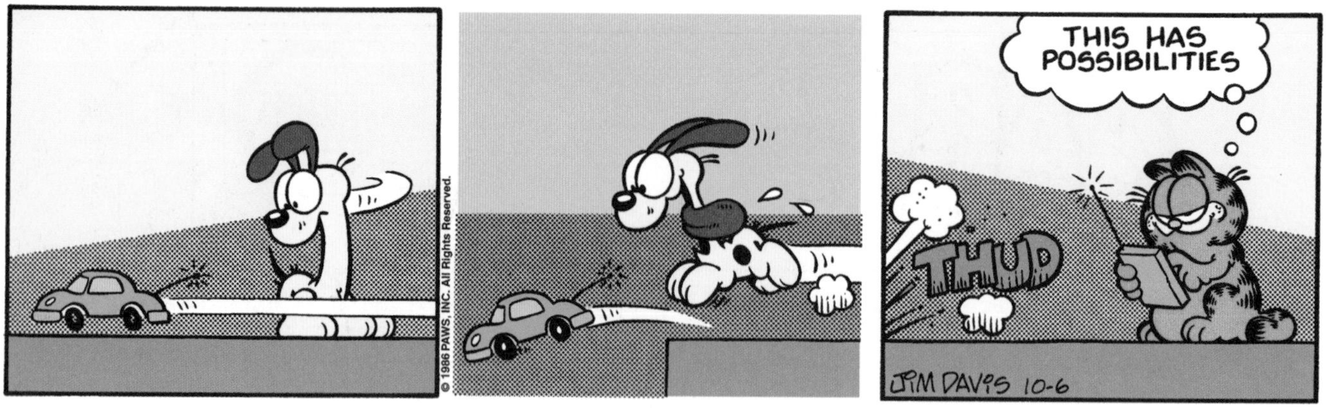
© 1986 PAWS, INC. All Rights Reserved.
THUD
THIS HAS POSSIBILITIES
JIM DAVIS 10-6

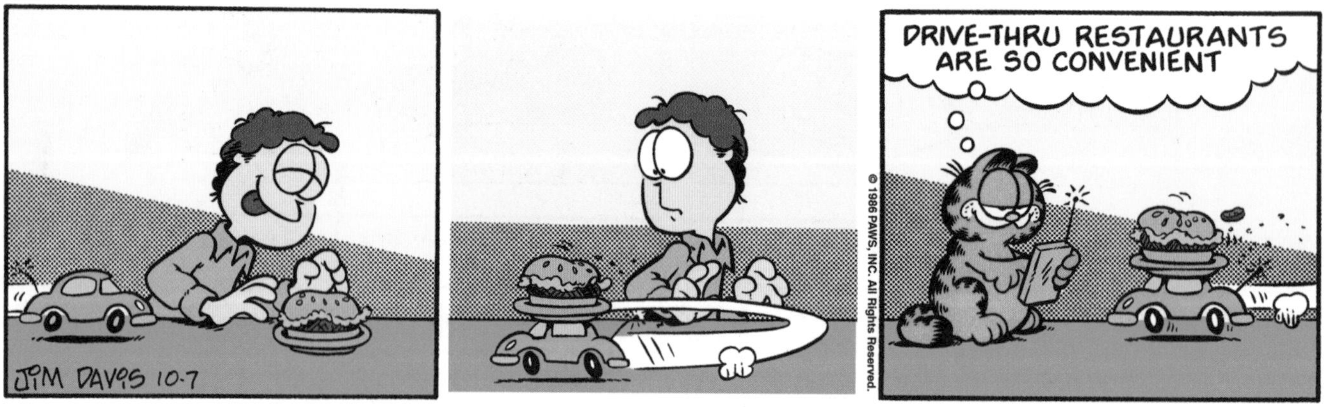
JIM DAVIS 10-7
© 1986 PAWS, INC. All Rights Reserved.
DRIVE-THRU RESTAURANTS ARE SO CONVENIENT

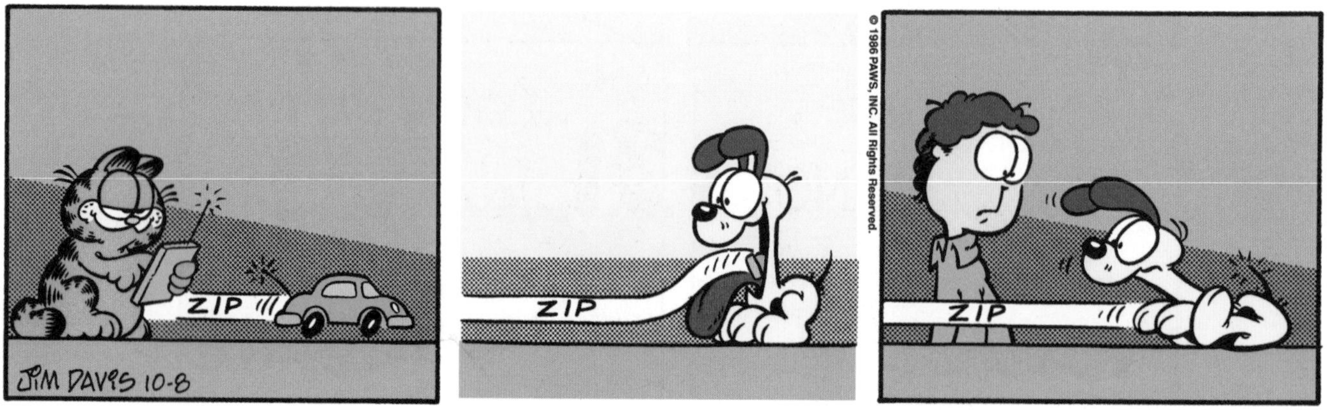
ZIP
JIM DAVIS 10-8
ZIP
© 1986 PAWS, INC. All Rights Reserved.
ZIP

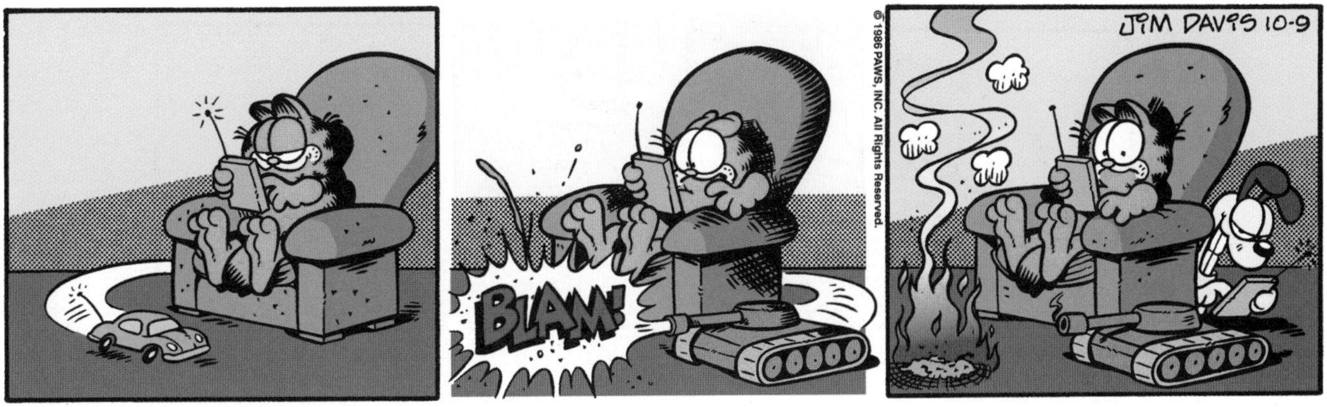
BLAM!
JIM DAVIS 10-9
© 1986 PAWS, INC. All Rights Reserved.

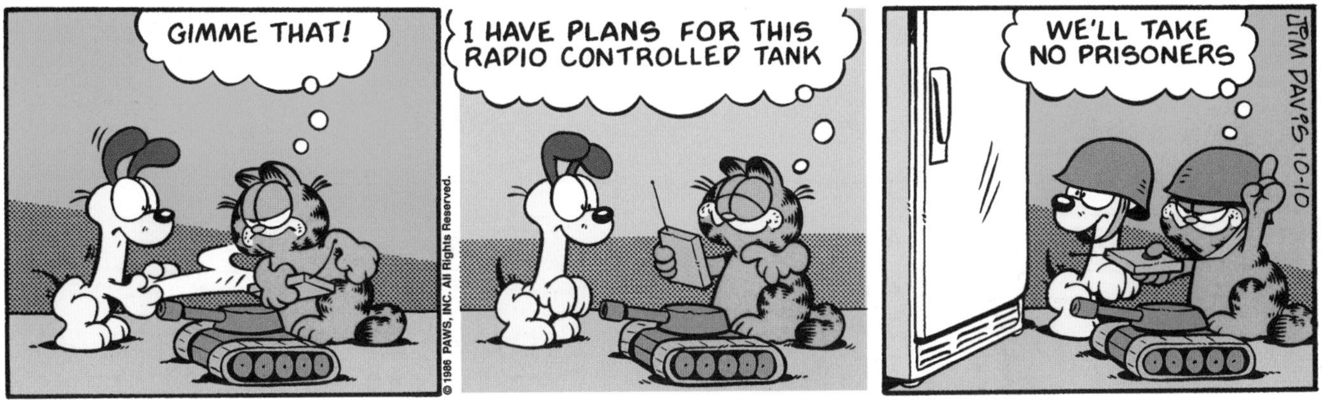
GIMME THAT!
© 1986 PAWS, INC. All Rights Reserved.
I HAVE PLANS FOR THIS RADIO CONTROLLED TANK
WE'LL TAKE NO PRISONERS
JIM DAVIS 10-10

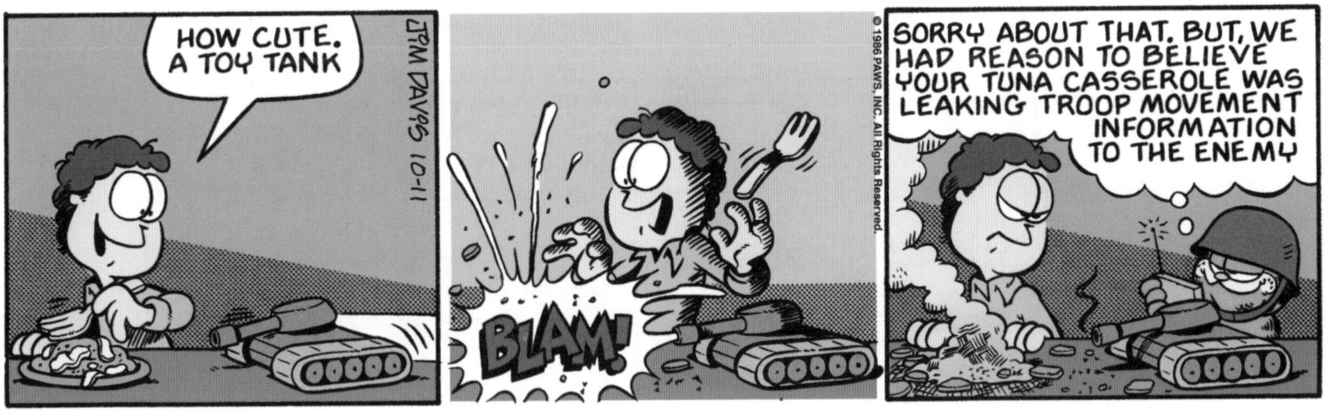
HOW CUTE. A TOY TANK
JIM DAVIS 10-11
BLAM!
© 1986 PAWS, INC. All Rights Reserved.
SORRY ABOUT THAT. BUT, WE HAD REASON TO BELIEVE YOUR TUNA CASSEROLE WAS LEAKING TROOP MOVEMENT INFORMATION TO THE ENEMY

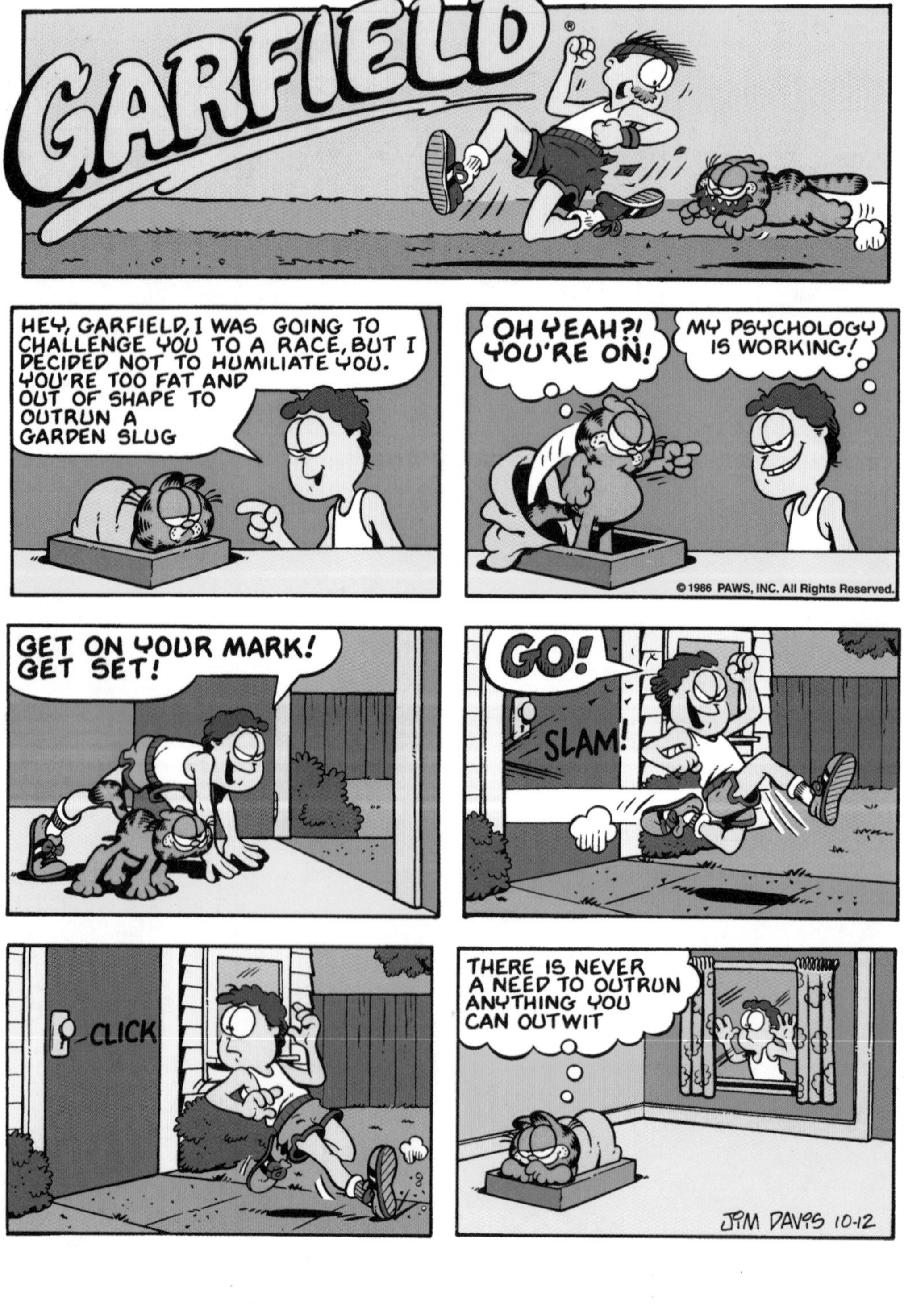
GARFIELD
HEY, GARFIELD, I WAS GOING TO CHALLENGE YOU TO A RACE, BUT I DECIDED NOT TO HUMILIATE YOU. YOU'RE TOO FAT AND OUT OF SHAPE TO OUTRUN A GARDEN SLUG
OH YEAH?! YOU'RE ON!
MY PSYCHOLOGY IS WORKING!
© 1986 PAWS, INC. All Rights Reserved.
GET ON YOUR MARK! GET SET!
GO!
SLAM!
CLICK
THERE IS NEVER A NEED TO OUTRUN ANYTHING YOU CAN OUTWIT
JIM DAVIS 10-12